D0240026

I Spend, Therefore I Am

I Spend, Therefore I Am

The True Cost of Economics

PHILIP ROSCOE

VIKING
an imprint of
PENGUIN BOOKS

VIKING

Published by the Penguin Group
Penguin Books Ltd, 80 Strand, London WC2R ORL, England
Penguin Group (USA) Inc., 375 Hudson Street, New York, New York 10014, USA
Penguin Group (Canada), 90 Eglinton Avenue East, Suite 700, Toronto, Ontario, Canada M4P 2Y3
(a division of Pearson Penguin Canada Inc.)
Penguin Ireland, 25 St Stephen's Green, Dublin 2, Ireland (a division of Penguin Books Ltd)
Penguin Group (Australia), 707 Collins Street, Melbourne, Victoria 3008, Australia
(a division of Pearson Australia Group Pty Ltd)
Penguin Books India Pvt Ltd, 11 Community Centre, Panchsheel Park, New Delhi – 110 017, India
Penguin Group (NZ), 67 Apollo Drive, Rosedale, Auckland 0632, New Zealand
(a division of Pearson New Zealand Ltd)
Penguin Books (South Africa) (Pty) Ltd, Block D, Rosebank Office Park,
181 Jan Smuts Avenue, Parktown North, Gauteng 2193, South Africa

Penguin Books Ltd, Registered Offices: 80 Strand, London WC2R ORL, England

www.penguin.com

First published 2014
001

Copyright © Philip Roscoe & Company Ltd, 2014

The moral right of the author has been asserted

Set in 12/14.75 pt Bembo Book MT Std
Typeset by Jouve (UK), Milton Keynes
Printed in Great Britain by Clays Ltd, St Ives plc

A CIP catalogue record for this book is available from the British Library

ISBN: 978-0-670-92282-6

www.greenpenguin.co.uk

MIX
Paper from
responsible sources
FSC
www.fsc.org FSC™ C018179

Penguin Books is committed to a sustainable
future for our business, our readers and our planet.
This book is made from Forest Stewardship
Council™ certified paper.

To the boys – grow up brave and kind

And Atlas through hard constraint upholds the wide heaven with unwearying head and arms, standing at the borders of the earth before the clear-voiced Hesperides; for this lot wise Zeus assigned to him.

Hesiod, *Theogony*, 507f.

At any rate, the international press made a great hue and cry about this 'find'. Handbooks, anthologies, surveys, 'literal translations', authorised and pirated reprints of Mankind's Greatest Masterpiece filled the world, and still do. Almost immediately, reality 'caved in' at more than one point . . . Contact with Tlön, the habit of Tlön, has disintegrated this world.

Jorge Luis Borges, 'Tlön, Uqbar, Orbis Tertius'

Of what happened later in the evening nothing definite can here be stated. None of the guests later on had any clear remembrance of it. They only knew that the rooms had been filled with a heavenly light, as if a number of small halos had blended into one glorious radiance. Taciturn old people received the gift of tongues; ears that for years had been almost deaf were opened to it. Time itself had merged into eternity. Long after midnight the windows of the house shone like gold, and golden song flowed out into the winter air.

Isak Dinesen, *Babette's Feast*

Omnia vincit Amor; et nos cedamus Amori.

Virgil, *Eclogues*, X

Contents

INTRODUCTION

1. I Spend, Therefore I Am

Imagine that you set off to buy flowers for your beloved. Perhaps you want Himalayan orchids – nothing but the best for the special one in your life – or perhaps something quieter, more restrained. You have some time on your hands, and you go from shop to shop, examining the different goods available. The supermarket offers you a selection of ready-made bouquets, cellophane wrapped; the price is good, though they are bright and loud under the strip-lighting. The perfumed boutique of the artisan florist has a bell on the door that tinkles as you enter; buckets overflowing with luxuriant blooms promise superior quality and bespoke arrangement. But the tissue paper wrapping and intricate ribbons will cost you plenty, so if you prefer, the cheerful dodger on his market stall will sell you a bunch of daffodils and wrap it in newspaper for the journey home. In each instance you judge quality and set it against price, performing a careful calculation of expense and return. With enough time on your hands, you would visit more shops, comparing identical bouquets across different supermarkets, setting one florist or costermonger against another, determined to find the best price for the same goods.

This is a natural enough way to act, you might think. The transaction in the flower shop is by its nature economic – understood as such by law, custom and by both parties to the deal. You will be required to hand over payment, and in return you will expect goods of the best possible quality for the price. You are free to select in a rational manner, maximizing your return, and once the purchase is completed you have no obligation to the florist, nor they to you. The shopkeeper – for you have settled on artisan chic – understands this arrangement well, and will try to sneak some social obligation back in, to intertwine your economic exchange with non-economic elements, such as good service, a little conversation, courtesy and a smile. The barrow boy might have offered cheerful banter. Had you opted for the busy super-market, you would have gained no such society, scanning your flowers and shoving banknotes into the slot of an automated till. The supermarket's appeal is solely to your economic faculties: more flowers for less money.

The giving of the blooms to your loved one is another mat-ter, though: a gift, an act of altruism made with no expectation of return. You seek nothing more than the sight of a smile illu-minating the recipient's face. Of course, dear reader, you don't believe that; you understand full well the implications and entanglements of the gift. As anthropologists have been telling us for years, gift-giving confers its own obligations; gifts demand repayment in kind, and personal relationships become entangled with chains of reciprocity.

Economic transactions, then, are ones in which these chains of reciprocity are broken: the swapping of money in return for services or goods severs, rather than reinforces, all extraneous ties. As an object is purchased it is transferred from one owner to another, and all claims of previous labour, time and entitlement are set aside. Unlike you and your beloved, the parties to an eco-nomic transaction are permanently quits.

In this book I argue that the act of purchase – of spending, if you like – is the distinguishing characteristic of contemporary life. We spend, and so we are. A purchase is a solitary ritual, governed by its own rules, epitomized by our imaginary hunt through the flower shops, chasing quality and value at the same time, purging interactions of social relationships and obliga-tions. When we spend, we gather information and subject it to a cool, calculative assessment of what is best for *us*; we become, for that moment, self-interested economic woman or man; we weigh costs against returns, we transact, and we move on.

Economic relations have been praised for many years for this ability to liberate us from the heavy hand of communal life, to pluck us from the small world of the pre-industrial village, where the minutiae of personal life – an individual's work, marriage, even death – was subject to collective scrutiny, and transport us to the anonymous freedom of the city. At its simplest, then, a purely economic society is one in which everyone is free of such obligations; one that is, instead, organized by self-interest alone.

According to economics, this is the natural state of things. In 1954 the British economist Sir Dennis Robertson gave a lecture at New York's Columbia University, commemorating its two hundredth birthday. He asked what the economist economizes, and answered that the job of economics was to 'economize on love, that scarce resource'.[1] By love, Robertson clearly meant civic virtue, or altruism. Because we are naturally self-interested, economics can and should instead provide a system of rewards that would motivate individuals to perform valuable social duties, without relying on 'love'.

Robertson's conception of love is a strange one. It works from the premise that there is only so much altruism to go round, and that if we squander it on trivia there will be none left when it is really needed. But selfless behaviour and acts of good-will are things that flourish, the more they are given and reciprocated: one good turn, as the saying goes, demands another. In Robertson's manner of thinking, however, when civic relations break down, when people act selfishly, attempt to free ride or take an excessive share, the problem is not that there is too much economics, but that there is *too little*.

Let me offer another example. This morning I drove to work. Immediately behind me, filling the rear-view mirror and my conscience, was the bus, making the same twenty-minute journey. By taking the car I contributed to traffic, noise and pollution, and used precious global resources. I do not dislike the bus on principle; it is simply cheaper for me to take the car. But the car is only less expensive than the bus because I am not liable for the full cost of using it. If I were forced to be responsible for the full cost of the additional traffic, of the pollution, the noise and the consumption of resources I would find the car infinitely more expensive than the bus. In fact, the argument goes, if drivers were forced to pay the full cost of car ownership, only the richest could afford to drive.

In the language of economics, the noise, traffic volumes and pollution in this example are known as 'externalities', meaning that they sit beyond my immediate decision. The economist's answer to the problem of externalities is a simple one. You should give someone or some organization ownership of air, of noise and of traffic volumes, and entitlement to charge for their usage. Once someone is forced to bear the cost of users' depredations, such actions will stop being 'externalities' and so impinge on our decisions; problems persist because the market does not go far enough. As Robertson argued, reliance on human goodwill is insufficient, and we must instead take refuge in market exchange and self-interest. This line of thinking has become a commonplace in contemporary society. The optimistic belief of Enlightenment economists such as Adam Smith in the fundamental good nature of ordinary man has given way to a profound despair: collective action is increasingly considered impossible due to the base self-interest of mankind. I have even heard an eminent moral philosopher advocate the drugging of the water supply to mitigate our selfishness.

My argument runs in the opposite direction – economic reasoning *allows* me to come to the conclusion that the car is cheaper than the bus. My conclusion is a product of economics' ability to strip the chains of social obligation away from my transactions, leaving only a tight focus on immediate financial considerations. The calculation is made within a tightly economic realm of cost and benefit, and the outcome is simple: the bus is too expensive. Moreover, as the distinguishing characteristic of economic exchange is quits, there is a secondary outcome of any extension of market principles. Once I have paid the charge for pollution I am free, and I can pollute as much as I wish, so long as I continue to do so. Payment, like a caricature of confession, absolves one of all further responsibility.

A theory of life

In 1932, two decades before Robertson's address, another British economist published an essay on the future of economics. Lionel Robbins argued that economics could do more than study trade and taxes. He dreamed of an economics that could offer a single, unified theory of human action, a meaning of life expressed in economic terms. Eighty years later his dream is coming true.

A flourishing economic theory of marriage testifies to the unbridled ambitions of the discipline. Like much of the economics of human behaviour, this stems from the pioneering work of Chicago economist Gary Becker, who won the 1992 Nobel Memorial Prize for his demonstration that economic analysis can be used to give an account of competitive relationships outside of the economy. In the economic theory of marriage individuals calculate the gains to be had from possible partnerships and act accordingly. These gains could be anything – their precise nature doesn't matter for the theory – and result from multiplying the 'quality' of the two partners. As gains increase exponentially with the quality of mates (just as five multiplied by five is far greater than two multiplied by two) it follows that the highest 'productivity gains' would be experienced if highest quality partners paired up across the market, leaving lower quality partners to fend for themselves.

Becker's economic theory goes on to analyse what happens

within a marriage: once paired off, partners then compete with each other for a division of the spoils. So, using for a moment the somewhat simplistic descriptions of 'quality' employed by relationship economists, the wealthiest man should marry the most beautiful woman in order to maximize gains from the pairing (five times five being much higher than other possibilities). On calculating his share of the spoils, however, he may in fact choose to marry a less attractive woman in order to grab a higher proportion of the gains available in the union (five times three may yield only fifteen, but if he can take it all he is still better off than with half of five times five).[2] Self-interest and competition are sharp enough tools to analyse not only marriage formation, but how the relationship then develops and concludes – there is, of course, an economics of divorce. It may seem strange to think of marriage as a competitive relationship, but selfish competition is the essence of economic theory; there really is no difference between the calculations concerning which flowers to buy and which person to marry.

The economics of marriage is only a theory. Like all economic theories, though, it is making its way into real life. Economic models such as this are often criticized on the grounds that it is very hard to foresee the consequences of all possible actions, and therefore also hard to calculate what the rational, maximizing course of action actually is. Nowhere can this be more the case than in marriage, where couples grow together over the years in response to the many unpredicted things that life may put their way. It must be almost impossible to judge the future 'rents' from a successful pairing. Moreover, it is very hard even to appreciate all the qualities, good or bad, of one's partner on first meeting; these are discovered serendipitously over weeks, months and even years. Unless, of course, one joins an online dating site.

Here we find economic reasoning incarnate. The machinery of online dating sites – questionnaires, descriptions and rankings – breaks us down into our fundamental attributes, which can then be sorted and ranked. Similarly, those who use the sites lay themselves out for selection like goods on a market stall, labelling themselves with their vital statistics, qualities and preferences. It is unsurprising that those advertising themselves online are prone to the petty dishonesties of hustlers and salesmen: they grow taller, slimmer and smarter, and, judging by the briefest perusal of advertisements, display a universal enthusiasm for open fires and cosy evenings. Nor is it a one-way process. Through breaking *oneself* down into a list of attributes, and through the constant comparison of those attributes with others', one becomes aware of one's own value, and the value of others in comparison. Then, and only then, is it possible to make a rational choice as to the best of all possible partners.

I hope it is uncontroversial to say that, whether in love, work, or care, human goods are *relational*: care and kindness, affection, love, generosity and support, are mutual endeavours, things that can come about only through relationship and community with others. They simply cannot be built single-handed; they cannot be driven by self-interest, for they involve giving, receiving and returning. In this book, I hope to show that online dating represents just one example in a steady process of social change that we have collectively undertaken, and the consequences of which will not be fully understood for many years. Our personal relationships have been redefined by economics, manifested in particular ways of talking, thinking and doing.

Another example central to my narrative is health care, where the growing discipline of health-care economics has had an enormous impact on the provision of care, the availability of treatments and the allocation of resources. As we enter a prolonged period of budget cuts and scarcity, economics' hold on the sector is only likely to grow tighter. Health-care economics claims to offer the most sophisticated, and therefore the morally superior, means of arbitrating over who should receive what treatment. But as I will make clear, it can only elaborate on the *most efficient* distribution of resources, and even then within the constraints of highly artificial assumptions.

Founding health-care economist Alan Williams is famous for advocating, for example, that we spend money on hip replacements rather than dialysis machines, because it is a more efficient use of the money. This, you might think, would be a judgement that should be debated through democratic means, not made on the basis of unelected expertise in a controversial discipline. Yet cost–benefit analysis is widely adopted in the governance and allocation of care, the provision of safety measures, spending on culture and education; when a politician says that he or she is obliged to spend money as *well* as possible, it almost always means as *efficiently* as possible. As we will see throughout this book, adopting efficiency as the prime virtue in all policy measures leads us to a society in which we might not wish to live.

The scope of economics

Some have suggested that economic organization is by its very essence immoral, treating human beings as means to the ends of bureaucratic and organizational goals. Yet, as Max Weber pointed out, bureaucracy succeeds not only because it is efficient, but because it is a useful and fair means of organization. It is objective in the sense that it treats everyone the same. Rational, economic decision-making is a cornerstone of bureaucratic organization because it is straightforward and transferable. It makes all kinds of problems and products commensurable, creating linkages and alternatives that did not previously exist; between dialysis and hip replacements, between educational institutions, even potential spouses, and rare landscapes and shopping trolleys.

But in what sense is such a comparison objective? As we will see throughout the book, equating 'objective' with 'impartial' or 'unbiased' brings its own problems, but more often economic decisions are considered to be objective in the sense of being scientifically, and therefore incontrovertibly, true. This is utterly incorrect, and when applied to economic reasoning it is truly damaging.

We must, for this reason, contend with one central argument. We address it at the beginning of this book, and we return to it at the end: is economics not simply a science, and a successful one at that, a theory that has been compared to the theory of evolution in its reach and explanatory power? Does it not simply describe? No. There is no such thing as a purely descriptive science. Sociologists of natural science have recognized that the act of inquiry is closely linked to the object being investigated. Our knowledge of the sub-atomic particle investigated under the huge 'microscope' of a particle collider is as much a product of the machine, the research protocols and the teams of scientists who have spent whole careers working on this sensitive equipment, as it is of quarks, muons or bosuns themselves. The argument is equally true of social science. The agent that forms the very basis of economic investigation – the rational actor, instrumentally pursuing its ends, always searching for more and better – is itself a product of economics.

I will argue throughout that economic reasoning is a technical performance, one that comes into being in specific places as a result of the language we use and the tools with which we are equipped. Often, both are provided by the organizations which benefit from their use, just as a supermarket provides shopping trolleys. I will show you this phenomenon in everyday settings: shopping, buying a house, gaining an education, trading the stock market, falling in love, falling ill, even in dying and in the arrangements we make for our body after death.

Through its language and tools, economics brings into being the agent about whom it theorizes: self-interested, calculative and even dishonest. We may believe that these qualities are natural aspects of humanity – indeed, schooled in the conception of enlightened self-interest inherited from Adam Smith, the father of modern economics, we find it hard to consider that humans have ever acted any differently – but there are many reasons to believe that this is not the case. Native self-interest is too vague a concept, too animalistic a motivation to explain the complexities of decision and organization that we daily encounter. Self-interest for the twenty-first-century economist means something quite particular, something technical and rational.

Consider the many realms into which we compartmentalize our lives. Family life, for example, is different from our working existence. We are liable to complain if a colleague brings too much of their personal life into work or a spouse brings too much of the workplace home at the end of the day. Intimate relationships in the workplace are taboo and bureaucratic or commercial relationships feel out of place in the family home. Such distinctions look to a broader division that runs across our social world, where we habitually separate economic and non-economic transactions: the buying of flowers from the giving of them. Different rules apply, as do different criteria of right and wrong, and conceptions of value and worth. In the realm of the economic, we are concerned with value for money, with efficiency and return on investment, whether specified in the rule-of-thumb estimates of everyday life or the complex mathematical models of economics.

It is not that the spaces of economics are artificial and our personal relationships somehow natural and pristine. In each case boundaries and modes of behaviour are *built* through careful organization of the world around us. They are the result of hard work, and maintaining them takes effort too. In the economic realm we are bound by legal constraints, for example, expecting to pay for and take delivery of goods that we have purchased; laws, social constraints, systems of valuation and even money are all part of the technical apparatus of economic life.

The influence of economics is spreading. We do not need to look far to see its domination of politics. In Europe, those nations still solvent install economic technocrats as heads of state, managers whose job it is to impose harsh sanctions and austerity measures upon populations who, one might infer from the policy response, have misbehaved and must be reprimanded. There are riots in the streets and shortages in the hospitals. Were the military actions of a despotic regime to produce the same consequences, stern speeches would be made in global assemblies and soldiers dispatched. When dictated by economic policy, suffering is allowed; harsh medicine, but it must be taken. In the bubble that preceded the crisis, and the hard times that must follow it, economic models, theories and even ideologies have become our representatives in Parliament.

Economic ideals have diffused through government offices and public services. For any administrative area, one can find a branch of economics that will advise on the efficient allocation of resources and check the worth of public expenditure or the return on time and effort invested: there is an economics of health care, of the environment, of risk prevention and safety.

We have let economics rule our political decisions, and it is coming to govern our personal interactions. There is an economics of marriage, as we have seen, and even an economics of suicide: did you know, for example, that the 'costs of suicide include transaction costs in the form of the money costs and time costs of effecting departure from the world', or indeed, that 'there is a difference between the long run and short run price elasticities of suicide due to a lagged adjustment to equilibrium taking place'? (In other words, if an easy means of suicide is taken out of circulation, then suicide rates fall as 'effecting departure from the world' becomes just too much trouble.)[3]

Economic practices creep into everyday life through the mundane apparatus of everyday life – shopping trolleys and price-comparison websites, for example – and in the language and justifications that we use. We have even invited it into the most intimate corners of our lives, where we allow it to arbitrate over our lovers, our loved ones and our bodies. It is a powerful and parsimonious analytical technique, yet, more and more, we are taking it as a doctrine of behaving, of choosing and of being. Here, economics is in danger of making us forget how to have solidarity, compassion and empathy. It is at war with the goods of life. At a time when the challenges facing our world do indeed require collective action instead of a reliance on the enlightened self-interest of individuals, economics may yet be our greatest obstacle to change.

Economics has made good on its promise to deliver prosperity and democratic freedom to much of the world, but in doing away with the age-old problems of humanity, it has opened up a crisis of an entirely new variety. The discipline's Enlightenment pioneers would have struggled to imagine a world where more prosperity, more goods and more wealth could somehow impoverish us, but contemporary psychologists have proved what philosophers have long claimed: increases in wealth and status can make us unhappy.

Economics has taken, like Atlas, the burden of the whole world upon its shoulders. Alas, they are too narrow. We must question the foundations of the economic endeavour, and be brave enough to insist that its science of efficiency is not enough – necessary, perhaps, but not sufficient – to govern and to discipline our world. Perhaps, as I explore towards the end of the book, it will be possible for us to imagine an economics of flourishing, one that supports the virtues and goods of life, if we allow ourselves radically to rethink the nature of the economy. For the moment, though, I have a story to tell: how economics burst its chains and escaped the laboratory, and how much that has cost us all.

PART ONE

2. From Truck and Barter to the Meaning of Life

In Great Britain in the last three decades there has been a profound change in the way that property ownership is understood. Not so long ago, housing was part of the contract between state and citizens. After the Second World War, successive governments built hundreds of thousands of state-owned houses, designed to provide cheap, long-term accommodation with a security of tenure for the occupiers. Housing was understood as a social good, to be supplied and owned by the state, and by the end of the 1970s approximately 40 per cent of the population lived in 'council houses' owned and maintained by the local authority.

In the early 1980s, though, under Margaret Thatcher's radical programme of market-focused reforms, many of these houses were sold off. In 1980, the Housing Act established the 'right to buy' which allowed tenants of at least two years' standing to buy their property at a substantial discount. Right to buy proved one of the most successful and popular policies of the Thatcher era. According to the free-market orthodoxy of the time, by dismantling state-owned housing provision 'the government divested itself of money-losing facilities, eliminated costly operating subsidies, received current income from the sales proceeds, and made independent home owners out of formerly dependent government residents'.[1] In other words, efficiency and cost saving, together with a novel doctrine of personal empowerment through property ownership, were considered the prime virtues of this – and, by implication, all – governmental action.

Other motivations also informed this strategy: for example,

many council estates had become decrepit, and the new think-ing held that once transferred to private ownership, these houses would be looked after by their purchasers. Moreover, as the state of repair of neighbouring houses could have an effect upon the monetary value of these newly owned properties, it was expected that the proprietors would lean upon their neighbours to tidy up rubbish-filled front lawns and mend broken windows. Property ownership became infused with a moral weighting that goes way beyond the primary purpose of providing accom-modation and security for the occupants: Britain would become a better place if more people owned their houses, while a tiny part of state responsibility, security and policing, was trans-ferred into private hands. In the broadest political terms privatizing housing stock meant undoing the post-war settle-ment of state support and state intervention in favour of a market-driven system, dismantling a social contract and replac-ing it with a market.

There was also a transfer of risk from the government, which received payment in cash, to the home owner, who became a speculator on the improvement of the locality. Many – the majority, perhaps – have benefited from a thirty-year rise in house prices, fuelled by the widespread demand for ownership that Thatcher's reforms had encouraged. Of course, on the mar-gins some have still suffered; many of the worst estates have deteriorated so far that they have been pulled down, and empty houses are being sold off for renovation at prices far below the market level. In Stoke-on-Trent, one of Britain's most deprived cities, houses in some streets are being offered for £1 in an attempt to regenerate the area.[2] Those who purchased proper-ties in streets like this thirty years ago are now locked in by ownership of an unsaleable asset and must be bought out by the state.

The next step in this programme of economization came in

the mid-1990s, when buy-to-let mortgages appeared for the first time. The buy-to-let was a device concocted by the Association of Residential Letting Agents and a group of mortgage lenders, with the intention of reviving the residential letting market, by this time in the doldrums following Thatcher's drive towards home ownership. Whereas previously mortgages had been intended as a way of allowing purchase of the single dwelling inhabited by the mortgagee, now mortgages could be raised on properties in which the owner had no intention of living. The buy-to-let mortgage was phenomenally successful: by 2006 12 per cent of the UK's population was living in buy-to-let accommodation.[3]

For those who took them up, the new wave of buy-to-let mortgages severed any remaining bond between the house purchased as a home and the house purchased as an investment. Properties bought-to-let are necessarily understood in economic terms: the cost of the mortgage must be set against the likely income generated by the property, itself dictated by the number of bedrooms and other amenities on offer; improvements to the fabric of the house will be driven by purely financial considerations, how much they will add to the capital or rental value of the property. The capital value itself becomes less a measure of the desirability of the property and more a factor of the possible rental income. Home owners are free to become landlords, borrowing over and over again, spreading the equity – the share of the value that is owned, not borrowed – accumulated in the properties already owned between more and more houses to build a teetering empire of rental properties. The process was aided by, and largely contributed to, a booming property market; television programmes promoting get-rich-quick home-makeover schemes blossomed and everyday conversation was filled with the buzz of who made what on the property ladder. Exceptional examples became well known: the former maths teachers from south London who built up a portfolio of nine hundred properties with a rental income of £1.5 million.[4]

But there are other effects, too. A growing pool of borrowers provides a lucrative opportunity for lenders, and credit flows into the market, expanding the available money supply. More credit drives prices upwards, increasing the equity available to owners. Fortified by these capital gains, landlords can borrow still more, while new buyers are priced out of the market and forced to rent, providing ever more juicy returns for property owners. Throughout the early 'noughties', credit manufactured by Wall Street financial engineers fuelled the flames. We have the making of a classic speculative bubble where existing owners flourish and new buyers suffer. In effect, this is a tax levied on the young by the old, by those who own property on those who do not. I am one of the guilty, just old enough to have bought a house in what, back in the late 1990s, already seemed like an out-of-control market; I don't know how those just a few years younger will ever manage to do so. Those who did buy in the boom years in the mid-noughties will for years live with a millstone of debt round their neck; in Ireland, where the bubble became truly manic, and competition and cronyism drove prices far beyond any reasonable level, many have been permanently ruined.

Housing forms one of the central examples in this book. It is a meeting point for politics and regulation, for the novel schemes of entrepreneurs – whether residential letting agents or Wall Street bankers – and for the personal lives and life projects of those who live in them. It shows markets doing what they always do, left unsupervised: transferring wealth from those who have little to those who have more. Thatcher's reforms drove a slow transformation of the house from one category – a home, pedestrian, cheap, often state-owned, viewed in terms of its function and social benefits of safety, security, dwelling – to another – an article of private property expected to generate profit and viewed in terms of its economic return. Housing is the visible tip of a leviathan: the economic theory of neo-liberalism and the political and technical apparatus that backs it up.

Private ownership of housing was just one aspect of Margaret Thatcher's endeavour to transform Britain in the 1980s. She also pursued private ownership of state-controlled utilities, market deregulation and an unwavering belief that national prosperity depended upon the productive efforts of individuals: in her words, a fair day's work for a fair day's pay. Her policies might have been taken one by one from a book called *Capitalism and Freedom*, Milton Friedman's handbook of 'neo-liberal' economics. On the other side of the Atlantic, Ronald Reagan's 'Reaganomics' also embraced this free-market ideology, and brought about tax cuts on the basis of the Laffer curve, an economic theory purporting to show that lower tax rates could generate more revenue. In the USA and Britain, politicians championed the 'trickle-down effect', where letting the rich get richer was the surest way of bringing prosperity to the poor. By the middle of the 1980s economics – a very particular kind of economics – had transformed the economies of the English-speaking world, and had woven the threads of economics into the fabric of society.

The idea of self-interest

Such policies are built upon an unshakeable belief in self-interest, paired with a dim view of what mankind is capable of without an immediate incentive. Housing reform and associated policies presume, for example, that an individual can be persuaded to maintain a home only if there is the prospect of immediate financial gain. As the example shows, such policies soon enough bring into being the kind of self-interested economic man that they first supposed, reinforcing the initial belief of policymakers.

Yet the modern economist's idea of self-interest as the eternal and universal motivation of man has, in fact, quite specific historical origins. The ideas that grew into our contemporary association of free markets with democracy, and of rational self-interest as the basis for moral and personal freedom, began to emerge in the seventeenth century, during the European Enlightenment, when they were first invoked by the radical liberalism of the English in the work of the seventeenth-century philosophers Thomas Hobbes and John Locke.

In *Leviathan*, published in 1651, Hobbes argued that a self-interested pre-social man traded a life that was 'solitary, poore, nasty, brutish, and short', for the stability offered by government and social institutions. John Locke reasoned from 'natural law' to a social contract under which rational, self-interested agents accepted governments in return for 'life, liberty and the pursuit of happiness', a phrase later enshrined in the American Constitution. Hobbes and Locke both envisaged that man had 'natural rights', that, before the coming of society, man lived in a 'natural' world where he had freedom to do as he wished, and take what he wanted. But such total freedom (or anarchy, as we might call it) inevitably brought strife, and mankind had accepted a social contract as a means of avoiding it. However, the natural rights of man as sovereign individual in his own person remain unencumbered: society, in any form, is a matter of an original, individual choice. Replacing the older conception of the divine right of kings, the language of individual freedom as a God-given right, the most basic right of all, which is so influential in American political debate today, is a direct descendant of Hobbes's and Locke's thinking.

It was Adam Smith, a member of the eighteenth-century

movement known as the Scottish Enlightenment, who breathed life into the idea of self-interest as a motivating force in economics. He argued in *The Wealth of Nations*, published in 1776, that man had a 'propensity to truck, barter, and exchange', and told us that it was the self-interest of the baker, brewer and butcher that would provide our supper. The ability of mankind to organize exchange is what distinguishes humans from the animals: 'Nobody ever saw a dog make a fair and deliberate exchange of one bone for another with another dog. Nobody ever saw one animal by its gestures and natural cries signify to another, this is mine, that yours; I am willing to give this for that.'[5] Smith's writing is a tribute to unintended consequences and the power of indirect causes; a God-fearing man writing at a time when Providence was still regularly blamed, or praised, for its interference in the natural order of events, he believed that nature, left to its own devices, would channel economic activity in the most beneficial manner: 'By directing that industry in such a manner as its produce may be of the greatest value, he intends only his own gain, and he is in this, as in many other cases, led by an invisible hand to promote an end which was no part of his intention.'[6]

Adam Smith's name regained prominence in the 1980s as the champion of free markets, the classical economist who first pointed out the 'invisible hand' of the market, which became the best, if not the only, justification for notions like the trickle-down effect: the idea that a healthy market will, left to its own devices, self-regulate and turn competing self-interests into wealth for all. These twentieth-century Smith revivalists invoked the invisible hand as a powerful rhetorical device; I am sure I'm not alone in my mental image of a huge hand pointing down from the sky, part Monty Python, part Michelangelo, a higher intelligence directing the market, turning private vice into public virtue.

But trickle-down and virtuous free markets are twentieth-century interpretations of Smith's writing. Smith never mentions *the* invisible hand, only *an* invisible hand, and then only in passing, once in the *Theory of Moral Sentiments* (1759) and once in *The Wealth of Nations*. Indeed, the Enlightenment thinkers inherited a respect for the hierarchy of family, civic institutions and the state. Apologists for Smith argue that self-interest is a broad term that includes the interests of family and local community; certainly it seems the case that Smith's idea of self-interest is not the narrow, calculative meanness that characterizes twentieth-century economic man. Economist and Nobel laureate Amartya Sen puts it well: some men are born small, some men achieve smallness and some men have smallness thrust upon them.[7] Smith, by all accounts, is one of the latter.

Smith is hardly advocating untrammelled self-interest, then; he is making a theological point about the immanence of divine intention in nature, and therefore in the world. Nature intended mankind to be productive and wealthy, and will ensure that a productive, wealthy world is the best of all places. His faith in the providential alignment of natural causes and economic preferences assures him that an individual's self-interest is the same as the natural interests of the community and the state.[8] In the *Theory of Moral Sentiments*, Smith goes so far as to say that even tyrants will be governed by the invisible hand; when they cannot eat any more, when they are absolutely sated, then they have no option but to redistribute wealth to the needy. Smith's passage may strike us as absurd, Polyanna-ish; yet, ironically, the sentiments expressed here are almost identical to the ideas behind 1980s trickle-down theory. The philosopher Immanuel Kant, who dedicated his life to the rational elaboration of Enlightenment values, looked forward to an eternal peace driven by market exchange, a view that rings true in modern liberal economics too; Fritz Koenig's sculpture *The Sphere*, which stood in the courtyard of the World Trade Center buildings in Manhattan, was a giant bronze globe, symbolizing world peace through trade. It is telling that Kant's vision of eternal peace is also justified by an appeal to nature: exchange had enabled mankind to colonize the world, and is therefore somehow natural.

Nature is an exemplar for the Enlightenment economists: in endless balance, blind and without purpose. Smith argues that it is precisely the inability of individuals to contemplate the purpose of the whole, but only myopically to pursue their self-interest, that will make the machine of the economy run so well. The invisible hand is a vision of nature written into economics, where the market is a wonderfully benevolent natural machine, capable of transforming self-interest into the common good. For the Enlightenment thinkers it was nature, not scripture, that offered mankind comprehension of the Divine; the laws of heaven were written into the laws of nature, and thus into the wonderful, ineffable operations of the market. The words of the great Victorian hymn –*Immortal, invisible, God only wise/ In light inaccessible hid from our eyes* – apply just as well to the Enlightenment vision of the market.

Metaphors of bounteous nature were not the only ones in circulation. The previous generation of economists, known as the Mercantilists, had preferred an economics of war. They believed that there was only so much wealth in the world, and that the role of nations was to amass as much of it as possible. Trade was an exercise in selling goods in return for gold, the enriching of one state at the expense of another: throughout the sixteenth and seventeenth centuries European nations struggled to export as much of their manufactured produce as possible, while limiting imports and stockpiling bullion.

The Mercantilists' agonistic economics was countered by a biological one. In the second half of the eighteenth century François Quesnay, doctor to Louis XV in France, led the 'physiocrat' economists, who saw the social body as akin to the human body; following the demonstration of the circulation of blood, they theorized that wealth circulated likewise, and that economics was the physiology of society, nourishing the organs of industry and trade. David Hume, the Enlightenment empiricist, attacked Mercantilist theory with technical arguments about the circulation of money.

These biological metaphors shifted economic thinking from the *doux commerce* of Smith and Kant to something altogether less generous. In 1786 an Anglican cleric named Joseph Townsend enjoyed a temporary fame when he published an essay titled *A Dissertation on the Poor Laws* (subtitled *By a well-wisher to mankind*) in which he campaigned for the abolition of these and all welfare measures. Invoking notions of natural balance and order, Townsend tells a parable of goats and dogs, set on Robinson Crusoe's island in the Pacific Ocean. According to Townsend, a handful of goats landed by a Spanish sailor, Juan Fernández, as a self-sustaining supply of food for future visits had come to be a reliable source of sustenance for the English privateers who preyed on Spanish shipping. The Spaniards retaliated and introduced a pair of dogs, greyhounds, which ran wild, multiplied and decimated the goats. The remaining goats learned to stay on the cliffs, out of reach of the dogs, and a 'new kind of balance was established'; the agile, energetic goats and dogs survived while 'sooner or later, the lazy will be left to suffer the natural consequence of their indolence'.[9] Townsend concluded: 'Hunger will tame the fiercest animals, it will teach decency and civility, obedience and subjection, to the most brutish, the most obstinate and the most perverse.'[10]

Townsend is now little remembered. Nevertheless, his work was widely read and debated in its time, and perhaps more than anyone Townsend introduced these naturalist ideas into English thought. Charles Darwin and Thomas Malthus, two of the greatest thinkers of the era – of any era – took notice of this obscure cleric's parable of natural balance and necessity, based upon the immutable laws of physiology. Malthus wrote it large onto the human world, and Darwin developed it into the theory through which we understand the evolution of life on earth. In economic thinking, the social reformer and utilitarian zealot Jeremy Bentham sided with Townsend and saw the threat of poverty as a necessary motivation for his grand industrial plan to function. For Bentham the near-poverty of the many is a necessary predicate of the prosperity of society. Self-interest must be enforced by hunger, a harsh discipline backed by the highest moral high ground of all, because 'the laws of commerce were the laws of nature and consequently the laws of God'.[11] The sharpness of these biological metaphors is far from the prosperity, empathy and eternal peace envisaged just a generation earlier.

The Enlightenment thinkers discerned unchanging natural laws that stretched back to the dawn of time. History and literature suggest otherwise. In medieval times the circulation of wealth was driven by war. Lands and weapons changed hands on the battlefield and the king controlled the flow of wealth through his superior military power; medieval economics does not look so different from the exchange of goods we can discern in the ancient Greek world of the *Iliad*, where warriors pause in the midst of battle to strip gleaming bronze armour from those they have vanquished, and King Agamemnon offers the sulking Achilles a bribe of precious metals, lands, horses and women to return to the field.

It is anthropology, though, that demonstrates, most clearly of all, the local and specific nature of economic activity. According to the great economic historian Karl Polanyi, the evidence of anthropology suggests that these 'laws of commerce' were far from being natural or immutable or universal, or indeed anything apart from the product of learned behaviours born out of local cultural norms.[12] From the 1920s until the middle of the twentieth century, economic anthropology – as the discipline became known – produced more and more evidence that aboriginal arrangements simply did not look like Western market economies. Anthropologists argued that the notion of profit was alien to these cultures, and that reciprocity instead was the social glue that bound their societies together. In the Kula ring of the Pacific Islands, studied by Bronislaw Malinowski in the 1920s, islanders made elaborate exchanges of shells with counterparties on other islands, binding each other into webs of obligation that stretched far back into the past and into the future. The legendary ancestors who had begun the tradition were thereby linked with future generations as yet unborn; such reciprocity stretched through time as well as between people and places. In the extravagant potlatch of the indigenous North American people, wealth was, and still is, redistributed and destroyed through a gift-giving ceremony, shoring up the social structures of the tribes at the same time.

If the Kula ring and the potlatch scarcely resemble contemporary Western economic arrangements, neither did the economies of pre-industrial Europe. The village was the basic unit of subsistence in a largely agrarian society. Manufactured items were supplied by monopolistic guilds; in seventeenth-century London guilds held rights to supply almost every conceivable commodity. Polanyi argued that the economy as we know it is the result of the extraordinary social changes – 'The Great Transformation', as he called it – that swept across Europe, and particularly Britain, in the space of a few years in the middle of the nineteenth century.

This transformation was a deliberate re-engineering of civil society. The enclosure of common land displaced families formerly dependent on largely self-sufficient village communities.

Why did they not revolt, like their French counterparts? A basic welfare state, embodied in the Poor Laws, held off starvation in the short term. Constructed as a wage supplement, this dole ensured that workers would receive a minimum no matter how hard – or little – they worked and how little the employer paid. It took two decades, according to Polanyi, for the rural poor to become demoralized and small-scale industry to be ruined. When the Poor Laws were repealed workers flowed into the new cities, where they were forced to work for starvation wages and in appalling conditions. Hunger did indeed tame the fiercest animals and teach deference and civility to the most perverse. The idea of the rational, self-interested individual, a creation of the Enlightenment thinkers, had been enacted by the creation of the labour market and enforced by the ever looming threat of starvation.

The nineteenth-century economy – our modern economy of industrial capitalism – emerged, then, not as a worldly manifest-ation of transcendental economic rules, nor as the inevitable result of a Darwinian evolution of society, but as the outcome of deliberate innovations in law: the abolition of assistance for the poor, the construction of robust property rights over land and capital, together with the technological and organizational innovations of the industrial revolution – machines, fearsome engines, factories and dark Satanic mills – and the displacement and near starvation of an entire agrarian population to trans-form a rural peasantry into a source of industrial labour, all of which was supported by a conception of the market as a mirror of nature, of laws physical and therefore divine, and as a site of *truth*. In the middle of this transformation there comes about the economic man, driven by self-interest, abstracted from bonds of family, church and state, endlessly seeking efficiency in the face of universal scarcity brought about by the market-based exchange-ability of all things.

Polanyi has been condemned as a primitivist, representing a romantic tradition that harks back to ancient society as harmonious and peaceful, based on reciprocity, and solidarity. Indeed, Polanyi does warn that contemporary man will lose 'the imaginative wealth and power of his savage endowment', and is guilty of setting up an unrealistic idea of the noble tribesman.[13] But there is more at stake here than the respective merits of 'primitive' and 'modern' societies, or whether gift exchange is a more natural and authentic means of economic interaction than the market: the anthropological endeavour, whether among ancient societies or modern-day financial colossi, has been to show that *each and every* form of economic interaction is the product of specific, historically, culturally and geographically located organization. This is as true today as it was in the nineteenth century.

It follows that there are particular characteristics attached to our industrial, market society: that *all* goods and products are organized for sale and purchase through the market, that they are *only* available through the market and that people using the market must act, not as primitives, but as distinctive, modern creatures, economic men and women. In the words of George Dalton, a prominent anthropologist: 'It is market organization which compels its participants to seek material self-gain: each must sell something of market value to acquire the material means of existence.' The 'economic man' of nineteenth-century economics had turned from an idea into a 'succinct expression of this institutional fact'.[14]

The economics of freedom

For the Enlightenment economists, the market became a site of truth, a mirror of nature, a liberating force against the repressive social relations of the pre-industrial village. Self-interest, the private pursuit of profit, was the wellspring of public virtue through the benign mechanisms of trade. The project of English utilitarianism, conceived by Jeremy Bentham and elaborated by John Stuart Mill, sought to translate these virtues into law, reforming prisons and schools along the lines of the new market economy. So matters held until the arrival, in the late nineteenth century, of the fathers of modern economics, the Austrian 'marginalist' revolutionaries: Carl Menger, Joseph Schumpeter, Ludwig von Mises and, most famous of all, Friedrich von Hayek. Together with the Englishman William Stanley Jevons (to whom, I was delighted to discover, I am distantly related) and the Frenchman Léon Walras, they recreated economics as a mathematical project.

Economics had never before been exposed to serious maths: Adam Smith and his fellow Scots were philosophers and literati as much as economists, concerned with good governance and the proper conduct of mankind. Jeremy Bentham's intellectual endeavours were directed by the taxonomic conventions of eighteenth-century biology, and his dream of a grand utilitarian calculus that would render all the virtues and vices in the world commensurable was dismissed by his successor John Stuart Mill as a rhetorical ploy.[15] In the nineteenth century, though, there arrived the notion that a good's usefulness could be expressed as a continuous mathematical function, when, working independently, Jevons, Menger and Walras 'discovered' the theory of marginal utility.

These two small words have wielded a disproportionately large power over the organization of the twentieth century. 'Utility' simply means 'value', or 'usefulness', but it differs from all previous definitions of the word in two important ways. First, this usefulness can only be seen, or understood, as it influences human behaviour. The usefulness of a thing is shown by the degree to which humans act out of desire for it. Second, that utility can be expressed in a single numerical function. The analyst need no longer be concerned with philosophical bickering over the nature of the good, and simply recognizes that people value things in different ways and this is reflected in their behaviour.

'Marginal' – concerning the margin, or edge, of availability – deals with the change brought about by an additional unit of a good. The change can be positive or negative. When manufacturing, marginal costs may fall as you produce more, but are likely to rise again beyond a certain point, as inefficiencies creep into the process. According to textbook economics, you should stop making a product when the additional marginal cost equals the additional marginal revenue. Perhaps the most important aspect of marginalist thinking is the recognition that the utility of any good diminishes with every additional unit of it: this is the concept of 'diminishing (marginal) return'. The second slice of cake, for example, delivers fewer benefits than the first, the third and fourth still less. We can immediately see problems with taking this argument to an extreme: for the condemned man, each day of reprieve may have a great marginal utility. But as a rule of thumb for analysing consumption it is useful enough, and the intention of the movement was to arrive at a manner of thinking that was mathematically productive. Jevons and others at the forefront of the 'marginalist revolution' demonstrated that these diminishing returns may be predicted arithmetically, and so turned the mathematics of value into the centrepiece of twentieth-century economic science. The theory behind the so-called trickle-down effect, for example, held that money had a 'marginal utility' like anything else; it had less value to those who had more of it, and they would spend rather than invest, stimulating the economy.

The leap to mathematical formalism did many things to economics. For a start, it elevated economics to a new standard of mathematical proof. An economics that looked like physics – queen of the sciences for most of the twentieth century – commanded considerable authority in the real world. And mathematical economics did look like physics, very like physics in fact, for the simple reason that it *was* physics: nineteenth-century heat equations served as the intellectual model for the marginalist revolutionaries.[16]

The outbreak of the Second World War helped to build economics' institutional standing further as the mathematical processes of the budding discipline were swept up into the war effort. Economic scientists found themselves working on computational problems such as code breaking, early computing and artificial intelligence, used in applications such as bomb sights and automated anti-aircraft gunnery. Some of the greatest twentieth-century economists, such as John von Neumann, were mathematicians, operations researchers and atomic bomb designers too. This fusion of projects persisted after 1945 as mathematical economics found itself allied with the military-industrial project and the United States' efforts in the Cold War, with military-industrial funding swelling the university departments and the ranks of practising mathematical economists. Military-industrial laboratories such as the RAND Corporation, a think tank formed by Douglas Aircraft Company to perform 'Research ANd Development' for the United States military, saw algorithmic computation and economic reasoning – game theory and behavioural simulations – join together to plan out scenarios for the always possible nuclear Armageddon.[17]

The linkage between economics and the Cold War effort against Soviet totalitarianism was perhaps a natural reflection of the political dimension at the heart of this twentieth-century economic doctrine. Despite their insistence on mathematical abstraction, its founding thinkers such as Hayek and Friedman made far-reaching claims about the interdependency of market

relations and democratic freedom. Economics may be an explora-
tory engine, but it came to be the centrepiece of a complex
political doctrine, too: neo-liberalism.

Friedrich August von Hayek came to London in 1938, seeking
refuge from the Nazis. He had taken up a chair at the London
School of Economics, secured for him by Maynard Keynes, and
when war broke out the great English economist took Hayek
away from the dangers of London to Cambridge. Hayek volun-
teered for air-raid duty and, so the story goes, spent many cold
nights on the rooftop of King's College, listening for the distant
drone of German aeroplanes. As he sat among the spires, he set
to wondering what had brought the Nazis to power. His answer
was simple, although unexpected: the Nazis had been elevated
by socialism. While Keynes and others had looked on Nazi central planning, protectionist policies and monetary expansion as
some kind of economic monstrosity, brought about by a despotic regime, Hayek saw the causes reversed. For him, the rise
of the Nazi state was a necessary consequence and inevitable
outcome of socialist economic doctrines. The state corporatism
of the far right is, after all, not so different from the socialist
Utopia. The Nazis pursued central control, vainglorious building and vast architectural development, and a sense that the
body of the state was more important than the bodies of those it
comprised; we can find these very same things in the contemporary communist regime of North Korea, for example.

The Road to Serfdom sets out Hayek's historical-economic
theory. It was published in 1944 and sold so well that it became
unavailable owing to paper rationing; it was only with the publication of the Reader's Digest version in 1945 that the book
became more widely accessible. Hayek echoes what has become
known as the 'socialist calculation controversy' first sparked in
1920 by Ludwig von Mises, who argued that the absence of the
monetary valuation provided by a market would make calcula-

tion impossible, and thus questioned the possibility of a centrally planned and organized economy.[18] Mises's point is simple: prices tell us what people want, so that entrepreneurs can provide these goods. Without prices neither entrepreneurs nor the state can possibly divine the consumption requirements and preferences of individuals. The calculation controversy raged in the post-war years in an intellectual environment that was broadly supportive of interventionist politics and central planning. Hayek agreed with Mises that socialist central planning was unable to compute the infinite permutations of supply and demand that are required to manage a national economy, and took the argument further to examine the consequences of persevering with the model of central planning. Unable to accurately assess demand, the planned state would commandeer labour to produce goods that were unwanted while failing to produce those that were greatly needed. People would lose their freedom to work as they please and to buy the goods that they choose. The centrally planned economy will always run behind the needs of the world, with its organization mired by committees and bureaucracy, petty squabbles and struggles for power. Eventually, often sooner than later, the economy will collapse and there will be shortages combined with other crises such as the hyperinflation in 1930s Germany. The people will demand action, and into this gap will step a despot. Democratic rule will cease. There will be crimes of hate and, in an Orwellian touch, language itself will be subverted. Work, wages and even leisure will be planned activities. Hitler was just one example of what Hayek held to be a timeless historical mechanism, as socialism consumes itself again and again: 'democratic socialism, the great utopia of the last few generations, is not only unachievable, but to strive for it produces something so utterly different that few of those who now wish it would be prepared to accept the consequences'.[19]

These same principles informed Milton Friedman's work,

some twenty years later. In the preface to a later edition of *Capitalism and Freedom*, a book that became an enormously influential popular work of neo-liberal economics, Friedman reminded its readers of the intellectual climate into which the book was first launched. In the 1950s, he said, the intellectual orthodoxy was socialist in its outlook, and those who were 'deeply concerned about the danger to freedom and prosperity from the growth of government, from the triumph of the welfare state and Keynesian ideas, were a small and beleaguered minority regarded as eccentrics by the great majority of our fellow intellectuals'.[20] On its initial publication in 1962, the book was ignored by the review columns of the major publications in the US and was covered only by the *Economist* in London. The book has since sold 400,000 copies and is still in print fifty years later, a testimony more to the sea-change in political orthodoxy than Friedman's stolid prose. Friedman was an American and the nation's constitutional language of liberty speaks strongly in his writing, but at the heart of his book lie the axioms of liberalism. We can see the shadows of Mill, Locke and Hobbes: 'to the free man, the country is the collection of individuals who compose it, not something over and above them', writes Friedman in its opening lines.

So, what can perform the superhuman tasks of organizing the distribution of goods and the allocation of labour? What will succeed where central planning must fail? What will save us from the horrors of socialism and totalitarianism? The answer to all such challenges was, of course, the market.

For Hayek, and those who inherited his ideas, the fundamental problem was that of knowing what other people want, how they value and choose. Their solution was to let people *show* what they value by paying for it. As money is a universal medium, it can rank not only all the preferences of an individual, be they for a heterogeneous selection of goods and services, but *all* preferences of *all* individuals. Need, desire, necessity are all rolled into one single measure, automatically worked out by the marvellous market.

This line of thinking continues: the amount a person, or firm, or other entity will be prepared to pay for something depends upon the value they think they can gain from it. In turn, such expectations depend upon their own productive capabilities, whether financial, intellectual, material or bodily. The crucial fact is this: if everyone competes for an asset on the basis of their own expected returns, the winners will be those who can make best use of the asset, and therefore the outcome of this competition will be best for society as a whole, at least in terms of providing the highest returns on its available assets. So, in the labour market, a 'higher quality' firm will pay more for a 'higher quality' individual, because they expect higher returns. We do not need to know which firm or which individual is highest quality in advance; the market will figure it out on its own.

The economics of the mid-twentieth century saw the final fusion of the providential assumptions of the Enlightenment and the mathematical aspirations of the marginalists. For the Cold War neo-liberal, the freely competitive market will protect democracy and ensure the world gets everything it needs. Competition is the only means of coordination that does not require coercion, and money is a great instrument of freedom, offering a means for people to express their preferences for a universe of goods and sell their labour as they please. The market is the only computer big enough to deal with this task; Hayek likens entrepreneurs to engineers who, watching a few dials, can adjust their activities to the data recorded by the price system.[21]

Let me offer an even simpler example. Imagine a remote, pre-modern, agricultural society, which has somehow adopted neo-liberal modes of organization. There are many farmers, but only one plough; some farmers have greener fingers than others, and the quality of the land varies. The farmer prepared to bid most for the plough is the one with the greenest fingers and the best land, because he can afford the highest price. He lays hold of the plough, and the whole community benefits. Imagine now a variety of crops. Each is priced differently in the market, as buyers consider their wants and needs; now the plough will go to the farmer who can produce the most of the most preferred good. The market will adjust to the climate, harvests and changing preferences. Even in a closed universe, the computation required to predict which farmer will generate the best return on the plough is already tricky. If we open it up to include other factors, such as the effect of trade and varieties of tool, the complexities soon become infinite. Hayek's argument is incontrovertible: the market *is* a wonderful computer.

Neo-liberal Utopias

For Joseph Townsend, author of the parable of the goats and dogs, and the liberal tradition that he inspired, all a government need do is step back and let natural processes take their course. For the neo-liberals, though, laissez-faire turned out not to be enough to bring about the competition on which the whole process relies. Indeed, establishing a stable pattern of economic exchange, whether altruistic, reciprocal or market-based, proved to be hard work.

In the 1950s and 1960s experts argued over the best way of helping Latin America progress through its economic difficulties.[22] One side of the debate favoured an interventionist politics involving import tariffs, exchange rate manipulations and fiscal measures to develop the internal market. The leading proponent of this 'structuralist' approach was the United Nations

Economic Commission for Latin America, based in Chile, and during this period it enjoyed a clear political dominance at home and abroad. On the other side were the neo-liberal economists who blamed exactly these kinds of interventionist measures and declared that the free market – a truly free market – was the only solution to the ills of Latin America.

By the 1950s neo-liberalism was a small, determined and well-organized political movement. It can be traced back to the 1946 'free-market project' of the University of Chicago Law School, and to the Mont Pèlerin Society formed by Hayek and others in 1947 in a Swiss village of that name. Its central endeavour was to promote democratic freedom and free markets. As we have seen, these two concepts had become virtually synonymous in neo-liberal thought: democratic freedom meant small government and fierce competition. In *Capitalism and Freedom* Milton Friedman, who came to be the society's most prominent figure, provided a list of government activities that he regarded as unjustifiable from a neo-liberal perspective. These included agricultural support, import tariffs and restrictions, output controls, rent controls, minimum wages, detailed regulation, compulsory social security programmes, public housing, national parks and military conscription. Cutting through traditional boundaries of left and right, particularly in its opposition to conscription, Friedman's list is an intellectually rigorous statement of the free-market democracy that sat at odds with much of the political thinking in the post-war years, revolving as it did around currency controls, the gold standard, Keynesian intervention and a social contract with those who had risked their lives in the Second World War.

The neo-liberal collective became skilled in advancing its agenda through political channels. The research backed think-tank of the Free Market Society (later the Chicago School of Economics) with its useful policy suggestions and its generous funding through relationships with corporations and the military-industrial complex, formed an easily replicable model that was taken up across the Anglo-Saxon world.[23] Together with the Mont Pèlerin collective it managed to promote the neo-liberal creed from the fringes of economic life to the dominant intellectual philosophy in politics and the social sciences at the end of the twentieth century. The extent to which these aims have been incorporated into everyday economic life, particularly in the United States, and the ease with which measures associated with the post-war settlement can be branded as 'socialism', show just how successful the neo-liberal project has been.

Perhaps the most infamous neo-liberal intervention came in 1955, when the economics faculty at the Catholic University of Chile in Santiago agreed a supervision arrangement with the Chicago School of Economics and over the next twelve years sent thirty of its brightest stars (twenty-nine men and one woman) to Chicago. Here the 'Chicago Boys', as they became known, fell under the spell of Friedman. Following the model of the Free Market Society, a neo-liberal think-tank – even today necessary for any group of proselytizing economists – was set up in 1968. For the time being, though, it remained peripheral to Chilean politics. In 1970 Salvador Allende was democratically elected by a growing socialist workers' movement, and from 1970 to 1973 popular support for his government rose as economic quality of life improved: in 1971 GNP increased by 8.9 per cent and unemployment fell from over 8 per cent to 3.8 per cent.[24] But politicians in the United States, at the height of the Cold War, were less than keen on a flourishing Marxist government in Latin America and in 1973 General Augusto Pinochet, backed by the United States, seized power through a military coup. The army installed a brutal regime that institutionalized torture and persecuted its critics. For a year not much happened on the economic front, as the army made only moderate changes, but international oil shocks and a collapse in exports gave the Chicago Boys their chance, and they persuaded the generals that they could supplement the regime's brute force with their own intellectual ability. By March 1975, when they organized a highly publicized seminar on neo-liberal economic policy, attended by Friedman himself, they controlled the Chilean economy. In the absence of any possibility of criticism – thanks to the brutal tactics of the army – an unrestrained experiment in shock liberalization began.

The reforms brought in by the Chicago Boys had a messianic aura. Rolling back the state takes more than firing bureaucrats. A free-market regime requires an infrastructure of regulation, particularly property and contract law, if it is to function. Certain kinds of transactions must be made legal while others must be forbidden. As the example of housing showed at the beginning of this chapter, introducing or developing markets is less a matter of deregulation and more one of re-regulation. So the Chicago Boys introduced 'seven modernizations', new labour laws, privatization of health care, shifting the organization of education and government to a local level and so forth. They also scrapped price controls, opened borders and encouraged exports, and privatized national industries, all positive interventions requiring new regulation.[25] The free economy is no less a product of careful organization than the command economy. What differs is the intention of the regulation: the neo-liberal regulates *towards* a free market rather than away from it.

If these reforms read like a synopsis of Friedman's recommendations in *Capitalism and Freedom*, it is unsurprising, as the book was adopted as a key text by the Chicago Boys, alongside Hayek's *The Road to Serfdom*. Hayek was by this time teaching in Chicago, albeit at the faculty of philosophy, and he too was a regular visitor to Chile and a supporter of the neo-liberal regime. Readers may be wondering how two of the greatest advocates of economic freedom as a means to individual liberty came to be outspoken supporters of the economic policies of a regime that habitually tortured and murdered its critics; Friedman took refuge in the oldest dodge of all (at least among the scientific classes), claiming that he rendered only 'technical economic advice' to the Chilean government, despite his 'profound disagreement' with its political system.[26]

The success or failure of the Chicago Boys' economic experiment is contested. In the short term, things were very bad. Exiled economist and diplomat Orlando Letelier, writing in *The Nation* in August 1976, gave witness to the pain that the shock therapy had inflicted in the short term: inflation of 341 per cent, and unemployment higher than 20 per cent.[27] By July 1976 roughly a quarter of the population had no income whatsoever, while humanitarian efforts aroused the suspicions and hostility of the junta's police force. The perfect competition dreamed of in Chicago was farcical in Chile, and as recently nationalized industries were transferred back to private hands, powerful and established economic interests took advantage of the process to secure their own prosperity. In this sense, writes Letelier, a confirmed socialist, the coup had been a success, a revolution led by the middle classes desperate to regain their prestige and capital from the workers. The high point of the revolution was a new constitution introduced in 1980, the 'Constitution of Liberty', a clear acknowledgement of Hayek's influence.

After the shock, matters improved dramatically: by the late 1970s inflation was low and the economy was in good health. But growth had been financed by foreign loans, which, combined with the light-touch regulation demanded by free-market ideology, provided fertile ground for financial speculation. In the early 1980s a speculative collapse and associated panic led to a sharp decline in national output and a temporary lessening in the power of the Chicago Boys when market mechanisms failed to restore equilibrium, as they had promised. By 1984, as an ever weaker Pinochet opened dialogue and cut deals with increasingly important opposition leaders on the political right and centre, the remaining Chicago Boys were removed from power. In 1985 another neo-liberal, Hernán Büchi, took over as finance minister, a job which he held until the fall of Pinochet's government in 1989.[28]

The return of a democratically elected government allowed Friedman to proclaim that free markets had worked a 'miracle' in its restoration, conveniently ignoring the fact that Chile had been governed democratically before Pinochet's intervention, or that tens of thousands had been tortured and imprisoned, many murdered, in the interim. Gary Becker described Chile as a 'role model for the whole undeveloped world'.[29] But the Chicago Boys' short reign had done more than introduce economic liberalization; it had fundamentally changed the way that government was done in Chile.

It is one of the axioms of the modern world that truth is to be found in science, and objectivity in numbers; that the authority of the scientific method transcends other knowledge. From the beginning, the Chicago Boys 'presented themselves as the bearers of an absolute knowledge of modern economic science, thereby dismissing the existence of economic alternatives'.[30] By taking this position, they could claim that opposing views or criticisms stemmed from ignorance and a failure to understand the true nature of economics. They allowed a brutal dictatorship access to reservoirs of respectable intellectual capital on the basis of which it could negotiate with foreign firms and bankers. Once the whole political debate had been dragged onto the terrain of scientific economics, opposition became possible only in the language of economic technicalities. Opposition groups founded their own scientific think-tanks and research institutes, and when Pinochet's government was finally replaced by an opposition regime, opposition economic advisers flowed in from the new institutes to offer their own brand of left-wing economic technocracy. Whatever else they managed, it is quite clear that the Chicago Boys achieved a permanent transformation of Chile's understanding of the relationship between economics and state: economic technocracy is now an established part of Chilean government.

For a neo-liberal such as Hayek, the market offers an alternative to the state; more market necessarily means less state. As the technocratization of Chilean government shows, the market is so much better than the state at doing state-like things that it becomes a yardstick to measure government. For the neo-liberal, markets are particularly good at stimulating competition and pursuing efficient solutions to allocation problems, and so competition and efficiency become the prime measures of state performance, and civil servants are scrutinized by measures that have been developed in market settings. We are so habituated to these criteria that we may fail to notice all the other things that a state could be doing: providing justice, looking after weaker, vulnerable or impoverished members of society, stimulating creativity or pursuing equality, to name just a few.

We don't have to look as far as Chile to see such transformations. Eastern Europe had its own shock liberalization in the 1990s, after the Soviet Union collapsed. In the United Kingdom, the transformation to a free-market society came through a repositioning of state-owned housing, infrastructure and national industries as privately held assets. In terms of government itself, we have seen an equally dramatic transformation of the principles by which decisions may be taken. For example, Dave O'Brien of London City University has studied policymaking in the UK's Department for Culture, Media and Sport.

He found the mandarins obsessed with notions of market failure and in thrall to the Treasury's Green Book, a set of guidelines that draws on economic frameworks to guide policy intervention in the 'market' for culture.[31] Indeed, the topic of efficiency in the provision of culture, and of return-on-investment measures in analysing the value of money spent on the arts, is a site of continual, bitter warfare between policymakers and cultural bodies.

An economics of humanity

Neo-liberal economics has been able to mobilize networks of capital and political influence, and to provide institutional entrepreneurs with levers that change, not just organizations, but whole nations. But twentieth-century economics did not stop at reshaping the social world. Economics has designs on the nature of humanity itself.

Lionel Robbins's 1932 tract, in which he dreamed of a unified theory of human action based in economics, was titled 'An Essay on the Nature and Significance of Economic Science'. Economics, he wrote, is 'the science which studies human behaviour as a relationship between ends and scarce means which have alternative uses'.[32] At the end of the previous century, Jevons and the other 'marginalists' had argued that the value, or utility, of any good diminishes with every additional unit. Robbins's new economics pushed even further, incorporating time into the analysis: 'When time and the means for achieving ends are limited and capable of alternative application, and the ends are capable of being distinguished in order of importance, then behaviour necessarily assumes the form of choice.'[33]

For Robbins, these 'ends' might involve work and leisure, or sustenance and sleep. What matters is that all are purchased with time, and most with labour, and mankind does not have a sufficiency of either. Once everything has been made exchangeable through the market, shortage becomes a logical inevitability; as Robbins notes, we have been turned out of Paradise. Economic man simply can never have enough, to the point where even human kindness can be seen as scarce. This is what allowed Robertson to remark in 1956 that the job of the economist is to economize on 'love'.[34]

Gary Becker has been the foremost proponent of the economics of human behaviour. His work has sought to apply the principles of rational decision-making to the everyday choices that people make. In the context of marriage, crime, schooling, or even death, Becker relentlessly drives through a notion of individuals as continually assessing the costs and paybacks of the various options available to them. Costs and paybacks do not have to be financial, for individuals 'maximize welfare *as they conceive it*, whether they be selfish, altruistic, loyal, spiteful or masochistic'.[35] Thus in Becker's work the full range of human attachment, experience and emotion is reduced to commensurable and scalar variables: to numbers.

The logic behind Becker's argument is disarmingly simple and seemingly incontrovertible. People always seek what is best for them out of the resources and choices available. Often other people compete for these same resources – jobs, school places, sweethearts – and markets form. In the end the individual who can make the best, most efficient use of the resources available will seize that resource, precisely because they will be willing to bear the highest cost. What is true for Hayek's entrepreneur is true for Becker's individual. This logic recasts every individual as an entrepreneur of the self. We should understand, not only our labour, *but every aspect of our person* as a future revenue stream; we can enhance these revenues by education, investing costly time and financial capital to build our human capital, intellectual or physical.[36] Our decision to do so must be based purely on our estimate of the future returns available on that investment; we become a productive machine, valued in the same way as any other business asset. Our decisions, choices and life plans become factors in the cost–benefit analysis that we must focus upon ourselves.

What began under Adam Smith as an analysis of trade and national wealth has come a long way. In the twentieth century it guided the reforms of Margaret Thatcher in Britain and Ronald Reagan in the United States; it underwrote the free-market upheavals in Latin America and the shock modernization of Eastern Europe. Adopted by politicians and institutional entrepreneurs, it has drastically shaped the world we live in, intervening in politics and in society.

But it has also set its sights on the greatest questions of human behaviour. Such an extraordinary step can only be based upon the belief that we find in economic exchange an existential truth about the nature of human beings. Where the Mont Pèlerin neo-liberals contented themselves with holding up the free market as the fount of democratic freedom, Becker and his intellectual descendants discover universal explanations of humanity in economic theory. Some, such as the philosopher Daniel Dennett, go still further. For Dennett, economic decision-making is the fundamental mechanism of evolution. Cost–benefit analysis turns out to be 'a general principle of practical reasoning' through which evolution operates, as life-forms compare costs and benefits of one action with another.[37] Economics has finally achieved the goal of those mathematical pioneers and blossomed into a grand science of everything. It is a big step to take, but once we agree that evolution and economics are one and the same we are just moments away from a grand unified theory that offers no less than the meaning of life.

Today economics is indeed presented to us as a science of

everything. Not only can it unseat politicians and compel nations, it has now become culturally and intellectually ubiquitous in its explanations. Bookshelves strain under the weight of the ever more confident 'economics explains everything' genre. Most famous, perhaps, is Steven Levitt and Stephen Dubner's *Freakonomics*, subtitled *A Rogue Economist Explores the Hidden Side of Everything*, but there are many others: Robert Frank's *The Economic Naturalist: Why Economics Explains Almost Everything*, or the second book in Tim Harford's enormously successful Undercover Economist franchise, *The Logic of Life: The New Economics of Everything*. There is a disconnect between the trivial nature of the questions asked – Why are cups of coffee in railway stations so expensive? Are swimming pools more dangerous than guns? Or, best of all, if attractive people are more intelligent, and blonde is considered attractive, why are there so many jokes about dumb blondes? – and the seriousness with which we are expected to take economics.[38] Perhaps this is inevitable: a science of all human behaviour will be a science of human trivia.

We should take it seriously all the same. If we do, we will see that an economics of everything rests on three cardinal assumptions. The first, explicit, claim is that people are self-interested and respond to incentives. Economic models have a mechanistic tone, with people assumed to react to stimuli with the same predictability and regularity as a motor and its switch. The second assumption is of fundamental individualism: the idea that people take their own decisions, individually responding to the incentives they find around them. All kinds of motivation, whether hunger, greed or malice, generosity, compassion or love, can be reduced to input variables in the model. These two assumptions are certainly fit for purpose, so long as the purpose is building models of how individuals respond to incentives; at the same time they are reductive, compressing the whole wealth of human experience, reason and decision into a single near linear scale.

But if economics were truly an objective, descriptive science, none of this should matter, for we would be insulated by the final assumption of the economist: that economics merely describes. It is this assumption that we must turn to now.

3. Economics Does

Consider Allie, the 'happy prostitute'. We meet her in Levitt and Dubner's follow-up to *Freakonomics*: *SuperFreakonomics*, introduced by way of a backstory of two boring marriages and a successful but dull career, military and civilian. She is:

> smart, capable, technically sophisticated, and she also happened to be physically attractive, a curvaceous and friendly blonde whose attributes were always well appreciated in her corporate setting. But she just didn't like working all that hard. So she became an entrepreneur, launching a one-woman business that enabled her to work just ten or fifteen hours a week and earn five times her old salary.[1]

For Allie, there is only one way to maximize the returns on her physical and personal attributes: to sell them. Levitt and Dubner tell us that, as Allie finds her way around her new profession, she conducts experiments in the elasticity of demand by raising the price that she charges. At $300 an hour she is overwhelmed by demand, so increases her price; at $350, then at $400 an hour she experiences no drop-off in demand. At $500 an hour she is just as busy, though taking block bookings where she gets more dinner and has less sex. According to Levitt and Dubner she 'learned to price discriminate, and understood well the market forces of supply and demand', putting up prices to chase off clients, though in this case 'demand appeared to be price insensitive'.

Levitt and Dubner sum up their section on Allie by asking why there aren't more women like her: they claim that the wages are good and the hours flexible, and opine that there is little risk of violence or arrest. There are, they say, sacrifices, such as not having a husband and the difficulty of making friends beyond her immediate circle of co-workers, but 'these negatives just might not seem that important when the wage is $500 an hour'.[2]

Only an economist could pose that question. It assumes that all factors of the decision are commensurable: that sacrifices – no husband, or friends – are negatives to be set against the positives of a high wage and that all can be worked out on a grand slide rule. Yet despite the stated advantages, high-class prostitution is a career that many women, I would venture, would find repugnant: selling sex challenges deep-seated cultural and moral norms that lie beyond the narrow framing of an economic choice. Economics would have to work hard to make such factors 'exogenous', or external to the decision, to be able to say that prostitution is like military service or computer programming, only better paid.

But Allie is different. She *has* made this choice – a wise one, in the view of the authors, it would seem. The reason, surely, is that Allie herself is an economist, or at least thinks like one. After all, she must have begun from an a priori expectation that high prices would lower demand for her services, because she certainly could not have discovered that from her own unsuccessful attempts at price discrimination: in her case increased prices failed to lower demand. (At the same time, they changed the content of the hours paid for: inference might have taught her something else, something much more subtle, about the relationships between money and sex: if one pays enough, perhaps, the act doesn't seem to be purchased at all.) It is, after all, an axiom of economics that demand falls as prices rise: the demand curve always slopes downwards. Allie has learned to talk and think in economic terms, even in the face of evidence to the contrary. Indeed, by the time she was introduced to

Levitt, she had a copy of *Freakonomics* on her coffee table, and when she retired from the oldest profession, we learn that she opted for the newest one, returning to college to study economics.

Allie's experiments in price discrimination are a synecdoche for the question at the centre of this book: does an intelligent, technically competent person, a woman such as Allie, infer the laws of supply and demand from the world around her, or does she act in a way that is already informed by economic theory? Are the laws of economics immanent in the world, eternal truths that we will inevitably encounter as we fumble our way through it, or are they useful, intellectual rules, created by economists, which can help us navigate the chaotic waters of everyday life?

Why does economics explain so well?

In Borges's fable 'Tlön, Uqbar, Orbis Tertius', the narrator stumbles upon an imaginary world of that same name. He discovers it at first through an encyclopedia entry, in a bootleg imprint of an American almanac, and then in more detail in the papers of his father's friend, Herbert Ashe, an engineer for the Southern Railway Company, now deceased. Tlön, it turns out, is the work of a secret society set up to imagine a new world from top to bottom, one where ideas are seen to be real and reality is uncomfortably false. For much of the story Borges speculates on the grammar and philosophy of Tlön. But then something strange happens. Artefacts from this imaginary world begin to appear in the real one: a compass with its dial inscribed with characters from the Tlönian alphabet, or a strange, impossibly heavy cone of metal, an image of the deity from that other world. In the conclusion of the story the narrator tells us that, as findings and details proliferate, our own reality has collapsed, with a history of Tlön now taught in schools and its language replacing French and Spanish. Mankind is unable to resist the rigour and logical splendour of this imaginary world: 'How could,' says the narrator, 'the world not fall under the sway of Tlön, how could it not yield to the vast and minutely detailed evidence of an ordered planet? It would be futile to reply that reality is also orderly. Perhaps it is, but orderly in accordance with divine laws (read: "inhuman laws") that we can never quite manage to penetrate.'[3]

Borges's story hinges upon the distinction between a world that is orderly because we have made it so, because the rules are the result of human reason, and a world – our world – that, if it is orderly at all, is governed by laws which remain all too often beyond our comprehension. Humans, Borges muses, are unable to resist such powerful, accurate, logical rules and fail to ask *why* they work so well; surely they do so because the world of Tlön has been imagined according to those rules, rules that produce at the same time as they describe.

Borges's fiction has a real-life counterpart: the economy. It is a world of seductive order and clarity, explained in great detail by a set of rules that we call 'economics'. Yet, it is precisely because the economy is governed, structured and organized by those rules that they explain it so well.

We are not used to looking at economics in this way. We are used to thinking of economics as a description of something that already exists and is independent of that description: we think of it as a science. Leaving aside the fact that all scientific description is as much a product of our own scientific methods and instruments and language as it is of the natural world, there is a crucial difference between natural science and economics. Scientific endeavour is continually disciplined by the world it examines; it hunts for causal relationships which existed long before science caught up with them. Where we can, we harness them and become engineers in the world – for example using Bernoulli's principle to make an aeroplane fly – but the air molecules that allow us to do so remain aloof, unchanged by our endeavours. Through this process, Bernoulli's explanation is tested against reality every time a plane sets off down the runway: if it were inadequate we would find out soon enough. Economics, on the other hand, examines the human world, focusing on things that exist within a specific historical and cultural context – ideas of value and worth, primarily – and the descriptions it offers bring about that world just as much as they describe it. Economics and the world it examines are tied together by obscure, yet powerful, loops of feedback and interaction.[4]

Like natural science, economics can never escape from the dense entanglements of expertise, instrumentation and language; unlike natural science, economics measures itself.

Positive economics and the power of language

To understand the scientific claims of twenty-first-century economics and why they are misleading, we must step back to the post-war years, where philosophy of science was dominated by Karl Popper, a Viennese philosopher who came to occupy a chair in the London School of Economics, and the Oxford philosopher A. J. Ayer, champion of logical positivism. Positivism is a tradition of scientific investigation, dating back to the Enlightenment, that privileges physical, sensory data over philosophical wrangling, while the 'logical' refers to the structure of language itself. Ayer and his fellows in the Vienna Circle hoped to purge language of what they called 'metaphysics': statements based on things such as feelings and emotions. What would be left, they hoped, was a clear, logical language (hence the name) that could be used to make a close and pure description of reality.

Specifically, Popper took aim at the everyday 'inductive' method of empirical science, where scientists observe regularities and from these formulate scientific laws. For example we may see on many occasions that water boils at 100° Celsius, and we consider it a rule. For Popper, an infinite number of observations did not logically entail a rule; there is no logical reason, on the basis of observation alone, why the next time water boils it should do so at 100°C. Indeed, adding salt or gaining altitude does change the boiling point. So the absence of counter-examples did not constitute a logical proof of their impossibility. Popper gave the example of black swans, unknown to Europeans until explorers arrived in Australia: it had never been logically sound to claim that all swans are white, and empirical evidence eventually arrived to confirm this. He argued that science should move forward by producing hypotheses and attempting to discredit them; we are never entirely certain, only becoming more specific in what we have not yet disproven.[5] We may only hypothesize that water boils at 100°C and we must endeavour to prove otherwise, by adding salt or climbing mountains, refining our hypotheses and assembling an ever more comprehensive picture of things that have not yet been disproven.

Popper's arguments have long been out of favour in the philosophy of science, and as you can imagine, this kind of philosophical finesse made little impression on the everyday practice of science. But it had a huge impact on economics. Most post-graduate students in economics have encountered Popper's ideas in the digested form of Milton Friedman's 'Methodology of Positive Economics'.[6] Friedman argued that economics was an engine for scientific investigation, a way of finding things out, based on the use of assumptions to offer empirically testable predictions.

Friedman went far beyond what Popper might have countenanced. In Friedman's writing there is a sense not only that

inaccurate assumptions do not matter, so long as they offer falsi-
fiable predictions, but also that assumptions may even be
virtuous – in the sense of explaining well – *because* of their inac-
curacies.[7] The book you are holding now is full of inaccurate,
but useful, assumptions, which steer economics' investigations
wherever it goes. Gary Becker's economics of marriage, for
example, is made possible by the assumption that men and
women rationally calculate the future gains from a partnership.
In other words, economic models of marriage operate *as if* this
were the case. Sometimes this can go terribly wrong: in the
run-up to the financial crisis of 2008, investors used 'as if' models that left them unable to comprehend the crash, even after the
event. Nonetheless, the argument that inaccurate assumptions
are useful inventions has allowed economics to perform a neat
sleight of hand: to rid itself of the obligation to base its theories
on observation of the world around it and yet at the same time
to claim the utmost standards of scientific rigour.

Underpinning this line of thinking was another yet more
basic assumption, upon which all of their arguments, and indeed
all other scientific methods, rested: the idea that it is possible
simply to describe the world. At the same time, there appeared
another thinker, Ayer's great rival in Oxford, who showed us
that this is not the case.

John Austin was an austere man, cold and forbidding, who
resembled 'an inscrutable crane, bald-headed and angular', and
had been a strategist in military intelligence, working for Eisen-
hower during the war.[8] He liked to play Bach partitas on the
violin at home and 'tended to write and speak of Aristotle as
though he were an interesting but slightly exasperating colleague living on the next staircase'.[9] He would gather together
the brightest young Oxford philosophers for Saturday morning
salons where he would shred their papers or, if he admired them,

pay them the compliment of ignoring them altogether.[10] He was, therefore, a man thoroughly of his time, but at the same moment he was a visionary, original thinker, who opened the door to a new intellectual age.

In 1955 Austin delivered a lecture series at Harvard, and the lectures became a short book, *How to Do Things with Words*. Over the course of twelve lectures he carefully dismantled the notion of a neutral and dispassionate language. Words, as his title makes clear, *do*: they act and intervene in the world.

Austin began by making a simple distinction between two kinds of statement. He described most phrases, such as 'the shirt is blue', as 'constative'; we might call them descriptive. These statements can be true or false; they can be proven or disproven. He then highlighted another kind of statement, which he termed 'performative', which cannot be proven or disproven: a performative utterance changes the state of the world by the simple fact of being said. Examples include 'thank you', 'I declare you man and wife', 'I name this ship', or 'arise Sir so and so', or even 'the London interbank lending rate for today is . . .' Performative statements are often moments of passage, such as the florid Latin pronouncements of graduation ceremonies. As Austin pointed out, these phrases have a social setting, a set of necessary conditions for their 'felicitous' (Austin's word) execution. At the University of St Andrews, where I work, the Latin that confers a degree must be accompanied by a touch on the head from an ancient scholar's cap, and take place in a graduation ceremony, presided over by the dignitaries and faculty of the university and flanked by three ceremonial maces, each over five hundred years old and symbolizing the power of the institution. The Principal's introduction speaks of transition: in the ceremony scholars become masters, masters doctors, and doctors professors. These are classic, felicitous performatives.

But Austin did not stop there. In the second half of the book he zigzagged towards a much fuller understanding of performative (a word that he described as new, and ugly, but 'at least not profound'), arguing that *all* statements are to some extent performative. For example, a simple description, such as 'my shirt is thin', changes the world in several ways: the speaker of this statement *becomes* a person who says their shirt is thin (irrespective of whether it is or not); the world *becomes* a place in which a shirt has been said to be thin. Meanwhile, the 'true' meaning of the phrase may have nothing to do with the thinness of the shirt in question: if it is cold, the person who says their shirt is thin may, in fact, be *complaining*; if it is hot, they may be *reassuring* their companion that they are comfortable; the statement might, in fact, be a *request* for a new shirt; or it might be a *refusal* to give their shirt away; whether the statement can be proven or disproven misses the point entirely, because the statement is not an assertion of fact but an action, one that has everything to do with the context in which it is uttered and may have nothing to do with the thinness of the shirt.

By this account, any description has the power to change the relationships between people and to change the world around it in infinite ways, and a 'true' understanding of a description depends entirely on who makes it and in what context. Imagine the power of some very simple phrases: 'I admit I did it' or 'I am not your mother'. If spoken in jest or to a friend, their meaning is nothing like as potent as if they were spoken in a courtroom or to someone who believes themselves to be your child. Above all, once such things have been said, they can never be unsaid: the action that they perform can never be undone, however much the speaker may later deny having spoken the words or insist they were misunderstood. Austin's innovation has run and run, sparking fierce argument in literary theory and elsewhere. For example, the famous queer theorist Judith Butler has even argued that gender itself is a performative, a cluster of social practices and values held in place by language.[11]

Austin's claims are more than relevant to economics. In 1998 Michel Callon published *The Laws of the Markets*, in which he made the radical claim that economics produces its own world. He suggested that the thing that we call the economy, the creature that academics and pundits discuss and politicians tinker with, is a product of (or, as he puts it, is 'embedded in') economics. By the same token, economic man, the instrumentally rational solipsist of modern economic theory, is a creature bred, perhaps even engineered, in the laboratory of the economy: a repertoire of social competencies held together, or in Austin's language 'performed', by a technical vocabulary, economic rules and procedures, and the material architectures of the economic world.[12]

For a very simple example, let's return to my choice of whether to take the bus or the car. The language of economics frames my choices in terms of calculations of marginal utility and opportunity cost – what each mode of transport costs me in relation to what it provides. It brings a particular state of the world into being: one where I have become a person who considers the problem in these terms. The very language of price, of utility, of value for money changes both me and the nature of the problem; irrespective of whether 'price' and 'utility' correspond to reality, the concepts themselves are alive and at work through me. The world caves in as the rules and reasoning of economics fill it. Economics tells us where the boundaries of a decision should be set, what matters and what does not: in doing so, it sets those boundaries. It is the language of economic rationality that makes it possible to compare, on a single scale, Allie's high wages and the sacrifices that she must bear to pursue her calling.

Making facts in the favela

In the 1970s the post-modernist turn took hold of the staid discipline of 'history of science' and gave birth to the 'sociology of scientific knowledge'.[13] Thinkers such as David Bloor in Edinburgh took issue with the idea of science as a process of discovery, where facts linger invisible until they are illuminated by the torches of scientific investigation. Nothing could be further from the case, he argued: facts are made. How could we not have noticed for so long? Even the etymology of the word 'fact' bears this out, for it is derived from the Latin *facere*, 'to make'.[14] At the cutting edge of science, facts are carefully assembled in the giant detectors of particle accelerators, on the laboratory benches of genetics workshops; they are debated by communities of experts and eventually appear in print on the pages of prestigious journals.[15] The hallmark of an accepted fact is that we are no longer concerned with the circumstances of its production; it is free to travel through the science columns of newspapers, for example, into the wide world. It becomes a building block for future scientific experimentation, and does not need to be replicated or re-proven.

If facts are made, are 'socially constructed' as a sociologist might say, it surely follows that nothing is certain, and everything is politics. Only by recognizing that scientists are one group of experts among others, one particularly powerful special interest group, can we begin to unpick the excessive influence that science exerts. Science is pernicious, unelected politics, clad in a laboratory coat. At least, this is what the sociology of science told us.

Forty years on, and we can see that the relativist approach gives us problems. If scientific knowledge is judged purely by 'expertise', then other groups of 'experts', homeopathists, for example, can argue their case: who is to say your opinion is better than mine? Medicine replies, of course, by citing data, methods and instrumentation; by showing exactly the dedicated spadework of experiment and trial that has gone into building medical practice. Homeopathists have picked a bad fight: medicine is a grimy, empirical discipline that eschews high theory for daily, practical evidence. But what about climate change? Or not so many years ago, the arguments over tobacco and cancer? Here again we have sceptics and self-proclaimed experts inveighing against a body of empirical data; industrial lobbies and special interest groups with huge political muscle leaning into a fight over what can be classed as generally accepted scientific fact. Scientists have no alternative but to fall back on their evidence, their data and instrumentation, the burden of proof that they have accumulated day after day, year after year. They have no option but to make public and defend their techniques and explain their instruments. This after all is what democratic science is about. They have, in the words of Bruno Latour, to *pay the price* of their accumulated knowledge, of doing science.[16]

So what are the processes through which economics makes its facts? Let us now test its claims to scientific objectivity not by disputing the theory on which it is based, but by investigating, in the following example, its evidence, its data, its techniques and instruments.

In the years up to 2004 the World Bank supported a programme in Peru to grant formal property rights to those citizens who had moved to the cities and had set up residence as squatters in large, unauthorized and unregistered shanty towns.[17] The plan was put forward by Peruvian economist Hernando de Soto, and its aim was to stimulate bank lending, and thus economic activity, by giving would-be entrepreneurs a source of collateral against which they could borrow. This programme spoke to one of the most deeply held convictions of the neo-liberal creed: the assertion that property rights are an inviolate and necessary basis for economic growth. The programme failed in its stated objective, which was to stimulate bank lending. Bankers, human after all, were unwilling to take security on the only asset of poor families, and the collateral was all but worthless. So there was great surprise and jubilation when Erica Field, then a PhD student in the economics faculty of Princeton University and now a tenured associate professor at Harvard, spotted something unexpected in the data.

Field showed that the inhabitants of those houses who had been granted ownership of their homes worked longer hours, while their children worked less, and offered an explanation for this finding.[18] The hypothesis that she tested through her carefully constructed 'natural experiment' was that squatters without title needed to stay at home to defend their property from robbers or rival squatters. Adults were better defenders, and so children had to go to work. Following the grant of title, adults could work, leaving children free to attend school. Her research made immediate headlines, discussed, for example, by Alan Krueger in *The New York Times*, who wrote that 'hard evidence suggests there may be something to Mr de Soto's argument, although for reasons he did not anticipate'.[19]

Field's study is exemplary, a master-class in economic analysis. She has thought through and tested every conceivable variable. She marshals convincing evidence that the dwellers in the shanty towns spend time and resources protecting their property from (other) squatters, theft and even government eviction, and that this substantially damages their ability to work away from home. She shows that land titling programmes lead to an additional sixteen hours per week of labour supply, mostly attached to adult males, while hours worked by children decrease, especially in smaller families (although she cannot be certain of the mechanisms behind this change). The size of households is important, according to Field, because large families are likely to have someone at home all the time, while small families must consciously opt to leave a guard at home. She also shows that there is a substantial increase in investment and improvement in homes following the titling programme. The 'hard evidence' referred to by Alan Krueger is Field's careful collation of data from 2,750 households, surveyed in March 2000 at the end of the project.

So de Soto's reforms and Field's analysis seem to confirm one of the great axioms of modern economics, that property rights are a necessary basis for economic action. De Soto's claims were widely accepted. For example in 2006, even before Field's study was published, de Soto's claims were reproduced in the World Bank's 'Doing Business' document, which advocated property titles as a boon to entrepreneurial activity.[20]

Yet at the heart of Field's analysis is an assumption: that it is the grant of title that *causes* the change. But it seems highly unlikely that the central mechanism posited by Field actually would have any such effect. The titling programmes would not change the geography of the city, or the location of the dwellings, which are in dense urban slums where regular police forces fear to tread. If there are no police to guarantee the security even of legally owned property, why would an otherwise identical property suddenly become less vulnerable once legally owned? And if the property were lost, such ownership would not equip the residents with any further financial and economic resources to seek redress through courts of law. Even if an entire neighbourhood were granted title at the same time, so that no one had any need to squat another's property, the study's findings rely upon – assume – a conception of brigand shanty-towns that must be guarded day and night until, on the granting of land title, they become magically law-abiding.

Real life is more complicated, and Timothy Mitchell, professor of political theory at Columbia University and whose example this is, makes an effort to show how factors that led to the change in working patterns – such as gentrification of neighbourhoods and improvement in infrastructure – happened in geographical and temporal parallel with the titling programme.[21] In short, the bureaucrats worked first in the districts where they felt most safe, because they were *already* improving: increased labour market participation was not caused by the bureaucratic allocation of formal land titles; instead *both* phenomena were *effects* of the same underlying causes.

The important lesson from Mitchell's vignette is that economics represents a sophisticated and ongoing project of measurement, testing and analysis that is entirely self-referential. Field's assumption was deemed useful by economists, irrespective of its accuracy, because it allowed her to construct an innovative and interesting economic experiment. Here again is the difference between economics and the natural sciences: the hypotheses of natural science are built out of existing, experimentally validated, scientific knowledge, while the hypotheses of economics are extracted from the founding charter of that discipline: rational choice, individual agency and property rights. Natural science regards inaccurate assumptions as a problem – assuming a change in the structure of air, for example, might predict that aeroplanes can fly more efficiently, but it is not an assumption we would like to see tested. Natural science tries to make its assumptions more accurate; economics moves in the opposite direction. Like Tlön, the image of the world constructed by economics is seductive in its order and detail, 'a labyrinth forged by men, a labyrinth designed to be deciphered by men'. Thanks to de Soto's experiment, economists 'know' something more about the economic consequences of property rights than they previously did; for the rest of us, for non-economists, the conclusion drawn from Field's findings is, as Mitchell politely puts it, 'utterly implausible'.[22]

Well, so what? At this point the sceptical reader might ask: 'Economic theory may be self-referential, but how does that affect me? Surely this is just an academic dispute?' But, as Austin has begun to show us, what we know and how we talk begins to change who we are. Adam Smith may have said that mankind was distinguished by its ability to truck, barter and exchange, but modern self-interest is a complex, technical achievement that hinges on the making of fact and the role of scientific practice. We will now look at the specific processes by which this achievement comes to affect us all.

4. Making Economic Man

Karl Polanyi located the birth of *modern* self-interest in the philosophy of the Enlightenment and the industrial revolution, while Timothy Mitchell puts it in the latter part of the twentieth century. Both agree that it is linked in some way to the structure of the market economy in which it functions, and that it is central to the strange creature that is *Homo oeconomicus*. Oddly, economists themselves are ambivalent as to the existence of economic man: it is a sociological problem, far beyond their interest. A neoclassical economist, if pressed, would probably tell you that the economic agent is an imaginary figure, an implausible but useful assumption. Behavioural economists have dedicated their careers to proving that economic man can never exist on the grounds that humans are systematically unable to overcome our evolutionary, prehistoric ways of thinking.[1] But at the same time, economists do behave *as if Homo oeconomicus* did exist, and as Allie's escapades and Austin's insights suggest, economic theory has a habit of bringing its predictions and assumptions into being. Is it therefore possible to claim, as a first step in the argument, that an economics based on self-interest is likely to encourage self-interested behaviour?

Is self-interest learned?

There can be no better place to investigate this process than in a university, where economics students may be compared with those who study other subjects, a natural control group that has not been habituated into economic modes of thinking, at least not in any formal way. Naturally, there have been a number of studies on how 'economic' these two groups of young people are compared to one another. One such comprised a series of experiments concerning the 'free rider' problem.[2] Standard economic theory suggests that, where possible, individuals will 'free ride' in the provision of public goods. This means that, if they can, they will contribute less than they owe to collective endeavours but still take their full share of the benefits. Their experiments on student guinea-pigs who were not studying economics showed that individuals would happily contribute 40 to 45 per cent of their available 'funds' to collective endeavours. When the payback was to be in the form of a good that could only be enjoyed collectively – in this case a music system or a dorm party, but potentially a park, or a bridge, or fresh air – the students contributed 84 per cent of their resources, even though they would be unable to choose how the money would be spent. Then the experiments come to the graduate students in economics, who offered an average of 20 per cent of funds, less than half the contribution of their peers, even though they expected to enjoy the music or the party just as much as those who had paid up. Free riding does exist, it seems, but only among economics students. One parallel study inadvertently shows us how much we inhabit different personae in different settings: to elicit a meaningful yes, test setters reminded the students that they were supposed to answer as economists, writing: 'How do we want you to play? YOU WILL BE DOING US A FAVOUR IF YOU SIMPLY SET OUT TO MAXIMIZE YOUR WINNINGS' in the instructions.[3]

Another example is offered by the well-known game of prisoner's dilemma, in which two criminals, partners in crime, housed and interrogated separately, may decide to hold their silence or implicate their co-conspirator. Each is faced with the same possibilities: if both criminals hold their silence, they both receive a light sentence; if one holds silence while his partner implicates him, the silent party receives a heavy sentence and the informer walks free; and finally, if they both implicate each other they both suffer a moderate sentence. Logically, each prisoner should assume that their partner would betray them, and so they should do the same, as it is the least bad outcome irrespective of what the other player actually chooses. Game theorists call this least bad outcome the 'dominant strategy' and management theorists teach students that it is the safest way out of the dilemma of business competition.

In life, though, logic may not be the best guide, and instinctively most people recognize this: there has always been honour among thieves. In experiments there is a tendency for people to keep quiet. Unless they are economics students: an experiment, conducted in 1993 by Robert Frank and his colleagues, showed that economics students are more likely to defect than other students, and concluded that 'exposure to the self-interest model commonly used in economics alters the extent to which people behave in self-interested ways'. In other words, self-interest can be taught and learned. Economics students know that the *rational* thing to do is to betray one's co-conspirator, even though it is the action that potentially results in *everyone being worse off*. And self-interest slides naturally into stratagems and even dishonesty: another set of experiments, also conducted by Frank, showed that economics students were more likely to take kickbacks from a tradesman at the expense of their friends.[4]

What conclusions can we draw here? At the very least we can say that 'one effect of economics training is to strengthen belief in the pervasiveness, appropriateness, and desirability of self-interested behaviour, which, in turn, should lead to exhibiting more self-interested behaviour'.[5] We can rule out the native selfishness of economics students as well. Frank's experiments have shown that even economics undergraduates, who may be quite self-interested to start with, can learn to be more so. He examined a cohort of students, one half of whom were taught microeconomics by a game theorist (who, by definition, bases all theories on the motivation of self-interest) and the other by an expert on economic development in communist China. At the end of the course, those taught by the game theorist showed a higher level of self-interest than the other group.[6]

More generally, though, there seems to be an acquired view among economists that self-interest is the only motivating force in the whole world. In addition, self-interest is a powerful behavioural standard, increasingly seen as the right way to act, to the point where people will retell genuinely big-hearted actions as motivated by self-interest, or justify prejudice on the same basis: another study showed that white Americans who opposed mixed-race school buses cited reasons such as children's safety and property values even though they may not have been parents or property owners.[7]

All interesting, to be sure, but to my mind these experiments miss the point. Perhaps that is because they have been conducted by economists, who are rooted to a second axiom, the individual nature of decision-taking. Real-life economic decisions, on the other hand, are embedded in complex networks of calculation, hidden in everyday devices; they happen in the world, not the laboratory. Such entanglements are missing from these experiments on students which take place in carefully prepared laboratories where the rules are made clear in advance: you should think like an economist.

It makes more sense, then, to pursue a different line of reasoning: we should not ask whether self-interest can be learned, but whether economic man, a creature defined by calculative, rational self-interest, can be *made*. To discover this, we should pay attention to everyday, real-world decisions and examine the entanglements and instrumentation that makes them possible. We must explore how we are governed by economics.

Jeremy Bentham, prison planner

There are three things one should know about Jeremy Bentham, an English philosopher and social reformer who lived from 1748 until 1832.

The first is that he believed the pursuit of happiness was the only thing that mattered in human existence, and on this basis he established Utilitarianism, the doctrine of the greatest good for the greatest number. Bentham, it should be remembered, was not averse to a bit of misery among the working classes; we have met him already advocating hunger as the essential basis for the smooth and prosperous operation of society.

The second is that he left instructions for his body to be mummified, dressed and seated in a glass-fronted cabinet the size of a large wardrobe. His peculiar creation, called the 'auto icon', is now in the possession of University College London. Like many of Bentham's eccentric schemes, the auto icon was not an unmitigated success. Thomas Southwood Smith, a friend and disciple of Bentham who had been instructed to carry out the mummification, employed novel, home-embalming techniques, and eventually produced a head that was more tribal artefact than philosophical shrine. The unpleasantness of Bentham's tanned and wrinkled visage has not, however, prevented generations of students from trying to steal it, and his head is now kept separately under lock and key.

The third thing that everyone should know about Bentham is that he designed a prison, and called it the 'Panopticon'. The plans epitomized Bentham's ingenuity as a social reformer. It was a prison like no other. Gone were the dungeons of old, with their stench and filth and rats, the crowded, dark gaols of popular imagination. His prison was light, airy and clean. Most of all, it was efficient. The building was to be circular, with the cells arranged round the outside. Only the smallest of windows would let light in from beyond the building, but the cells would be open on the inside, facing into a circular courtyard. The prison was to be several storeys tall, so dozens of cells might look down onto the central court, like alcoves in the Colosseum, gated on the inside. In the middle of the courtyard there was a tower, occupied by guards.

Bentham's special innovation was that the windows in the tower would be large enough to allow the guards to see the prisoners at all times but small enough that the prisoners could not see the guards. The prisoners must therefore assume that the guards are watching them at all times, and behave well, thereby internalizing the work of prison surveillance. Bentham's objective, of course, was to make the guarding process as efficient as possible; suddenly just a handful of guards can watch many times that number of men. Bentham thought the panopticon design good for other uses, too: factories and workhouses, for example, or any institutional building that required oversight and a degree of coercion.

Bentham never saw his panopticon built, though the design has inspired many buildings. Perhaps the most famous is the Statesville Correctional Centre in Illinois, built in 1952. Here, inmates are confined in huge circular buildings, their cells opening into a void under a vaulted roof and skylight, held under the constant surveillance of guards in a central, searchlight-studded watchtower. But examples can equally be found in industrial settings: Henry Ford's River Rouge plant featured surveillance galleries strung over the shop floor, and in our post-industrial era workers can be subjected to constant surveillance through electronic means. The intention is always the same, a 'state of conscious and permanent visibility that assures the automatic functioning of power. So to arrange things that the surveillance is permanent in its effects, even if it is discontinuous in its action.' In other words, those under surveillance come to supervise themselves.[8]

These words belong to the radical French intellectual Michel Foucault, who identified the panopticon as a metaphor for industrial society. Foucault argued further that contemporary society comprised a 'carceral archipelago' ('carceral' being related to the word 'incarcerate'), a whole series of panopticons through which we become useful members of society, and during the last years of his life he came to see economics as one of the most important of them.

Foucault begins his famous work *Discipline and Punish* with a harrowing description of the public execution of Damiens the Regicide, in 1757. Having attempted to kill the king, Damiens was sentenced to be executed in a graphic, horrendous way – the flesh to be torn from his bones with pincers, a caustic mixture of sulphur and boiling wax to be poured on the wounds, his body to be torn apart by trains of horses and the remains burned to ashes. Foucault delights in telling us that this pantomime of death fails. The specially made pincers will not bite and tear, despite the exertions of the executioner, the horses, not used to this gruesome work, fail, and throughout it all poor, brave Damiens clings to life and suffers, until the crowd are all sympathetic to the criminal and enraged against the king. Then Foucault skips forward, barely eighty years, to find prisoners institutionalized in Paris, rising at five, working, eating and praying according to the timetable of the prison authorities. The prison's coercion of hardened criminals into this other mode of existence is less graphic, more insidious, more effective and, most of all, more efficient than the spectacular revenge meted upon the body of the criminal by torture and execution.

We can follow Foucault and see analogies between the shift from public, dramatic punishment to institutional regimes, and the move from the market economy of the nineteenth century to the total institution of twenty-first-century economics. Indeed, it is possible to trace the development of this economic panopticon across the twentieth century quite precisely. Its completion, perhaps, is manifested in the figure of Allie, a woman who has internalized the regime of economic govern-ance so fully that she has become an entrepreneur of her own body, running a 'business' in a 'crowded market', experimenting on the price elasticity of her own person, and establishing the best possible return on her most intimate assets. At the other end of the twentieth century stands Frederick Winslow Taylor, the inventor of 'scientific management'.[9]

Frederick Taylor and the science of management

Frederick Taylor came from a privileged background but dropped out of school before ever reaching Harvard. Instead, he took on a craft apprenticeship, and so, in the early twentieth century, came to be managing a machine shop. Taylor's career bloomed just as systematization of production was beginning to sweep through America: Henry Ford set up his own firm in 1901, and his huge River Rouge plant, the largest of its kind in the world, was begun in 1917. Taylor stayed loyal to his roots, and throughout his time on the shop floor he saw the world from the viewpoint of the factory owners. In particular, he was convinced that the workers were guilty of 'soldiering', taking their time over jobs and deliberately lowering production.

Taylor recognized that the best way to get 'a fair day's work' from his men was to split up and routinize their tasks as much as possible, depriving them of their only source of power. Once craft skill became the property of the factory owner, rather than the worker, the price of labour could be pushed down, the worker having nothing left to sell apart from his own brute effort. 'A fair day's work' becomes the battleground between workers and employers: for the former it is reasonable recompense for the discharge of their skills and expertise during the working day, while for the latter it is the maximum amount of value that an employer can extract from a worker on an ongoing basis. If a manufacturer buys an expensive machine, he will want it to run for as long as possible and as quickly as possible without breaking. So it is with workers under scientific management.

The problem Taylor faced was that the tasks in the machine shop were complicated, and the tacit knowledge of the craftsman covered a huge range of operations. One of the notable early successes of management 'science' therefore involved nothing more complicated than an analysis of lifting and carrying.

In 1899 Taylor arrived at the Bethlehem Steel Company, clipboard in hand, to find 80,000 tonnes of pig iron heaped in a field next to the works. Pig iron is the name for the raw ingots produced by the blast furnaces; it is made by pouring molten metal down a central gutter from which small gullies lead to moulds shaped in packed sand. The whole thing resembles a sow suckling her litter. At the end of the nineteenth century, war in Europe had driven iron prices up and the owners of the pig iron wished to unload their holdings. Each of these ingots weighed roughly forty-two kilograms, and they were to be moved by hand from the heaps into railway trucks shunted down sidings built into the field.

Taylor quickly determined that each man moved twelve and a half tons a day – by my calculation some three hundred pigs, heavy enough work already. He somehow calculated that a handler 'should' be moving some forty-eight tons daily, four times the amount, and that if the process were managed correctly the men would be 'happier and better contented' than they were at the old rate of twelve and a half tons. He studied the seventy-five men in the pig iron gang, and selected four who appeared up to the task. Of these four, he chose one, named Schmidt, 'a little Pennsylvania Dutchman who had been observed to trot back home for a mile or so after his work in the evening, about as fresh as it was when he came trotting down to work in the morning'. Schmidt had bought himself a small plot of ground and was building a little house in the morning before work and in the evening afterwards. And most important of all, for Taylor's ends, he was said to be keen on money: 'a penny looks about the size of a cartwheel to him', Taylor had been told.

I shall spare you Taylor's excruciating dialogue (Schmidt: 'Vell, I don't know vat you mean . . . Vas dot a high price man?') (I don't know what that means, either). Taylor persuades Schmidt to shift the full load for an increased daily wage ($1.85, from $1.15), and he tells him: 'You will do exactly as this man [the foreman?] tells you tomorrow, from morning to night. When he tells you to pick up the pig and walk you pick it up and you walk, and when he tells you to sit down and rest, you sit down.' Under this direction, says Taylor, Schmidt loaded the truck and never failed to do so during the following three years.

In subsequent years, efficiency experts followed Taylor's example and discovered many more labour-saving devices. Among the most famous of those who imitated and developed Taylor's ideas was Frank Gilbreth, a contractor and self-proclaimed time-and-motion expert. With a truly scientific lack of irony, he began his time-and-motion career at the New England Butt Company, where he used a novel 'micro-motion' device, comprising a cinematic camera and a chronograph, to increase output in brick-laying and weaving. He used the micro-motion techniques to out-objectify Taylor, and his wife Lillian wrote books promoting her husband as the next great thing in efficiency studies, a mantle he held on to despite the lack of any real, actual improvements in productivity.[10]

The great Marxist labour theorist Harry Braverman makes Taylor a linchpin in his account of the 'degradation of work in the twentieth century' (his book's subtitle): distilling labour into its most abstract essence and determining the maximum amount that can be extracted in a given time are the essential modes of labour relations under capital.

I would like to take the argument in another direction and draw attention to the changing relationship between incentives, discipline and labour. Taylor's endeavours are based on the assumption that his workers can be encouraged by the promise of an increased salary. And yet he tells us quite openly that he has to search through the seventy men to find one who is interested enough in the higher wages to take so greatly increased a burden. Schmidt, meanwhile, is supervised on an individual basis and taught the correct way to organize his movements. Power is very much external and expressed in the permanent antagonism between Taylor and his men.

Taylor and his followers instituted a new kind of management, one where calculative regimes, be they clipboards and timers or the modern equivalents of suggestion boxes and productivity analyses, enforce a particular mode of being upon the worker. But these devices are external, still, relying on the close supervision and control of bodily conduct. Power is visible, external and hierarchical. The next step in the construction of an economic panopticon, the process of rendering power relations fully automatic and continuous, must be to make the individual internalize their economic subjectivity. Economics must control their actions through the shaping of their calculations and assessment of value – through changing, in other words, what counts.

From hunter to broker: the fisherman's tale

I have borrowed the following example from the work of the Norwegian scholars Petter Holm and Kåre Nielsen.[11] It concerns the implementation of fishing quotas in Norway in the 1990s, and it is one of my favourite studies, a splendid bouillabaisse of fishy cooking metaphors and careful scholarship. It is a story of how man lost another part, as Polanyi might have said, of his savage endowment: of how the noble fisherman, hunter of the high seas became, well, something else altogether.

The background to the story is a collapse in reserves of cod in the late 1980s due to overfishing of the cod and of their prey. Economics has long identified the 'tragedy of the commons' as a particular market failure; resources held in common belong to nobody, and therefore nobody looks after them. The collapse of fish stocks in the oceans, a consequence of industrial fishing, is considered to be one such tragedy. The Norwegian government therefore decided that the best course of action would be to establish quotas. These could determine how much a particular fisherman is able to extract from the ocean. In practical terms a quota is a property right, and when quotas are issued a commons becomes private property; a non-quota holder cannot just sail up and cast his nets. Quotas were therefore very good news for the fishermen, who suddenly became property holders.

But as we have seen, property ownership implies certain obligations and disciplines the owner in a particular way. When Margaret Thatcher transferred the public housing stock into private hands she handed over state responsibilities of supervision, maintenance and even policing. The fishermen suddenly found themselves subject to a new form of surveillance and governed by a different set of rules. As Holm and Nielsen write, 'Twenty years ago . . . fish were common property. The fisherman was a kind of hunter. Today . . . fish, or at least fish quotas, have become *property*. The fishermen have turned into quota owners and property managers.'[12]

The construction of this particular panopticon was far from straightforward.

Establishing property rights is never easy, especially where the property in question is slippery, elusive and at large in the depths of the ocean. Property rights refer to concrete items, things that can be identified by law, and located on maps and on plans. If a resource is to be shared out, then we need to know how big it is, and where we can find it. There may be, as the saying goes, plenty more fish in the sea, but how many, exactly? Economics provided a way of finding out: a method called 'virtual population analysis', a complex model based on birth and mortality assumptions, as well as the very solid technologies of spotting and tracking. But even once they *did* know just how many fish there are in the sea, how were they to know how many of them should be caught each year? To make that decision administrators developed, on the basis of yet more marine biology, more modelling and more statistics, the idea of the 'total allowable catch', a centrally determined quantity that, according to the model, could be sustainably fished.

The first quota measures, introduced in 1989, were crude and set a tight allowable catch. Once this had been reached, fishing had to stop. The effects of the communal allowance were absolutely contrary to the intention of the planners, though, for it gave a great advantage to larger, stronger boats with better equipment, able to head further out to sea and to fish earlier in the year. The first come, first served system led to an arms race of boatbuilding, squeezing out smaller vessels. The administrators, who were bound to economic ideas, saw this as wasteful, with money being ploughed into unnecessary resources, never mind the social consequences. In 1991 they introduced individual quotas, parcelling the commons into individual packets and allowing individual fishermen to catch a given number of fish each.

The individual quota completely transformed the role of the fisherman. When one owns something, one can sell it or dispose of it, just as easily as one can maintain it. Why go out into the freezing, violent North Sea when one can sit in an armchair and sell the right to fish – sell one's property – to someone else? Fishermen with a bigger boat, who can fish more cheaply and in relative safety, are likely to pay a good price for your quota. They might well pay you more than you can earn yourself, because they can make more profit on it. Like the farmers and the plough, in a free market, resources (in this case quotas) should flow to those who can make best use of them.

Another technical problem made the prospect of selling a quota even more appealing for the small-scale fisherman. The fish-processing industry relied upon a minimum level of catch for its business to make sense, but even with the technologies available to modern fishermen, sometimes the real fish made themselves too scarce. Restricting the amount that individual fishermen could catch was likely to restrict the total amount of fish brought ashore and thus increase the risk of not meeting the minimum catch required. So the sum of the individual quotas was made larger than the total allowable catch, assuming that no boat would be able to bring in its full share. Bigger boats once more gained the advantage under the system, and became even more efficient and profitable.

The closing of the commons shook the fishing communities and the total marketization of quotas was bound to upset Norwegian voters, who valued the idea of brave, communal fishermen. In order to mitigate against this, quotas could only be sold when attached to boats, a provision necessary so that retiring fishermen could pass on their only assets. But soon a market in boats and quotas sprung up; the brave, communal fisherman existed by that time only in the mind of the Norwegian voter. The sale of quotas now seemed inevitable, and indeed, in 2003, when a formal market in quotas was once again proposed, the Fishermen's Association, now a group representing quota owners and property managers, was one of its biggest supporters.

What does this tale of technical innovation, economic engineering, overflowing and unintended consequences tell us? First of all, that ownership is the neo-liberal panacea. When scarce resources become subject to market rules, sensible, docile and productive economic men and women can be relied upon to manage them appropriately. But ownership does more than enforce good behaviour: it redefines the world it has entered. Once the quota system is in place, there is no escape, no outside. The commons are enclosed, and the fisherman is constituted as something else entirely. A whole way of life hinged upon open access to the fisheries; fishing those northern waters is a difficult, dangerous activity, and was supported by tight, coastal communities. There were clear careers for men, at least, who could join the boats as youngsters and work their way up until they eventually owned and captained their own. The Fishermen's Association, formed in the 1920s, embodied coastal village values built around open access to a shared commons. The imposition of fishing quotas left nothing of this society unchanged.

These quotas certainly can be described as a panopticon. The fisherman internalizes the laws of the market; he adopts market-specific values and behaves accordingly. He prefers to lower risk and maximize return. He becomes, through the careful implementation of another 'complex of mundane programs, calculations, techniques, apparatuses, documents and procedures', the rational, instrumental, self-centred economic man, and as he does so, the life, the community, the whole world that he inhabits is transformed.[13]

The closed world of the private investor

So fishermen become economic men rather than social men; quota managers in soft armchairs instead of fearless hunters in the harsh northern seas. Yet entrepreneurial as they are, we can find an example of a more insidious economization closer to home, in the strange, closed world of the private investor.

Margaret Thatcher did not only sell off housing stock. She also turned thousands of individuals into shareholders through a series of massive privatizations. The wave of deregulation that she brought in to break up the sleepy monopolies of the City, known at the time as the 'Big Bang' of October 1986, opened London up to the brashness of Wall Street. It also made it possible for the 'man in the street' to buy and sell shares. In a few short years, Thatcher created the private investor.

In the United Kingdom, privatization was fronted by the iconic 'Tell Sid' advertising campaign, a pre-social-media take on a viral advertising message: a postman is knocked off his bicycle by an Everyman character, fresh from the pub, who says, 'I'm glad you're here, this will interest you . . . these British Gas shares, they come out in November . . . If you see Sid, tell him.' The postman relays the message to an elderly lady, with the additional flourish, 'They're really easy to do . . . if you see Sid, tell him.' The name Sid was well chosen, with its connotations of lower-middle-class solidity, the same staunch Thatcher supporter who had bought his own home not so long before, and at the weekend polished his beloved Ford Sierra to a perfect shine.

Private investors have always puzzled people who know about finance. They don't seem to do very well in the market, systematically underperforming the various benchmarks. In all fairness, most professional investors underperform the benchmarks as well, but that is an aside: private investors get dismissed as dumb, or reckless, or worse. Habits such as overconfidence drive returns down (men are much worse offenders than women here, and it costs them an additional 1.4 per cent a year in lost revenues).[14] But they persist in investing. Why?

As a doctoral student I set out to explore this riddle, one of which I had some personal experience. I had worked briefly as a stocks and shares journalist during the Internet boom years and ensuing bust; I had ended up on the board of a small quoted company that specialized in providing information on other small companies. It also specialized in spending shareholders' money more quickly than it made profits, and I walked the plank after just a few months at the helm. Nonetheless, that period gave me an insight into the world of the private investor: not dumb, not stupid, possessed of a solid pot of capital that had usually been acquired through a successful career somewhere else. Yet they were still investing in small companies like the one I worked for and the others I knew; two-bit outfits where good ideas and dreams could rapidly sour to losses and disappointment in the cold reality of commerce.

So I spent time with a clipboard, I conducted interviews and hung round investor shows. I discovered – and I'm pleased to say that others doing similar research in the United States and Australia at the same time drew similar conclusions – that private investors live their investing lives in a panopticon-like, self-contained world that directs and manages their investing habits. The same techniques, artefacts and devices that make it possible for individuals to participate in stock markets configure them in a particular manner, for better, or for worse; what it is to be a 'private investor' is inseparable from the world that they inhabit.

Their story was nearly always the same. People became investors because they were fed up with the poor performance and fat fees of the 'so-called professionals'. They sought to take responsibility for their own financial destiny, pulling their savings and investments, sometimes even their pension pots, out of mutual funds and embarking on a journey of financial self-education. Their projects are a manifestation of Thatcher's enterprise culture, which, in the words of the eminent sociologist Nikolas Rose, 'links up a seductive ethics of the self, a powerful critique of contemporary institutional and political reality, and an apparently coherent design for the radical transformation of contemporary social arrangements'.[15] And so they venture to go it alone. Once the step has been taken, they are sustained by a pervasive narrative of 'us against them', of outsmarting the financiers with their 'hundreds and hundreds of highly paid investment analysts . . .'[16]

Learning to invest is no easy matter. Before embarking on a career in finance one is expected to go to business school and learn the basics of asset pricing and portfolio management, but no such arrangements exist for private investors. Instead, you must educate yourself by attending investment shows, reading magazines or books, browsing online and chatting to others in the same position. Investment websites are thriving communities of chatter where individuals can share ideas, discuss strategies, celebrate success or commiserate over failure; the relationships formed with electronic others often do more to sustain investment practice than the real-world attachments they build up in shows and seminars. In this way investors learn how the market works and how they should understand it, and at the same time they purchase mechanisms for making the market visible and tractable. They may be 'chartists' who chase Fibonacci numbers through the financial market, or 'fundamental' investors hunting down hidden value in the smaller company markets; in either case they pay fees, subscriptions and commissions, and in return have the burden of market calculation lifted from them, enabling them to participate in the market.

As one might expect, there is nothing extraordinary about the technologies of governance that surround private investors. Some of them purchase computer programs that will analyse investment opportunities or draw elaborate graphs of share price movements, while others subscribe to tip sheets and magazines. Still others visit shows and speak to the management of firms seeking investment. Nevertheless, these mundane technologies, programs and artefacts enforce very particular ways of behaving in the market. Calculation is embedded in each of these devices, and serves to configure the investor who uses them in a specific way. Subject to this technology of self-entrepreneurship, they become not just economic men and women, but specialized economic men and women, positioned to offer maximum advantage to their curators – not the investors themselves but the owners of the technology that they use.

For example, one investor, whom I shall call Terry, told me about the magic numbers that he believed shaped the seemingly random movements of prices:

> Fibonacci ratios exist everywhere, they exist in art, they exist in the human body. If you measure the distance from your shoulder to your ankles, and then you measure the distance of your arm you'll see that that is a Fibonacci ratio, I think it's about 1.618, or .618, or your arm is a ratio of your body.

How does one discover such a complex code among the noise of stock market prices? It is, of course, invisible to the naked eye and the investor who wishes to find Fibonacci ratios must spend plenty of real money in the course of his pursuit. When I spoke to him, Terry had already spent thousands of pounds on training CDs, charting software and attending courses, and had invested most of his spare time for nine months on testing out new methods, with the hope of becoming a full-time investor in the near future. When one method disappointed he simply moved on to another, claiming that his system was not yet quite perfect and ignoring the other equally plausible explanation: that there are no magic numbers in the stock market, or at least, none magic enough.

The institution that surrounds private investors is so total that they are unable to see beyond it. The promise of the self-reliant, entrepreneurial future hangs in front of them, and combines with the sense that it really is their responsibility to improve their lot, to provide for themselves in old age, to take charge of their destiny and shape it accordingly.

Another told me in all seriousness that while he invested successfully in dividend-paying multinational corporations on behalf of his mother and his sister, his own investment activities in smaller, high-risk companies had 'always been a disaster'. When I pushed him as to why he kept on with this investing he replied that if he *could* just erase emotion, if he *could* act rationally, then it *should* be a good way of making money.

Private investors are outgunned on all sides by sheer calculative power: trapped between the professional investors with huge reserves of capital and 'all those PhDs' on the one side, and the investment service firms who will charge fees whether they win or lose on the other. Why do they continue in the market? Mental accounting, such as separating gains and losses, for example, and simple self-deceit carry a fair share of blame. I often heard statements such as 'excluding the bad ones, I did quite well', or 'the professionals had manipulated the market', or 'the very day I was intending to take profits, it collapsed'. More pernicious, though, was an underlying sense that the golden egg lay just round the corner, that success was only a few tweaks to the system or minor adjustments to strategy away, that it was the investor's fault for getting emotional, or attached to a share. The possibility of riches and success, or the idea of working on a laptop from a poolside at your tropical retreat, is strong enough to blind investors to the grinding reality of financial loss. The more exotic the product, the higher the risk, the stronger this motif of eventual breakthrough and escape became. Only in one instance did I hear an investor express any doubt in the *possibility* of making money from one particular branch of investment activity. And so, he told me as he sipped thoughtfully on his beer, he was becoming a chartist instead.

Interviewing people can be difficult. The dispassionate social scientist is not allowed to interfere, even when the pleasant man you are talking to tells you he is moving his pension fund into a spread-betting portfolio. And if I had rebuked him, he would probably have replied that professional fund managers had eaten up so much of his money already, he would rather lose the rest himself. I would have struggled to answer that. Private investors find themselves in a panopticon much more insidious than that of the fishermen; their aspirations, energies and personal savings tied into a system in which it seems they lose whichever way they try. There are some decent firms in the investment service sector, and I've worked for one of them, but no amount of decency can diminish the fact that there is a huge structural problem: individuals, failed by mainstream finance, are forced to fend for themselves in an unfriendly market where they become the prey of those very same financial institutions. Moreover, this arrangement is offered to us as part of a social settlement where we are expected to consider ourselves liberated and empowered in making arrangements for our own old age.

What do lifting pig iron, managing quotas and chasing value in small company stocks have in common? In all three cases there are unintended, painful consequences. Taylor showed generations of managers how to squeeze more value from labour, yet was shocked to see his higher-output workers treated like any other industrial commodity. In Norway, a well-intentioned policy move to preserve fish stocks ended up industrializing and economizing the fishermen, erasing a figure central to the Norwegian national identity. In the case of investors, the attempt to liberate oneself from the clutches of big finance, to take responsibility for one's future and to improve one's lot through intelligence and effort is likely to lead to a difficult and uncertain future.

The more important point, however, is that each case sees the nature of self-interested economic governance change. From the clipboard and stopwatch supervision of Taylor's men, linked directly to extra money at the end of the day, it becomes subtle, self-directed, and finally aspirational. Where Taylor presumes, against a career full of evidence to the contrary, that additional money equates to additional work and enforces his belief through explicit mechanisms of external surveillance, the other examples need no such coercion. Fishermen, redefining what matters – re-engineering administrative systems so that ownership and return on expenditure are the most salient factors in the decision over how to act – is enough to transform an occupation based upon the community and solidarity in the face of physical hardship and economic risk to a solitary, armchair pursuit of returns on capital. And in the case of retail investors, self-interest is recast as an obligation, one that promises and compels, even while it disadvantages those individuals.

These examples show that self-interest can be built. The governance of economics brings into being a series of closed institutions – panopticons – which discipline our daily behaviour. And within this panoptic archipelago, *Homo oeconomicus*, the rational, calculative, clinically self-interested economic individual, is brought into being. As we internalize the rules and expectations of economic governance – that, for example, we ourselves and no one else are responsible for the provision of our future wealth – so we become the very creature upon which economic theory is based.

But it is not enough to claim that economic man is the result of language alone, or of a dramatic politics internalized and enacted in our daily lives. We could not all be economic without the help of the everyday world around us. While grand structures such as work, politics and finance have contributed to the construction of the economic individual, much of the labour is done elsewhere, by the everyday devices and instruments without which we could not navigate the world. These material artefacts enact *Homo oeconomicus* in our daily lives, in shopping, learning, healing and loving. Let's now examine them at work.

PART TWO

5. Economics in the Wild

Let me return to a now familiar example and ask an elementary question: how is it possible to claim that the bus is more expensive than the car? The cost of the bus is straightforward enough: it is the cost of the ticket, charged in hard cash. The cost of the car is more complex, and I will need to do some maths. The tank of fuel costs such and such, and I get so many miles to the tank, or thereabouts, and the round trip to work is so many miles. A little arithmetic and I have my number. I could be more precise in my calculations if I wished; perhaps there is a little computer in the dashboard that will do the work for me. Meanwhile, I know that the tank of fuel costs such and such because there is a price per litre displayed at the filling station, and the pump measures the amount I put into my tank, and charges me accordingly. I can trust the pump because it has been tested by a qualified official according to prescribed weights and volumes. The instruments in my car are also calibrated by standard measures. There are road signs marked with distances, or I can consult a map, or a digital route planner. If I look at the map the scale requires a mathematical conversion, but Google or my satellite navigation system will do the job for me in a moment.

Even in this simple example, it is clear that such calculation goes right the way down, forming an endless regress where the only escape, eventually, is to trust someone else's judgement, expertise, or calculative skill. As systems become more complicated, we can do less of the calculating for ourselves. My grandfather, a physics don with a penchant for cataloguing, used to note down miles and petrol stops in a little notebook he kept in the glove compartment, working out his fuel consumption longhand. Now it is a matter of making a few checks on the dashboard display.

This may seem like a good thing. Less time scribbling in note-books means more time to do other, more pleasurable things. But, as Foucault never tired of reminding us, knowledge is power, even – especially – in its smallest and most tedious manifestations. Calculation is a form of knowledge, and becomes therefore a conduit for the exercise of power. It is the root of the panoptic archipelago discussed in the last chapter. It was calculation that enabled Taylor to drive craft out of the workplace: he may have begun with time-and-motion studies of lifting and loading but by the end of his career he had managed to systematize the lathe worker's craft. It took him twenty-six years, during the course of which he cut his way through eight hundred thousand pounds of iron, in fifty thousand tests, but he managed all the same. By 1906 machinists used his 'slide rule' rather than their own judgement. Still more complex calculation supports the transformation of Norwegian fishing: computation of fish reserves, of birth and mortality rates, of an acceptable return on capital. It is not the fishermen who calculate but the bureaucrats, and these equations embody and transmit their power over the populace. In the case of the private investor, the necessity of buying in much of the calculation required to invest places them at a permanent disadvantage to those who provide it.

Calculation is power

The sharing of calculation is all but inevitable. We manage to exist in a technologically advanced society only through the distribution of calculation to others; increasing complexity requires more delegation, and places us ever more in the hands of those to whom we give over our calculative efforts.

The phrase 'distributed calculation' was coined by the American naval scientist Ed Hutchins, in his fine book *Cognition in the Wild*.[1] He uses the example of a warship navigating tricky waters to show how complicated cognitive tasks can be broken up into simple stages, using specialized instruments and coordinated by systems and rules. On the boat, no one knows the whole picture. Below deck, sailors take readings of depth using a Fathometer, while elsewhere they record speed. High on sighting platforms others take bearings from landmarks on port and starboard sides. These readings are fed to the map room – and Hutchins is at pains that we should understand just how much calculative work is already buried in the maps themselves – where the location of the ship is plotted and sent upwards to the bridge. The whole process is coordinated by the Navy procedures set out in a thick handbook, and strengthened through repeated exercises, until a difficult calculative task is made robust enough to be continued accurately even in the heat of battle, even if individual crew members are lost.

The same thing happens in everyday life. The simplest choice, whether to catch the bus or the car, is only possible within the calculative infrastructure that is provided by economics. Economics 'in the wild' is a set of technical practices of measuring and calculating, embedded in and distributed among the artefacts and devices that surround us all the time: tickets, coinage, petrol pumps and mileage counts, signs and maps, multiplication and division. Economic man is a hybrid of all these, employing specific networks of artefacts for specific tasks, whose rational calculation is made possible through a constellation of instruments, measuring devices and calculators. Devices become, as Michel Callon puts it, 'prostheses' for economic action; in the sociology of markets we have adopted another word, 'agencement', to describe this constellation of humans and devices. It is a useful word because it reminds us that devices have agency: they *act*.[2]

Yet these 'agencements' rapidly become invisible. The example of the bus shows how quickly the hard work of calculation disappears into the background. Unlike the warship, where operational procedures are rehearsed through constant drills and practices – deliberately kept visible – the calculation that supports everyday life is hidden from us. Every technical innovation shuts away a procedure that might otherwise have been done longhand. Map, notebook and mental arithmetic segue into the dashboard computer. We can now do more. It becomes possible to devote much more attention to the fuel efficiency of one's car: my dashboard computer is much easier than my grandfather's longhand calculation. We begin to take the production of a fact – for that is what our fuel consumption figure is – for granted. We lose sight of how it is made and start to make use of it, even if it is only to support a bar-stool argument about the respective merits of various motor cars.

Another example is provided by our local supermarket, where we come up against calculative power that far outstrips our own: the wire shopping trolley. It is part carrier, but also part calculator, capable of exploiting our cognitive weaknesses. Supermarkets have long been mindful of the problem that careful shoppers may stop selecting goods before their budget is entirely spent, if only to avoid embarrassment at the checkout. The easily visualized volume of the trolley's basket offers a rule of thumb measure of expenditure, turns a difficult piece of mental arithmetic into a quick estimate, and deploys calculation to the shop's advantage, allowing customers to carry on loading up the products.[3]

Supermarkets are engaged in constant competition, and of late, with customers' purses tightened by recession, the battle for business is focused even more on price. Shops compare prices with their rivals, focusing their cuts on whatever their chosen customers perceive as important − white bread, frozen prawns or luxury orange juice − and claiming that they save each time they visit the store. But shoppers can never be expected to process cost comparisons across every good in the supermarket. That would be too onerous for the customer and risky for the store; if the shop handed its customers the numbers it would be handing power back to them, and running the risk that shoppers might come to undesirable conclusions.

So we receive single pre-processed facts, such as a till receipt that shows a notional saving of £2.78, or a percentage figure flashed across the television screen during an advertisement. These facts tell us something about how we *should* shop. If one shop is cheaper than its rival, then we should shop there, in the cheapest supermarket. We should be indifferent to all other factors, such as location, taste or social demographic. If these campaigns are successful, and their longevity implies that they are, it is because they have managed to insist upon the primacy of economic logic as a means of directing shopping choices. A hidden, distributed infrastructure of calculation transforms us into a different kind of shopper, one who focuses on price above all else.

As we wander up and down the aisles, our movement directed by the architecture of the shop, our attention is captured by the carefully coordinated offerings of products on the shelves. Labels and signs lead us around the store, and steer our assessment of products, easing comparison between rival goods. The labelling systems of supermarkets advance an inexorable economic logic, showing the price and weight or volume of the good, and facilitating comparisons not just across different versions of the same product, but of different goods entirely by translating that into a price per kilogram or similar. In the supermarket, we really can compare apples and oranges, as the price label is ruthless in its analysis.

A Marxist would urge shoppers to look past the artefact and see the labour relations embedded in it. These bananas do not really exist: they are the essence of exploited labour, taking the shape of a commodity. For many, that vanishing act is a step too far, and the bananas remain solid on the shelf. But try the same trick with a label and it works. By showing *only* the price of the goods being sold, the label can effectively purge every other factor from our decision, even if we know full well that the price saving offered in the supermarket is paid for elsewhere, in intensive farming, intensive labour, or exploitative working conditions.[4] It is the *label* that renders us blind to the circumstances of a commodity's production. It frames our decision, guiding us as to what matters and what does not.

This is why campaigners for better conditions for workers or for livestock, or for healthier food, recognize the battle for labelling as so important. As a counterfactual, try the trick of the label again, in reverse: this shirt was stitched by a woman in bonded labour. Her name is Runa, and she earns £7.95 a month. This phone was made by a man who took his own life: soiled goods, 25 per cent off. A 'Fair Trade' designation on packaging brings the subject of labour conditions back into the theatre of the supermarket, and a 'free range', or 'organic' label does the same for livestock and even arable crops. But it does so in a controlled manner in keeping with the economic nature of supermarket activity. Dealing with indentured labour and the products of sweatshops is no longer a matter of moral outrage – thou shalt not buy this shirt – but a fine, graduated consumer choice. Supermarkets offer established hierarchies of labelling where improvements in the quality of husbandry, or of a living wage, are reflected in increasing prices and consumers are free to establish the cost of their own conscience. In the supermarket, even moral virtue has an economic dynamic.

The supermarket is a theatre of economic activity, and in the theatre we must perform as an economic actor should. Vague worries over distant, uncertain labour conditions and mass production are pushed aside when we are faced with the immediate economic concerns articulated by the labels. There are rules to the ballet of a supermarket, as the French sociologist Franck Cochoy has observed; our interactions are with the shelves, the labels and the goods, not with one another, nor indeed with those who grew, reared, or stitched the products. It is, to borrow his metaphor, a garden of economic choice, tended by careful plantsmen and women.[5]

As I noted in the case of my bus ride to work, the economist sees externalities as market *failures*, places where the market cannot reach. Pollution, noise, exploited labour and intensive production – all of these would go away if the market were able to incorporate them fully in the cost of decisions – in other words, if we were to realize, fully comprehend and pay for the costs we impose on others by our actions. The example of the supermarket suggests otherwise: that the removal of the need to recognize, understand and pay for such costs is a triumph of the market. We must not be reminded of these costs, lest bad feeling get in the way of our spending. In this sense, turning something back into an externality is a useful result. Creating commodities, making them calculable and commensurate, turning everyday folk into calculative, rational agents – this is hard work. It is an organizational and technical achievement, a great success, not a failure. The supermarket frames the decisions that we take, and in doing so manages to exclude – to externalize – so many vital factors. And how is this done? By metrics, measurement and qualification, all crammed into a tiny, simple device: the label.

We can now recognize economics in the wild: planning, accounting, consulting, auditing and measuring.[6] We become economic, not through an act of deliberate choice, but through the systematic use of ordinary, everyday material devices: the very things that help us navigate the world.

Small but mighty: the FICO® Score

Reshaping an entire industry, purging it of social ties, emotion and affect, and repopulating it with economic men and women is a decades-long project. The transformation in our under-standing of houses – from places to live into investments; from a home into an asset – has taken roughly three decades. This would not have been possible without a radical restructuring in the provision of mortgages and insurance. When a person of my parents' generation wanted a mortgage, they went to see the bank manager. An important person in a small town, the bank manager had personal relationships with his clients and oversaw their current accounts. In my father's words, the bank manager 'knew what you were good for'. The old-fashioned bank man-ager had but one mandate: not to lose the bank's money. His job was to lend at interest, but carefully; he was obsessed with secur-ity almost as if the money was his own. In a manner of speaking it was, for he was lending out his savings and those of his neighbours.

In this, he had traditional economics on his side as well as common sense. Established banking theory tells us that lenders will do better to refuse risky loans than to offer them at higher interest rates, and that banking markets do not naturally 'clear', which means that supply does not match demand. For much of free-market economics, a 'non-clearing market' is a terrible problem, but banks have lived happily with it for many years. Banking is not a risk-sharing venture. A bank charging a few per cent interest every year can never afford to lose the capital of the loan itself (the 'principal') and will stay away from risky lending, even if the rates that could be charged are higher.[7]

Lending is what the Nobel Prize-winning economist George Akerlov called 'a market for lemons'. Buyers who cannot judge the quality of goods on offer will protect themselves by offering low prices, driving away the better-quality sellers, so that only the 'lemons' (the duff goods) will be left.[8] In order to stay in business, good-quality sellers can protect themselves with guarantees, develop brands and reputations, or build social relationships with their clients. In banking, where borrowers are the sellers and bank managers are the ill-informed buyers, the job of the bank manager was to assemble as much information as he could, and to entangle economic relationships with social ones. He would shake his borrowers' hands and look into their eyes, go to their cocktail parties and the weddings of their children, working to construct as much social scaffolding around the relationship as he possibly could. That way, the bank got its money back, for it is hard to default on social as well as financial obligations. Old-fashioned banking was a low-risk, low-return business, but done carefully and on a big enough scale it was a profitable endeavour.

Jump forward thirty years to my recent credit-card application. I visited an online comparison site to track down the best interest-free deal, clicked through to the provider's website, filled in my name and address, my annual income and some other peripheral details, and pressed send. Less than a minute later I had been accepted for a card with a credit limit of eleven and a half thousand pounds sterling at an annual interest rate of nearly 20 per cent. Low risk, low return this is not. Something profound has happened to banking.

Behind this dramatic change lies a shift in the way that credit applications are processed and in the kind of information banks consider important. The lender is no longer concerned with the individual circumstances of borrowers; the credit-card company does not know me personally, nor understand what I am 'good for'. What the credit-card company does know is the statistical likelihood that I will pay the money back. It has access to credit scores and population-level lending data, and employs an algorithm to make a decision on this basis. It no longer *avoids* risk on an individual basis but *manages* it across the population. The fundamental understanding of risk in lending has changed, and the story of this transition is not one of high politics but of technical ingenuity and entrepreneurship.

In 1956 two former military scientists set up a firm in San Raphael, California. These men were trained in the new discipline of operations research, where the power of algorithms and data analysis had been put to work solving the tricky computational problems that war had thrown up, such as aiming bombs and automating anti-aircraft gunnery. (It was complex stuff, and after the war, operations research laid the groundwork for modern computational economics and game theory.)[9] Shaped by their discipline, these men were committed to delivering practical solutions in which scientific method was built into functioning hardware. Their names were William R. Fair and Earl J. Isaac, and the company they founded was called Fair, Isaac & Company Inc. Today that firm is called FICO, is listed on the New York Stock Exchange with a capitalization of one and a half billion dollars, and supplies an essential part of the apparatus of American economic life: the FICO® Score.

The history of Fair, Isaac & Co. has been beautifully documented by the sociologist Martha Poon.[10] In its early days, the company built credit scoring systems for retailers in small-town rural America, offering its clients a chance to improve their business in the new area of mass-market consumer credit. Just as today, point-of-sale equipment needed to be straightforward, usable by clerks with no calculator and no statistical knowledge, so any system had to be built into the hardware with the difficult mathematics 'distributed' back to Fair, Isaac & Co. The firm developed a bespoke system for each client, using the existing records that its shops had accumulated. When the system had been delivered, the clerk would ask the applicant set questions provided by Fair, Isaac & Co., score the applicant's answers according to predetermined tables and add the scores up to arrive at a 'yes' or 'no'. Retailers could now see the probability of default compared with the existing client base: a little extra knowledge that allowed the stores *either* to increase their volumes at the same level of default *or* reduce defaults at the existing sales levels.

Poon is keen that we understand the physical nature of the credit scoring. This was not rarefied financial engineering in Wall Street skyscrapers. Young analysts, no matter how highly qualified, served time in the field hauling files from dingy rooms in remote shopping malls, photographing the records and sending them back to the firm's headquarters in California for coding and analysis. There, a team of housewives working in their homes converted the handwritten records into punch cards for analysis and the Fair, Isaac & Co. computers produced a final algorithm for the client. It really was economics 'in the wild'. Rarefied problems of sample selection and analytical focus were sorted out among the dusty cabinets, analysts making up the rules of this new research discipline as they went along, and the coding required care, skill and judgement as the messy data were corralled into a regular format.

Fair, Isaac & Co. soon moved on from the dusty graft of small-scale credit scoring. In the 1980s, firms in the booming but competitive credit-card industry wanted access to individual scores that would help them to sort out and stratify their market. Mass mailshots were common, but lenders could only then disqualify or accept applicants on the basis of whether they met a generic list of requirements. Far better for the lender to be able to calculate risk in a fine-grained manner, charging more interest where the likelihood of default was higher; a credit market that would 'clear' in this way would allow the lenders as much profit as possible. Suddenly, this was no longer a market for lemons, as buyers (lenders) could differentiate between good and bad sellers (borrowers). Risk could be managed and priced. So Fair, Isaac & Co. went to work to build a credit score on the basis of data collected by credit bureaus – the large firms such as Equifax that we know today – which maintained substantial records of missed payments and court hearings, together with information on regular payments but did not at the time offer a statistical analysis of this information. The new scoring system, known as PreScore, allowed for the pre-screening of mailshots and, as Poon points out, turned credit control into a marketing function. Lenders could suddenly see the universe of people who were statistically likely to keep up repayments on the cards and target them directly.

Yet Fair, Isaac & Co. was still making scoring systems. Its master stroke was a move, in the early 1990s, to a single numerical *score* for individuals, to sell data rather than technology. With a maximum value of 850, the FICO® Score is a continually updated, floating, consumer credit score. It expresses the creditworthiness of an individual as a single number: a fact. And as facts tend to do, it has travelled. It shook off the memories of its parturition – of dusty filing cabinets, of rural America, of hard-working young statisticians with their microfilm cameras, of economics in the wild – and moved on. In politics and high finance, where it made its new home, it became the basis for a sea change in lending activity.

On 11 July 1995 the giant government-backed mortgage lender Freddie Mac adopted 660 on the FICO® scale as its threshold for lending. A score of 660 therefore marks the lower limit of 'prime', and everything below that bar is described by a term that we now know all too well: 'sub-prime'. From 1995 the score worked exactly the same magic that Fair, Isaac & Co.'s scores had done in the credit-card market, making visible a whole new raft of consumers who could be targeted by lenders prepared to take on more risk for more return. There have always been bad borrowers, especially in times of house price inflation, but credit scoring made it possible for lenders to know exactly how bad they were, and efficiently target them at higher interest rates. Being a credit risk no longer meant being *excluded* from credit, but *paying more* for a scarce resource: a credit score imposes the laws of supply and demand, and risk and return upon an unwilling market.

When the credit crisis broke in 2007 we quickly learned that a central cause of the collapse was high levels of default among sub-prime mortgages. Of course, the other reason lenders were happy to target high-risk customers aggressively was because they were no longer lending their own money; in another set of extraordinary innovations mortgage risk was sold on to others, and the FICO® Score became one of the central devices in co-ordinating flows of risk and capital around the globe.

Policymakers and Wall Street engineers may have treated the FICO® Score as a useful fact. But for most people the credit score looks more like an asset, and FICO itself has been quick to see the revenue potential from this application. A visit to myfico.com, the firm's consumer facing website, allows US residents to discover their credit score and offers advice on how to manage it.[11] The incentives for doing so are both financial and practical. According to the website, a one hundred point difference in an individual's score could save $40,000 in repayments over the life of a $300,000 mortgage. I am told that young people wanting to rent an apartment need a healthy FICO® Score to get a foot through the door. Each year I ask the American students in my class if they know about the Score, and most do; to build a healthy rating, some of the wealthier youngsters have been given credit cards and have, from their early teens, carefully spent and regularly repaid the balance. A person's FICO®

Score is a personal attribute, something to be worked on and built up, a financial version of a university education or a washboard stomach.

The growth of credit scores exemplifies the move from lending as embedded in personal relationships to lending as an exercise in statistical risk management. The tools of economics, inscribed into technical devices as primitive as the paper scorecards of store clerks in rural America, or as sophisticated as the algorithms that lie behind the FICO® Score, have slowly severed the social bonds that served to stabilize the mortgage market in prior years. The growth of credit scoring was initially championed by governments pursuing left-of-centre economic policies of social inclusion. The bank manager and the store lending clerk were perceived as being too intimidating, and too exclusive. Relationships between bankers and clients were smothering, and the subservience to the small town peacock in the bank chafed. A bank manager's decisions could be erratic, based on physical factors, whether a customer came over as 'shifty', 'evasive', 'argumentative', of 'seedy appearance', or 'flashy'. He would sniff out the moral fibre of prospective borrowers and inquire as to the purpose of the loan, always on the lookout for domestic difficulties and extravagant spouses.[12] It was thought that financial inclusivity and opportunity could be better served by the objectivity of social science and that two birds might be killed with one stone: the problem of 'information asymmetry' that has bedevilled lenders from the earliest days (simply put, borrowers know much more about their ability to pay than do lenders) could be solved by statistical analysis and at the same time lending could be made available to everyone.

There are some problems with the credit scoring approach. Its dynamic response to recent activities makes for occasional collateral damage: an outbreak of loan delinquency among forty-year-old academics who buy their groceries online and my next credit-card application is out of the window. More important were changes in industry structure that followed, of necessity, the redefinition of the nature of risk. In British retail banking, the 1980s saw the traditional values of 'sobriety, convention, long and faithful service and skill in judicious lending' replaced by an emphasis on marketing, on selling, on customer service and quality.[13] The bank manager, where he still exists, has become a salesman. (As often as not, he is now a she: female employees, considered to have better powers of persuasion, have moved front-of-house.) Managers are subjected to competitive, target-driven employment policies. Banks, competing to increase shareholder returns through aggressive cost cutting, have closed underperforming branches and outsourced customer-facing roles to call centres abroad. The rise of 'objective' credit scores, instantly available, reliable and cheap, has been matched by the transformation of banking into a profit-focused sales industry. As one senior banker told me, banks simply could not make enough money by lending alone; not enough, anyway, to satisfy hungry shareholders and guarantee executive bonuses.

As ever, imposing targets and competitive reward structures make real the kind of employee that they presuppose, and the risk-averse credit manager is replaced by the sharp-selling hustler whose primary concern is to secure an annual bonus. The evidence for this in the banking industry is a wave of weighty settlements for mis-selling of financial products, investment schemes, payment protection insurance and, most recently, exotic derivative-based loan insurance that has cost small business millions.[14] It is more than culture that is amiss in banking. We have witnessed the complete reshaping of an industry along the lines envisaged by textbook economic theory, and at the heart of this transformation are the technical devices and material artefacts that hold together not only the industry, but also the people around it: the policymakers, central banks, ratings firms, depositors, borrowers and shareholders.

It is ironic and unfortunate that credit scoring turns out to be much less inclusive than its supporters had hoped. Credit scores rely on records of regular salary payments and existing credit obligations. Affluent and financially aware individuals, with good financial discipline, can instantly gain access to credit. Those who are off the grid, on the other hand, who have never been steadily employed and who lack a history of credit repayments are permanently excluded from participation in the new financial Utopia. The situation is compounded by the fact that the branches closed by the banks over the last thirty years – the less profitable branches – tend to be those in disadvantaged areas, exactly where the support of banks is most needed, and where the discretion of an insightful bank manager – a real person prepared to take a decision on the basis of a subjective assessment of character or intention – could have transformational effects.

A loan made by a careful individual to a well-selected borrower, even without a credit history, need not be higher risk than a statistically determined credit-card loan. Just look at the high levels of repayment among micro-finance projects; social relationships, as any good business person knows, cement positive behaviour and personal responsibility, encouraging individuals to pursue courses of action that may transcend self-interest in the short term. The global financial crisis and ensuing destruction of capital was not brought on by a few wonky loans to small businesses. Perhaps the instantaneous, depersonalized issuance of credit creates the very conditions that encourage default. Loans that are selected as commodities, through online comparison sites and application forms, or sold by unscrupulous intermediaries for their own short-term benefit carry no obligation beyond the legal claims that enforce them, and these have little value in a collapsing market. The 2005–6 housing market collapse in the United States showed the world what happens when financial obligations turn out to be supported by nothing more than paper. Wholesale default, with keys returned to lenders in the post, became normal.

In other countries, such as the United Kingdom, borrowers are not legally permitted to escape their debts in this way and must cling on, hopelessly indebted and struggling to make repayments on a property that is worth a fraction of the outstanding loan. In Ireland, those who bought properties in partially completed developments at the top of the bubble have seen developers walk away leaving them with little or no basic services, sanitation, drainage or street lighting. Denied a legal escape, Irish citizens struggle to support the vast debts of banks that are considered 'too big to fail' – another unabashed economic calculation – maintaining a bizarre, upside-down socialism where the poor must pay the price and bankers and bond holders find themselves comfortably protected. As we have all discovered, the rationality formed in the mould of online calculators, best deals, credit ratings, and an incessant short-termism of come-on prices, remortgages and refinancings is no basis on which to build a prosperous society.

Lists, rankings and the commodification of education

One could argue that the credit crisis was a freak event, an outlier. That is just what the banking industry did, of course, as it wriggled on the hook of the worst financial mishaps in decades. But there does not always need to be a calamity to make us uncomfortable. Let's turn to the case of higher education. In the last two decades, higher education in the United Kingdom has become increasingly market-driven. Universities have been transformed into a specialized service industry and a national corporate export. This reform has taken place under successive governments, but has reached a zenith under the stewardship of David Willetts, minister for universities and a leading intellectual in the Conservative party. Willetts's neo-liberal sympathies are clear – he is, for example, a member of the neo-liberal think-tank the Institute for Fiscal Studies – and he has pursued a progressive programme to introduce a market in higher education. Taking his cue from the Browne Review, commissioned by the previous Labour government and published in 2010, Willetts has greatly increased – trebled, in fact – the allowable tuition fees paid by students in England and Wales. Fees are just one part of a broader repackaging of education as some kind of saleable good where students are recast as customers. The following is typical Willettspeak:

> We have therefore increased choice and flexibility. We have also transformed the amount of information that is available for prospective students, which we believe will drive up standards in universities as prospective students think about what contact hours they will have, what the class sizes will be, how universities score on the national students survey and, crucially, how universities score on employment outcomes for graduates.[15]

Willetts's argument is clear: making students into consumers will somehow make universities *better*. If students have to pay fees the market will spontaneously arise, as universities compete with one another for 'customers'. Access to higher education will be determined by individuals' own assessment of their talent and possibilities, expressed in the willingness to borrow and pay fees; all that matters will be the eventual combinatory effect of intellect and degree quality on the student's earning power. Degree quality will be signalled by visible indicators of quality, such as school rankings, and (importantly) lower-quality institutions will charge lower fees. In other words, the market for higher education will come to resemble one envisaged in the opening pages of an economics textbook.

A market arrangement demands that the benefits of education are seen in the same way: the student, a person responsible for the management of his or her economic career, receives the bulk of future benefits, and so should bear the costs while seeking to maximize returns. We can trace these ideas to the predicates of neo-liberalism in general, and particularly to the Chicago School of Economics, where they find a formal statement in the work of Gary Becker. During his early career, Becker developed a theory of human capital, and analysed the individual-level returns on the investment of public funds in education. His figures rapidly became a benchmark that policymakers used to determine the effectiveness of education spending, helping to institutionalize and reinforce a myopic understanding of the point and purpose of education.[16]

This axiom of higher-education planning is self-evidently false. We all benefit from good teachers, nurses, civil servants, research scientists, chaplains, bureaucrats, administrators, town planners, sports coaches and so forth, all of whom have received a university education and many of whom will be hard pressed to recoup the fees and living costs that they have incurred. Moreover, students are already facing substantial opportunity costs: costs of time, of missed wages, even of missed unemployment benefits. It is an aside, but forcing students to take on a huge financial commitment for an education pushes them towards the few areas where they can, they think, be sure of making enough money to repay their debts, such as banking and law. The resulting surplus of bankers and lawyers means that many will be underemployed and, more importantly, all our talent will be in the wrong place.[17]

Better information is a central plank of market-driven reforms, allowing students to make improved, 'more rational' decisions.

A presentation given by the Institute of Fiscal Studies had this to say about 'information problems' in the higher-education market: 'To make *rational* decisions, individuals must be perfectly informed about: the nature of product (university quality, HE experience); prices (fees, living costs and lost earnings); and future (earnings and debt repayments).'[18]

Rationality is important, because, once the first step has been taken, once we have agreed that students educate themselves to increase their own capital and derive higher future earnings, then it is clear that the fee-paying student should seek out the highest return on those fees. The student, a young person struggling to map out a future, needs to become cool and calculative in choice of subject and institution, and, as the IFS points out, rationality can't happen without information.

Fortunately, students can make use of the paraphernalia of rankings, scores and quality measures that surround the contemporary university to assess the future returns on investment of both money and time, not to mention forgone earnings. Rankings distribute the effort of this enormous calculation – the work of comparing the many qualities of many institutions against one another – across expert groups and established metrics, assembling the potential student as a dispassionate, rational hybrid, an economic chooser of educational pay-off against cost.

But this is not all that rankings do. They are powerful creatures, and at the same time as they assess, university rankings tell students how institutions *should be* assessed. The American sociologists Wendy Espeland and Michael Sauder have shown that law schools in the United States have actually become more like the ideal institution on which the rankings are based.[19] As rankings become increasingly important in student decisions, faculty administrators will deploy resources and funding in such a way as to improve the ranking. The more rankings pull in other stakeholders, the more powerful they become.

Employers, for example, are likely to be convinced by the prestige of an institution, often seen in terms of rankings, and some career pathways really do close to students who fail to get into the upper echelons of the educational establishment. Telephone-number salaries paid to those in prominent positions in the financial industry, or corporate law, for example, attract floods of young talent, and as Robert Frank and Philip Cook note, the doors are already closed for those who have not been undergraduates at elite institutions. Frank mentions a student from a small Florida college, with a straight-A transcript and described in references as the best student her professors had ever taught, rejected by Harvard's graduate economics programme. Successful applicants also had straight-As and glowing references, but came from schools such as Stanford and Princeton. As he puts it, university administrators are 'forced to play the odds, which tell us clearly that the best students from the best schools are better, on average, than the best students from lesser schools'.[20]

Employers' decisions feed back into the figures for the increase in salaries provided by a particular degree, and strengthen the ranking still further. Institutions, aware of the relationship between rankings and applications, pressure faculty to produce work that fits an appropriate disciplinary mould and publish that work in outlets ranked high in discipline-specific lists. Institutional expenditure on research is expected to be manifest in a steady stream of publications, and academic achievement is likely to be accounted for in terms of concrete measures such as the 'h-index' (a citation score indicating how many publications cited and how often, and one means of indicating academic worth: an h-index of 10 means ten publications each cited at least ten times) rather than in the vague terms of reputation. Citation indexes and journal rankings make visible certain aspects of scholarly activity, and thus shape hiring decisions, reorganizing the labour market for academics.

None of this is expected to devalue, or even change, the central task of the university: education. How can that be the case? If one of the leading rankings of universities incorporated the score for, say, neon signage – an absurd example – campuses would resemble Las Vegas within weeks. This process does not just happen in universities: city rankings, for example, have tremendous influence over the decisions of town planners.[21] If administrators are worrying about signage (perhaps not neon, but branding does seem to matter to those at the top) or visible architecture and facilities, then there is a real danger, especially in institutions where funds are short and institutional positioning is precarious, that these things will draw money from less visible – less immediately accountable – purposes, such as teaching and teaching support. Moreover, administrators will come to understand their role as focused on improving rankings, rather than dealing with the central issues around learning and pedagogy. For example the National Student Survey in the UK consistently reports that students are dissatisfied with the length of time it takes to get feedback; a possible solution would be a heavy reliance on automated multiple-choice tests, where feedback is instantaneous. Could we really consider that to be a pedagogic improvement, even if it is what students *want*?[22]

Beyond the ubiquitous student experience surveys – and that 'student experience' carries a subtle repositioning of education as some kind of experiential commodity, like a safari or an adventure day in a hot-air balloon – universities are subjected to all kinds of other assessment. Accreditation by professional bodies, driven by a desire to offer students more workplace-relevant qualifications, places demands on institutions and may reshape their curricula and hiring strategies. Subjected to constant surveillance in research and teaching, faculty will play safe, offering conservative scholarship and low-risk traditional teaching. And who can blame them, with their jobs on the line if they fail to deliver good publications and systematically reach high teaching feedback scores? Where academic labour is reduced to the attainment of ranked publications *and nothing more*, it is inevitable that those academics prepared to play the game will abandon long-term attachments and circulate in the market, moving from institution to institution in pursuit of higher salaries. The losers, of course, are their students.

The same transformation that has overtaken many corporations has begun to reshape the academic career. The American tenure track system, where young academics must hit certain targets to secure a permanent post, increasingly resembles the 'rank and yank' system, where employees openly compete for preferment and to avoid dismissal, prevalent at the sharp end of the private sector, though perhaps without the commensurate financial rewards. We know that incentive systems, just like institutional rankings, will bring into being the kind of employees that they imagine: if the only way to survive in the tenure system is to combine technical excellence with an avoidance of risk and, perhaps, a willingness to strategically manipulate one's partners in research to one's own advantage, then these are the characteristics that will appear. Individuals who survive the private sector's 'rank and yank' may be exactly the kind of hard-nosed, savvy strategists that a corporation demands, but they may not improve a profession that is fundamentally based upon trust, empathy and pastoral competence, that is for many a calling as much as a career.

A market system also reshapes the priorities of students. When students are recast as customers they start acting like customers. But often they do not see that there are different kinds of customers; that buying a tin of beans from the supermarket is a profoundly different transaction from embarking upon a process of education that requires them to participate to the limits of their ability, imagination and emotional reserve. Of course, the tin of beans model is much easier, and many students prefer it. There is a resistance to understanding education as a process that involves reflection, trust, empathy and risk. Instead, many students see education as a set of targets, of boxes to tick, of work carried out at a particular level that will result in a qualification of a certain kind, where the student has simply to consume and regurgitate pre-digested chunks of knowledge. Students will choose modules that they perceive as easy, in order to get higher grades, which are worth more in the purely external sense of better employment offers and better salaries. Learning becomes about memorizing and reproducing, while the higher-order pedagogic goals of synthesizing, critiquing and evaluating – skills that we really need our young people to have, that are more useful and more worthwhile to the students themselves in any context beyond the shortest of short term – are pushed to one side.

As students take on more and more debt they become risk averse in their learning and their choices; in the twenty-first century, debt serves the same purpose as hunger did in the nineteenth, taming the fiercest student, teaching docility and civility to the most obstinate and perverse. In such a system, opportunities for developing as a thoughtful, reflective and self-aware individual are missed and education exists in the most limited form. The guiding principle of student satisfaction turns out satisfied students, yet a satisfied student is impossible to teach. We should aim instead for dissatisfied students, unsettled by what they have learned and driven to a critical examination of their preconceptions.[23]

Finally, a market in education will do what markets always do: allow benefits to flow from the weaker to the stronger sellers, from less affluent to more affluent buyers. Institutions at the top of league tables can strengthen their position further, and as the most elite institutions increase their prestige so young people with more resources – not of ability, as supposed, but of capital, education and class – will claim more of the benefits. Like individuals, universities are under pressure to generate returns from their activities. One avenue for doing so is the construction of a supportive alumni network, and this might even come to influence entry to an institution, determined by the possible future contribution to an alumni dividend. Such a tendency will militate against broader access and shore up the entry prospects of those already advantaged by wealthy backgrounds.[24] Rather than opening up access, commodified education seems only to widen inequality.

The commodification of university education has many consequences. Not least of these is the reduction of a social good, rich in intrinsic worth, an essential part of the apparatus of human flourishing, to an instrumental, short-term lever for personal advancement. This extraordinary, momentous transformation, a chasm rent in the post-war social contract, is held together by a most simple device: the list.

In the economic world, scale refuses to stay in place. Tiny numbers have huge effects. Credit scores can transform an industry, and institutional rankings shake up a sector. Yet some economic devices, hardly larger, wield the power of life and death. When economic analysis, embedded in cost–benefit ratios and efficiency tests, begins to dictate how we should protect and care for one another, we might pause to wonder just how much sovereignty we are prepared to surrender to these equations. We might even ask if there is a point beyond which we no longer wish to be economic men and women. In the next chapter we will see how economic analysis allows us to set one life against another, how it puts a price on life, the most priceless thing of all.

6. The Price of a Life

In W. W. Jacobs's classic story *The Monkey's Paw*, a sergeant-major returns from India with tales of dark magic, carrying in his pocket a shrivelled monkey's paw. He tells the ageing, avaricious Mr White that it will grant three people three wishes, but at a cost, for fate rules people's lives and those who interfere with it do so 'to their sorrow'. Later that night, Mr White wishes for £200 to clear his mortgage and the money soon arrives – as compensation for his son Herbert's fatal accident at work. The power of the story flows from the juxtaposition of £200 (perhaps £20,000 in today's money) and the pricelessness of Herbert's life; the paw is evil in its willingness to reduce the beloved Herbert to a mortgage repayment. So you may be surprised to hear that in the USA in 1973, the Federal administration officially valued life, not at £20,000, but at $200,000.

How much is life worth?

In early 1972, or perhaps in the tail of 1971, an ordinary American family purchased a Ford Pinto. The car suffered from a faulty carburettor, and was prone to flooding and sudden engine failure. On 28 May 1972, Lilly Gray set off in the six-month-old Pinto to Anaheim, taking her thirteen-year-old son Richard Grimshaw. She was on the way to meet her husband, but she never arrived. On that day the car chose to stall in the central lane of the freeway, coasting to a halt in heavy traffic. The vehicle immediately behind the Pinto avoided it, but the next, a heavy 1962 Ford Galaxie, slammed into the stationary car, crushing it and pushing the rear axle up against the fuel tank. Protruding bolts on the differential housing punctured the tank and the force of the impact sprayed fuel into the passenger compartment. As the Pinto crumpled up it exploded, and the passengers were severely burned even before it had come to a halt; by the time they escaped from the car, their clothes had been burned to nothing. A few days later Mrs Gray died from heart failure, while the young Grimshaw was severely disfigured, losing fingers, part of his left ear and much of the skin on his face.[1]

Grimshaw and Mrs Gray's family took legal action against Ford, alleging that the car was fundamentally unsafe. In 1978 Grimshaw was awarded $2.5 million in compensation and a further $125 million in punitive damages, later reduced to $3.5 million. The judge commented that 'Ford's institutional mentality was shown to be one of callous indifference to public safety'.[2] The court decided that Ford had been aware of the hazard and had chosen not to introduce a relatively cheap production fix; in other words that they had somehow compared human life and profits, and preferred the latter. Court documents list the possible options: reinforcing pieces at $2.40 and $1.80; $4 for a protective suit around the tank; a double tank placed over the axle at $5.79; a bladder in the tank at $8; placing the tank above the axle with a protective barrier at $9.95; a smooth differential housing at a cost of $2.10; a protective shield at $2.35; a bumper reinforcement at $2.60; eight inches of crush space at $6.40. Ford fitted none of the above, and the story has grown to be a legend of corporate immorality, trotted out to business ethics students: corporations prefer money to saving people's lives.

The legend needs a bit of debunking. At the time of the crash, the Ford Pinto had only just come onto the market, having been rushed to production in two years, roughly half the usual time.

Lee Iacocca, Ford's chief executive at the time, had been personally responsible for a project to introduce a car that could compete with the new, small foreign imports that were proving popular as oil prices suddenly soared, and the Pinto was his response: designed to weigh less than 2,000 pounds and cost less than $2,000. Margins were very slim. All the same, it does not seem to be the case that Ford deliberately ignored the possibility of fuel-fed fires. The firm's chief engineer, who had lost his own father in a Ford fuel explosion, was convinced that it would be dangerous to locate the fuel tank anywhere nearer the passenger area of the car. Engineers and regulators had not fully got to grips with the new crash tests and doubted that throwing a car backwards into a wall at thirty miles an hour reflected a real-life situation, so were not disturbed by the high failure rates. The rush to production, with factories being set up before design had been completed, meant that the basic design of the car was locked at an early stage. Most importantly, Ford engineers and managers saw small cars as inherently unsafe, with lightweight metals and innovative methods of construction, so understood the fire risk, not as a defect or problem, but as an unavoidable consequence of the car's small size. Complex organizational cultures and competing divisions added a final layer of uncertainty; marketers, for example, had learned that 'safety doesn't sell' following a previous disastrous attempt to make safety the centrepiece of a marketing campaign.[3]

Dennis Gioia, then an idealistic young man who worked as recall coordinator for Ford during the period, has written a sharp and self-aware account of the case. Reports of Pintos 'lighting up' (as the sales force put it) after low-speed collisions 'trickled in' but failed to cause alarm. Gioia was sufficiently shocked by the sight of one Pinto carcass in the accident salvage depot – known by workers as the 'Chamber of Horrors' – to instigate a recall meeting. But the reports of occasional, if terrible, conflagrations did not fit the pattern of incidents that necessitated recall. The panel, including Gioia, voted against recall, not once, but twice; according to firm protocol, recall cases needed high-frequency and traceable causes. Again, organizational divisions hindered information flow. For some reason the recall department did not know about pre-production crash test data which suggested that there may have been a more systematic problem with the design of the car, and the engineers had bigger problems, such as the absence of safety glass in the entire Ford fleet. During this whole period Gioia drove a Pinto, and sold it to his sister.[4]

The eventual recall, the largest in automobile history, came in 1978 only after an exposé by the journalist Mark Dowie – 'Pinto Madness' – which followed the enormous damages in Grimshaw's case, and another accident in 1978. The second accident resulted in the death of three teenage girls after their Pinto, pulled over at the side of the road, was struck by a van travelling at fifty-five miles an hour with a rigid plank in place as a bumper. The driver of the van, who was thrown out of the vehicle and died in hospital, was probably unfit to drive: police found beer bottles, caffeine pills and marijuana in the wreckage. Despite the van driver's obvious culpability, state prosecutors decided to pursue Ford for reckless homicide – the first time that a corporation had been prosecuted for a criminal offence – a decision which led to a high-profile trial, and ultimately a media circus. Ford employed the Watergate prosecutor James Neill as counsel for the defence, and was eventually acquitted.

So far, this looks like a case of organizational failure rather than a pathological focus on profitability. What was it that so infuriated the journalist Dowie? He alleged that the car was uniquely dangerous, that decision-makers had been aware of the car's problems, and that executives and engineers focused on cost rather than risk. Dowie included something else: a smoking gun in the form of a memo circulated at Ford that, he alleged, directly compared the costs and benefits of re-engineering the Pinto. Its central calculation ran roughly as follows:

Costs: $137,000,000
(estimated as the cost of production fix to all similarly designed cars and trucks with the gas tank rear of the axle: 12.5 million vehicles times $11 per vehicle)

Versus:

Benefits: $49,530,000
(estimated savings from preventing: 180 projected deaths times $200,000 per death; 180 projected burn injuries times $67,000 per injury; 2100 burned cars times $700 per car)[5]

This trade-off concluded the now infamous 'Grush/Saunby report', written in 1973 by two Ford engineers. A cost–benefit analysis, it appears to say that it would be cheaper for Ford to pay damages than fix the Pinto. The company, according to the myth that has grown up in business ethics classes and popular culture, chose the cheapest route: profits over safety.

We can only make sense of the Grush/Saunby argument within the intellectual tradition of neo-liberal economics. Remember that competition is the essential mechanism through which the market achieves the best allocation of goods. Through the invisible hand, the economy translates private vice into public virtue, self-interest into the common good. It follows that in order to maximize the common good, one must pursue private self-interest with as much vigour as possible. Milton Friedman had this in mind when he wrote in a *New York Times* article of 1970 that the only social responsibility of business was to compete as fiercely and as openly as possible. If you follow this line of argument, diverting resources to other activities is at best unelected taxation, and at worst theft.[6]

Friedman articulated the business climate of the time, and the automotive industry was doing as he suggested, competing with vigour against a flood of foreign imports. Grush and Saunby argued along the same lines: that the cost of modifying every single car and light truck on the road would far outweigh the benefits of the modification. The general economic pie, shared by everyone, would be lessened by such a move, in the same way that other restrictions on free trade, such as tariffs, shrink the total economic welfare available.

By this logic, as the economist Ronald Coase demonstrated, the cost of fixing social problems should be borne by the party who can do so most cheaply, on the basis that the less that is spent, the more *everyone* benefits. Coase's rule does not take into account any considerations of blame or justice: only the total saved matters, not the distribution of costs and benefits, so in the eyes of the cost–benefit analyst it is better that a few bear a high cost and many make small savings, even if the cost is being burned alive.

Yet, the designers of the Pinto never saw the Grush/Saunby report.[7] It was written three years after the first Pintos went into production, and did not deal specifically with the petrol tank on these cars, but addressed a proposal by the regulators for the installation of a valve in *all* cars and light trucks that would prevent fuel spillage in the case of the vehicle *rolling over*. It was written by two scenario planners – two 'eggheads' in another unit of the firm – as part of an intellectual engagement with the regulators over what the industry saw as a wasteful regulation.

It is safe to say that Ford engineers and executives had no desire to see customers killed or injured. Even Harley Copp, the Ford engineer who supervised crash tests and became star witness for the prosecution, never claimed this much. It is more likely that organizational failures and industry preconceptions prevented executives from seeing the full extent of the danger and a fix was never made. By this account, it is a problem of organizational blindness, or at least myopia. In hindsight, Dennis Gioia bitterly regretted not ordering a recall; the true proponents of a cost–benefit solution can never allow themselves such a sentiment.

It was later discovered that the Pinto case was not an isolated incident. In his excellent book *The Corporation*, Canadian legal scholar Joel Bakan tells the story of Patricia Anderson versus General Motors.[8] It follows what is by now a depressingly familiar pattern. Anderson was driving home from midnight Mass, on Christmas Day 1993, with her four young children in the back of her ageing Chevrolet Malibu. The car was struck by another vehicle, driven by a drunk, and burst into flames. As in the Pinto accidents, the family were horribly burned. When Anderson took legal action against General Motors it transpired that in the early 1970s the firm had been aware of problems associated with fuel-fed fires; the fuel tank in these vehicles was closer to the rear bumper than the firm's own internal directive suggested, and a protective metal brace had been removed from that year's model. In 1973 Edward C. Ivey, a General Motors engineer, had been asked to analyse this problem. He calculated that, with a total of five hundred fatalities due to fire, each costing $200,000 in damages, spread across the 41 million vehicles in service, the cost of damages equated to $2.40 per vehicle. The cost of prevention, on the other hand, would be $8.59 per vehicle, and the company chose to leave the design as it stood. Once again, the jury took exception to the calculative association of human life and economic cost and awarded punitive damages of nearly $5 billion, reduced to $1.2 billion in a later settlement.

In *The Monkey's Paw*, Morris – the sergeant major – told Mr White that the things he had wished for happened so naturally that one could, if one so wished, attribute them to coincidence.

But the characters in the story are not allowed to believe in chance, and neither may we. In the same year, in the strategy departments of the two leviathans of the American automotive industry, two reports were written, each pursuing the same logic, and each using the same number as a value for human life. At the heart of the Grush/Saunby memo, and Edward Ivey's calculation also, is a single figure: $200,000.

It is no coincidence. The figure of $200,000 was suggested by the National Highway Traffic Safety Association as appropriate for calculating the cost to society of each and any death. This cost was derived on the basis of lost future earnings, the loss of a productive member of society. In 1990, the NHTSA used a figure of $1.5 million, updated but based on the same assumptions: medical costs, lost earnings and damage to property.[9] While a person may be priceless, risk prevention is not, and in the face of so many conflicting demands regulators rely on cost–benefit to determine the usefulness of potential changes. The regulators are subject to judicial rulings that require 'objective' assessment of safety benefits, but industry will complain that excessive regulation makes it uncompetitive and shareholders will bewail lost profits, so the regulators are also placed under political pressure to justify the cost effectiveness of any requirements – hence the Grush/Saunby report.

The cost–benefit calculation shows us two things, then: that economics demands that we put a price on everything, even human life, in order to think about it; and that, if the analysis is to be a real decision-making tool, there must necessarily be the possibility that, having seen the costs – the 180 deaths, the 180 disfigurements, the 2,100 ruined cars – we might *still* accept them. We must equate a human life to $200,000, and we must then contemplate the possibility that this is an unaffordable amount.

The rational buyer of risk

Whenever we get behind the wheel of a car, whenever we pick up a kitchen knife or a garden tool, whenever we go to work in a factory, on an oil platform or down a mine, we take risks. Even the idealistic young Gioia was aware that in getting behind the wheel people took on *some* degree of risk. We can pay money to lower those risks: we can buy a more expensive car with lots of safety features, hire a man to take down the tree in the garden rather than wielding our own chainsaw, or settle for work that is less well paid but less dirty or dangerous. Alternatively, we can insist that the makers of cars and garden tools, factory and mine owners spend their own money in order to protect us. Either way, the avoidance of risk is a cost, and by accepting risk ourselves we are free to spend more on other things: driving a car with fewer safety features, or cutting down our own trees, may allow us to enjoy a better holiday, or a more substantial dinner.

For this reason, neo-liberal economics finds fault with a calculation along the lines of the NHTSA's $200,000, representing costs of an accident *to society*. Such a measure is not *individual* enough. Nor is it objective enough: it has been criticized for being a product of accounting, crafted by a government official. Neo-liberal economics analyses us as consumers, and it is no different here. We are rational buyers and sellers of our own safety; no one is better placed to judge our own demands for safety than ourselves. The better way, surely, of analysing risk is to discover how we price it ourselves, to uncover the price of risk as a natural, objective, fact.[10]

Economists have therefore developed a measure known as the 'value of statistical life', or VSL. It is possible to use data from activities which involve or avoid quantifiable levels of risk to estimate the cash value that individuals put on safety, to calculate how much we will pay to avoid risk or demand to confront it. So, for example, wages for work that involves a certain amount of risk can be compared with similar work that contains none: the premium that a painter working on a suspension bridge or an oil platform earns over the person who paints fences and railings gives an indication of how much money we need to take on risk. Consumer goods can be analysed to see the value placed on safety features in vehicles or appliances. From this it is possible to ascertain the rate at which a population will exchange wealth for small increases in survival probability. If I am prepared to pay £1,000 to avoid a single fatality risk of 0.0001 per cent, then my VSL is £10 million.[11] Inevitably, there is much controversy over the exact way of calculating these figures, but in the United States a figure of just under $7 million is used in policy decisions, while in the United Kingdom it is a paltry £1 million.

Using these numbers, manufacturers, employers and operators of utilities and transport networks can determine the level at which they need to implement safety devices. If a modification to a factory might save half a life during the period of its operation, it must be cheaper than £500,000 in the UK or $3.5 million in the US to be installed.[12] To put that another way: the owners of the plant need only act if the cost of safety improvements is less than the benefit, understood in terms of our own individual, albeit unwitting, willingness to pay for safety.

In *The Monkey's Paw*, a company representative comes to tell the Whites that Herbert has suffered a terrible accident, crushed in the machinery. The firm wished him to convey their deepest sympathies to the bereaved parents, that Maw and Meggins admit no liability at all, but to present a certain sum as compensation: the £200, of course, that Mr White wished for the previous night. As the distraught old man examines his son's mangled body – recognizable only by the clothes – he might be cheered to reflect that at those prices Maw and Meggins could compensate several more such deaths before they need contemplate expensive improvements.

An economist might argue that we are irrational in the way that we perceive risk and direct resources, wasting money that should be better spent elsewhere, and so imposing real costs on others by our choices. As the philosopher Jonathan Wolff notes, rail safety improvements often cost far more than £1 million for every life saved, as railways are relatively safe and improvements are expensive. On the roads, a similar expenditure might save many more people. In airports, increased safety procedures are likely to send travellers to their cars, indirectly leading to many more fatalities. Exploding cars and train crashes are high-profile, vivid events and we think them much more likely than they actually are. The starkest statement of this argument comes in the case of global warming, where some economists have provocatively argued that money would be better spent on infrastructure projects to offset the effects of global warming in the developing world than attempting to turn the tide of rising temperatures at vast expense and with uncertain outcomes. In each case the underlying argument is the same: we need economists to help us figure out what to do. We need cost–benefit analysis and the VSL in order to help us make better decisions. But these arguments miss a vital point.

When it comes to managing risk, cost–benefit analysis, applied through techniques of increasing sophistication, appears to tell us what we ought to do. It does not. Social contribution-based measures, such as the NHTSA's price-of-life figure, can only tell us what we should do if we have already decided that what matters most is maximizing a nation's wealth. Modelling risk as a consumption activity is to claim that our preferences over how much risk we accept in one part of our lives can be used to judge the obligation of others towards us. Yet someone might economize on a car, for example, because she is underpaid and has a family to feed: is it right that those who are richer and more powerful than her, be they employers or the transport company that delivers her to work, may find their obligations lightened by her decision?

In 1994 I went to work as a building labourer. Revising for my student exams I had watched the scaffolders working in the sunshine and decided that manual labour would be a suitable antidote to a long season hunched in the library. Once I had packed up my studies for the summer, I scanned the small ads in the London *Evening Standard*, and found a request for new hands in Harrow, not too far from home: the applicant should bring his own boots, but gloves and helmet would be supplied. I called the number listed on the advertisement and reported the next Monday, with a dozen or so others, to a red-faced foreman who scowled down from the steps of his Portakabin in the warm July sunshine.

So it was that I found myself part of a demolition team, cutting down a large concrete building from the inside out. It was arduous work. At times, five of us stood in a line, wielding pneumatic hammers. These were heavy pieces of steel, each comprising a tube the size of a large rolling pin with a floating chisel at the front and an air powered piston inside. They rattled in your hands, and made your fingers swell so that you struggled to close a fist. After an hour or so of use, the hammers would get hot enough to scorch our heavy gauntlets. One lad, working shirtless in the heat, touched the steel to his stomach and burned away five inches of skin. He said nothing and came to work the next morning all the same, the huge blister covered with a makeshift dressing. The pressurized air that powered the hammers escaped through nozzles near the bit and blasted the desiccating, bitter-lime concrete dust back at our flimsy masks and goggles; the compressors clattering behind us filled the building with the stench of diesel fumes. Occasionally a hose would burst with a colossal bang, like a giant party balloon rupturing, and we would have to pause while new hoses were hauled in and connected. And the noise, my God, the noise: you could hear, no, you could feel, the rattling of the hammers in your sleep. Once we had demolished a wall, we had to shovel it into wheelbarrows and empty it into huge skips, tonne after tonne. On the first day, a couple of new recruits asked an old hand when would be time for the afternoon tea break. He looked at us balefully, and spat: 'There is no fuckin' tea break.'

It was dirty, dangerous and unpleasant work, and all of us knew it; there was no irrational risk-blindness at work on that site. In my first week, I narrowly avoided a falling wall. The foreman, a giant, cheerful, Italian-cockney named Jimmy, shouted for me to get out of the way. He said afterwards that he had thought it was going to be another 'everyone 'ome early day'. A chunk of masonry landed on Jimmy a few days later, about a dozen bricks, enough to finish a normal mortal. It had been clinging to the ceiling as he took down a wall, and as he leaned forward after a heavy hammer blow it came down squarely between his shoulders; he shrugged it off, but I think it hurt him all the same. During our short breaks we lay on the grass in the sun, and as we chatted I learned that everyone knew of some fatality or other. The story that stuck in my mind was that of the poor soul who fell down an open lift shaft in a half-completed tower block. He managed to clutch the edge of the hole and hung there; when they pulled him out and stood him back on his feet he was so shaken that he staggered sideways and fell down the shaft a second time.

I kept it up for a couple of weeks but couldn't take much more. I was about to give up when, by chance, I was transferred to another site, a relatively gentrified renovation job in Chelsea where Wet, Wet, Wet's theme tune to *Four Weddings and a Funeral* played incessantly on the radio as the August rain streamed down outside. Even two hundred yards from the King's Road there were moments of danger and unpleasantness.

According to the economic notion of a positive relationship between risk and return, this work should have been very well paid. It wasn't. Not only was it the most unpleasant job I ever did, it was the least well rewarded. We earned £40 a day for ten hours' work, six days a week, with no prospect of promotion or improvement. And to cap it all, we were paid a week in hand.[13] Mick, a 'groundsman', earned £60 a day, a sum whispered in hushed, reverential tones. He was a long-limbed, rangy, red-headed Irishman who worked with a wild savagery and at break time fretted about the cost of his daughter's ballet shoes. Just getting through the world seemed to take its toll on Mick.

Willingness-to-pay models such as the VSL base policy costings on the assumption that we are best placed to calculate our own tolerance of risk. But they are blind to the impact of necessity. My comrades in arms included an ex-felon (I suspect), a former drunk who claimed to have kept up work while living on the streets, and men like Jimmy and Mick who were struggling to bring up families on pitiful wages, but who took pride in their freedom from the welfare state. There was Declan, a kind-hearted, toothless, ageing Patrick Swayze, whom I placed at fifty but later discovered to be twenty-nine. He had been working on such sites for fifteen years already. And finally there was a student, a constant liability to himself and everyone else, who commuted back daily to the leafy suburbs, shoulder to shoulder with pinstriped city folk, covered in dust and filth. On one occasion, for obscure and improbable reasons, I made the trip home with a large dirty shovel in the luggage rack. Small wonder that the pretty advertising intern who shared my carriage would never talk to me.

The experience of those who have to work like this every day, year on year, might at the very least suggest that their willingness to pay to avoid risk is constrained by their ability to pay. A neo-liberal economist would argue that such real-world data are valid for just that reason – it reflects the real world, rather than another set of ideal choices. Boundaries must be drawn somewhere, they might say. But following this line of argument sees a social injustice done twice, a 'double jeopardy' for society's least fortunate. The economists Richard Thaler and Sherwin Rosen, who pioneered the VSL, state that the data for risky work are clear and systematic, and this is doubtless the case.[14] But the existence of good data does not mean that we are compelled to act in a certain way. People often accept risk because they can't afford to avoid it, and, when their wages are factored into the pricing of risk, their lives are literally cheapened: compensation for harm is likely to be lower, and risk avoidance, now relatively expensive, becomes less necessary. Value-of-life measures therefore fail to protect those who most desperately need them, those for whom the scarcity of resources has become so acute that there is no real choice at all.

Cost-effectiveness and the allocation of care

Thaler and Rosen begin their analysis from the position that our behaviour, in aggregate, can reveal an objective, scientific price for risk and that, in their words, 'the value of a life is the amount members of society are willing to pay to save one'. But – as their forty-odd pages of dense economic prose, not to mention three decades of subsequent modelling, testing and debate show – the VSL is itself an artefact embedded in an intellectual and technical milieu. It is manufactured according to a particular ideological agenda, and in that sense it is just like the $200,000 figure, and like another, equally curious, set of calculations developed in Great Britain in the 1970s to arbitrate on the best — the most useful — use of medicine.

Every day, doctors and health-care administrators face terrible questions. They must decide who receives treatment and who does not, a question that at its worst becomes a decision over who should live and who should die. If resources are always scarce we should, the argument runs, focus on what is most useful for the money available, understood according to some standard metric or other. Thanks to the growing discipline of health-care economics, a barrage of measures has grown up to help practitioners decide on the most useful allocation of treatments. Pre-eminent among them is the Quality Adjusted Life Year (QALY).[15]

In outline, a patient's QALY is calculated by the number of years of life they are expected to have left, multiplied by the expected 'quality' of those years, with 1 being perfectly healthy, 0 being dead, or even -1, worse than dead. As always, calculation rests on more calculation: the measure of 'quality' is itself a hybrid of distress and disability scales, carefully quantified and developed through survey work, which then vanishes into the background as the measure becomes ever more widely accepted.[16] To give some examples, 'severe distress' with full mobility makes little impact on the quality of life (0.967), while being confined to a chair and bed without distress score 0.875 and 0.677, respectively. The combination is much more damaging: confinement to a chair with severe distress, and to bed with moderate distress both score 0, equivalent to being dead, while being confined to bed with severe distress, or being unconscious both score -1, much worse than being dead. These figures develop unhelpful equivalences from the outset. For example someone in the later stages of terminal cancer scores the same as someone in a coma; someone with a migraine also scores worse than dead. Though clearly quite different, all three of these conditions become commensurate through the quality measure.

The next step in the QALY's logic is for doctors or administrators to compare the change in the QALY brought about by a given treatment to the cost of the treatment to derive a cost-utility score. Using the QALY, administrators can see which treatments represent better value for money understood in terms of quality-adjusted life years per pound. When arbitrating between different treatments for the *same* condition, the approach is useful, for health-care resources are always tight and should not be wasted. However, the more usual purpose of the QALY is to examine cost–benefit not in the case of different treatments for the same condition but across *different, otherwise incommensurate* ailments and conditions. The QALY and its sibling the DALY (Disability Adjusted Life Year) urge managers to prioritize treatments that present best value for money. It is this elevation of cost–benefit to a principle of universal moral reasoning that has led to John Harris, the editor-in-chief of the academic *Journal of Medical Ethics*, to describe the QALY as 'potentially a life-threatening device' and more recently 'wickedness' and 'folly'.[17]

Some examples will illustrate why Harris and others worry about the QALY. The measure is based on the truth, or at least the plausibility, of the idea that a person would prefer a shorter, healthier life to a longer life spent in severe discomfort and disability. This may or may not be true. A terminally ill patient in great pain may still cling to their final months and the possibilities they offer. In fact, it is easy to see that someone in their final months may value each day at a much higher level than those of us who drift casually from one week to the next. Moreover, as Harris points out, even if we accept this rule for ourselves, that does not mean that it transfers across persons; I might well prefer my own life to be long and uncomfortable to somebody else's being short and healthy.

If seven individuals have no life expectancy without treatment, but following surgery six could expect a happy year, and the seventh, seven happy years, the life-year-based allocation scheme will save the seventh. On a population level, this may be the best outcome for everybody but it can hardly be welcomed by the six soon to be deceased, and their many friends and relatives. There is something personal and individual, something important about life that the QALY fails to recognize. Life is, as Harris says, the *sine qua non*. Imagine, then, that an administrator must choose between a hip replacement, dialysis and continuation of life-support. A hip replacement is cheap and brings about a measurable improvement in quality of life, giving a low cost per QALY. Dialysis is expensive, and prolongs a life of moderate discomfort. By cost–benefit analysis standards, hip replacements are a much better treatment than dialysis, because the QALY treats the unpleasantness of dialysis, preserved year after year, as a *cost*. It is likely, though, that the patient considers the likely alternative to dialysis much worse. As for the unfortunate soul on the life-support machine, a QALY of −1 suggests that money spent on preserving their life yields negative benefits – worse than nothing – and the machine should just be turned off.[18]

Immediately, we can see that a management regime that prefers cheap, efficient fixes at the expense of costly interventions can cause problems. The focus is on life years, not lives; benefits, not need. It prefers low-risk treatments with more certain outcomes. The ageing, terminal cancer sufferer can expect little sympathy. The wretched victim of a motoring accident, left burned and in horrible pain, faces a 'double jeopardy' with their quality of life already reduced to such a level that the cost-effectiveness of any treatment they might receive falls automatically.[19] Does this happen in practice, you might wonder. Indeed it does. In 2006 the UK's National Institute for Health and Clinical Excellence (NICE) suggested that treatment for Alzheimer's disease and dementia, although effective, should no longer be provided by the National Health Service on cost–benefit grounds.

It was this decision, in fact, that drove Harris to the indictment of cost-utility treatment as simply 'wickedness' and 'folly'. But the argument of the health-care economist is equally simple. We live in a finite world, so any course of action has costs – resources taken away from other projects.[20] Giving a treatment to someone means taking another treatment away from someone else. We need a clear and transparent yardstick. The defenders of NICE's decision argued that there must be some point at which a treatment is considered too expensive – what if a single treatment cost more than the entire NHS budget, for example? – but the pressing problem is to determine just when that happens. What makes the discussion particularly bewildering is that they are all, in their own way, arguing about equality of access. For Harris, the philosopher, equality means removing barriers and offering all persons the same chance of treatment, irrespective of cost. For the health-care economists, equality means generating as much 'health' as possible for the available funds by making sure no one is too greedy in their treatment.

Consider NICE's ruling on IVF, that it should be made available only to women aged between twenty-three and thirty-nine as treatment is most likely to be effective in this age bracket. If we want our IVF pennies to generate as many babies as possible, NICE's decision makes sense; if we believe that the purpose of IVF is to offer infertile patients a better chance of conception in place of none, then it makes no sense at all. How we choose to allocate health-care funding speaks directly to our understanding of what health care is all about: what *goods* do we expect it to deliver?

The defence of the QALY is, of course, that it saves us from the arbitrary nature of human judgement, preferring the scientific rigour of numeric analysis. But calculation goes all the way down and there is much hidden work behind the QALY. If we pursue and identify each of the decisions that has gone into its construction, we will arrive at moments of expert judgement and, equally, arbitrary assumptions. The claim of objectivity, central to health-care economics, is undermined by the inescapable presence of judgement at some point in the chain of calculation. That is true more broadly, whenever we make judgements over the viability of risk prevention or the appropriate allocation of scarce resources. Even in the simple example of the farmers and the plough, market outcomes are driven by the farmers' own judgement of the possible future returns they can generate based on their resources. In complex organizational settings, calculation becomes ever more rarefied and complex, and hides more and more of those expert or arbitrary judgements from the ultimate framing of any decision. After all, how is it possible to accurately determine the quality of life enjoyed by an individual, and the improvement in that quality offered by a drug or surgical intervention? People vary, physiologically as well as psychologically. Exogenous details – networks of family and friends in particular – will make a real contribution to the quality of life encountered. And distribution according to utility alone neglects other virtues that we might regard as equally, or even more, important: appeals to justice, perhaps, or an obligation to treat those who suffer particular pain.

The rallying cry of health economics is 'evidence-based policy', and there is certainly a role for evidence. But there is also a role for judgement, for recognition of the role of expertise in health care, and most of all for a democratic, open discussion of the goods that we expect health care to deliver. Only when we have decided what we want health care to do can we decide what data to gather and what evidence is required.

When the debate over the QALY first exploded into the media in the mid-1980s, it was associated with the people who had invented it, and particularly Alan Maynard and Alan Williams of the University of York. The 'blue-eyed, blue suited' Williams became a media pin-up as he sought to present his rational analysis of health-care problems. The comparison of hip replacements and dialysis was Williams's own, a provocation for rational budgeting: in 1986 dialysis cost £14,000 a QALY and hip replacement just £750 per QALY. Williams told the media that we should not shrink from the conclusions to which the economic approach leads us: we should turn off dialysis machines and spend the money on other things. As it happens, the science studies department at York was also booming during the 1980s and, in 1989, three sociologists published a book on health economics which characterized Williams, Maynard and their colleagues – notice that this is suddenly a narrative with people and place – as (just) another special-interest group focused as much on their own self-advancement as the objective truth of their measures.[21]

Thirty years later, Williams and Maynard have proved successful enough to have vanished from the story. Cost-utility is simply an established, reliable measure: publicly, NICE decrees that Alzheimer's disease should no longer be treated; in my own research I have found that, behind closed doors, the liver-transplant community experiments with simulations of population levels and life years to determine the optimum allocation of organs.[22] The colourful, local characteristics of the QALY's invention have fallen aside and it has become an accepted methodology, another precedent in the growing case law of bureaucratic governance.

This is a dangerous road to follow. The economic approach shifts focus to the treatments and the money spent rather than those who are being treated. Patients become obstacles to the smooth functioning of administration, the most efficient return on resources as understood in beds visited per pound sterling, or some equivalent measure. If the logic of cost-utility is applied systematically enough, if it is sufficiently normalized in everyday practice, quality of care comes to *mean* cost-saving. Private contractors will, and do, compete for contracts on the basis of the efficient provision of services, and there we see another facet of the same problem: it is much *easier* to communicate cost savings than it is to demonstrate intangible factors such as compassion or care, and if we insist upon an environment where every single factor is ranked and weighted, attention will soon enough gravitate to efficiency.

According to a recent editorial in *The Lancet*, one of the world's leading medical journals, the UK government's positioning of the NHS as a failing business is 'one of the most cynical, and at the same time cunning, ways by which the government abdicates all responsibilities for running a health-care system that has patient care and safety at its heart'.[23] *The Lancet* argues that economic virtues have been allowed to colonize the health service to such an extent that doctors are expected to be businessmen and administrators first and foremost, with efficiency, cost-saving and financial solvency their primary concerns.

In the UK in 2009, the NHS was rocked by the scandal of an appalling lack of care in the Mid-Staffordshire NHS Foundation Trust. Patients suffered systematic abuse, left in their own excrement for hours on end, abandoned in corridors, neglected or maltreated by carers. When it was investigated by Robert Francis QC, the first 'Francis report' pointed at target-driven priorities and notions of competitiveness as central to the problem. Yet a second report subsequently identified the problem as stemming from the Trust's organizational culture, and demanded a tool such as 'a cultural barometer' to measure the 'cultural health' of all parts of the system.[24] Since the Mid-Staffordshire scandal, eleven other trusts have been placed into 'special measures' on account of their unacceptably high mortality rates. This proliferation of failing in the NHS indicates that something has gone terribly wrong, and that the values of economics are a cause, rather than a cure. Those who have worked on organizational culture in the NHS argue that any attempt to measure 'cultural health' will just reduce it to another box-ticking exercise, another variant of cost–benefit utility.[25] Instead, a healthy organizational culture needs time to grow and space to flourish; culture, like responsibility, is hard work.

The ranking has been able to reorganize the higher-education sector, and transform what it is to be a student. Credit scores have linked borrowers and lenders in previously unimaginable ways and facilitated financial engineering on a disastrous, global scale. In the management of risk and the provision of care, economic ways of visualizing the value of life have transformed how we allocate resources and manage problems. Risk has been transformed into another consumer good, while health care has been recast as a commercial enterprise with a focus on cost saving and efficiency. Each of these transformations has been driven by an underlying political sense that the market, and the mode of relationship that the market embodies – fierce competition, the mores of consumption, and the cost–benefit analysis of any decision – are the only appropriate means of evaluating what is just and what is right.

Such questions, discussions about how we organize our society and what we value, are surely a matter for public debate, and numbers will always be part of that conversation. Yet economics is ahead of us, working to bring about a world where economic valuation is the only discourse that matters. The expertise, judgement and sense of obligation to our fellow human beings, on which care and risk prevention must centre, are pushed to one side, as economics models and analyses, bringing facts into being, colonizing our language, changing what we know. In the next chapter we will see economic reasoning at its most raw, as it investigates the buying and selling of our bodies, and ask the question: is everything for sale?

7. How Not to Pay Your College Fees

It is common practice to work while a student, and it is not unusual for students to take on unpleasant and menial jobs, as my own story shows. In a mode of thinking where education is regarded as a collective good as well as a personal one, where the lines of causality between personal investment and personal pay-off are not so clearly drawn, this work might have been regarded as part of a young person's education: diverting, informative, or even character building. There might also be a limit as to how far an individual might reasonably be expected to go to serve the collective good: one might not be expected to damage, use up, or corrupt oneself; to really, personally, pay for that education.

The neo-liberal conception of the world washes away any such distinctions. According to its thinking, we are productive machinery, docile bodies earning revenues and bearing costs. Not one part of our person escapes this economic analysis. We comprise varied endowments of intellect, skill and physical attributes; we are free to shift capital from one endowment to another, in order to generate the best returns on our entire person. An attractive but unintelligent man might parley his looks into wealth via a modelling career or a careful marriage; equally, a clever but unattractive man might, for example, divert revenues from his well-paid job to a new wardrobe, perhaps even undertake surgical enhancements, in pursuit of better clients, social status, a more attractive spouse and so forth.

The neo-liberal, like Marx, understands productive activity as the essence of humanity. The neo-liberal, however, does not condemn the exploitation of the self, but *mandates* it: we must be entrepreneurs of our own persons at all times. We must all be like Allie, all of the time, making businesses out of ourselves, competing in crowded markets to return maximum value on our assets.

By this account, as we have seen, students who pay for an education are investing in their intellectual endowments to maximize future returns. They will harvest the benefits, and therefore they must shoulder the costs. By the same token, then, an attractive young person, possessed of his bodily capital, might sell it in various ways to fund tuition. He might sell sexual services to pay his way. He might, alternatively, part with a kidney or a lobe of his liver in exchange for his college fees. I have read a serious scholarly paper suggesting such an exchange could be institutionalized at a national level in the form of a scholarship.[1]

The neo-liberal economist can hardly object to these transactions; economic exchange between two consenting adults, where both maximize their utilities and express their preferences through price, is the root of democratic freedom.[2] The free-market enthusiast must therefore dismiss any repugnance to such an exchange as irrational and find no moral difference between risky labour, prostitution and kidney sale.

Leaving aside protestations of moral outrage, just as the neo-liberal economist does, let us focus our attention instead upon the processes of commensuration and commodification that make these transactions possible. It is not the transfer of money itself that should catch our attention but the shift in thinking that makes it possible for the transaction to take place. We should question the ease with which we can now shoehorn future salary, university education and kidney sale into the same sentence, and examine how it has become so commonplace to debate – and acquiesce in – the moral feasibility of such a linkage.

The cost of a corpse

Powerful arguments against markets in organs come from those who have witnessed first-hand the misery and exploitation caused by illegal organ traffic.[3] Inevitably, the sale of an organ is contemplated only by the very poorest and most economically desperate, who receive only a pittance for their sale and suffer in the absence of aftercare and support. Many seem to have been misled or tricked into donation. Anthropologist Nancy Scheper-Hughes, founder of the anti-trafficking organization Organwatch, sees the illegal trade as symptomatic of the greatest evils of globalization: 'In general, the circulation of kidneys follows established routes of capital from South to North, from East to West, from poorer to more affluent bodies, from black and brown bodies to white ones, and from female to male or from poor, low status men to more affluent men.'[4] Evidence shows that, rather than starting a business or paying for education, money is swallowed by repayments to moneylenders, with the balance spent on basic necessities such as food and clothing.

But what about a legalized trade, one that is conducted not by criminals but under the auspices of the law? In Iran, where vending is legal, poverty makes follow-up care inaccessible for a great majority, and vending leads to severe depression, marital problems and social stigma. Donors find themselves weak and unable to work, and thus even more impoverished; some even wonder how they can sell their second kidney. A survey of 300 vendors in Iran did not discover a *single one* who had reported a positive improvement in quality of life.

Empirically, then, it seems very hard to sustain the argument that the wealthy kidney buyer and the poor kidney vendor can engage in a transaction that is equal, fair and mutually rewarding. On the contrary, organ trade as it exists exemplifies everything that is wrong with markets: the rich get more and the poor end up with less.

How might a free-market enthusiast reply to such evidence? They might, and invariably do, cite need. The developed world is desperately short of organs for transplantation: as the procedure has become more routine and reliable so waiting lists have swollen. In the UK, for example, some 7,000 people await a kidney transplant, and many will die without ever receiving one. The USA has 119,000 individuals awaiting a transplant out of a population of 313 million, a proportion nearly four times higher than the UK.[5] Waiting lists are swollen by society-wide problems such as obesity, which leads to diabetes, renal failure and fatty liver disease. The demand for organs is high, but it is not being met. Donating an organ is encouraged, of course, but selling organs, even if they are your own, is still illegal in the UK, North America and elsewhere – Iran being the only country to have a legal market for organs. So the question is: if we started to allow people to sell their organs, would it solve the problem?

We cannot take it for granted that the market would increase supply. The anthropologist Richard Titmuss studied blood transfusion policy and in 1970 argued that paying people for blood would 'crowd out' those who voluntarily donated.[6] Now that blood transactions have been legalized in many countries, there is empirical work to support his suggestion: paying for blood seems to change the supply rather than increase it, leading to lower-quality suppliers who change more rapidly. Quality goes down, monitoring costs go up and supply stays the same.[7]

Despite this uncertainty, the challenge for the economist is merely to show that a free market in kidneys, if it were permitted, would be a more efficient solution, and that everyone would benefit accordingly. A sophisticated economic model could help by showing how much, in dollar terms, we could gain through legalized organ markets. In this sense, defeating the moral argument against such a market becomes an exercise in quantitative modelling: will organ markets be *good enough* to overcome the principled objections to them? To answer that, we need to know the price of kidneys.

David Kaserman, who passed away in January 2008 at the age of sixty-one, was professor of economics at Auburn University in Alabama. He had been a government economist, and as an academic became a recognized authority on industrial organization and anti-trust economics. He was, according to his obituary, a fine scholar and a decent man to the end. He comes into this narrative as one of those unfortunate many who have suffered kidney failure and undergone dialysis, and the more fortunate few who actually received a kidney transplant. It must have seemed natural to employ the resources of his professional training to advocate what he saw as a better way of organizing the transplant system. Kaserman and the colleagues with whom he worked on a series of papers wanted to show that social welfare would increase – the whole world could be better off – if a market system was introduced.

It is an axiom of classical and neoclassical economics that the wealth of nations – as Adam Smith put it – stems from specialization and the exchange of goods based on differing skills and resources. For the neo-liberals, free exchange of goods and prosperity are necessarily linked; in classes on international trade, economics students consume supply-and-demand graphs which demonstrate that the removal of tariffs raises general wealth. Kaserman and his colleagues reasoned that what is true for the goods trade would be true for organ trade too: take away the barriers and everyone gains.

The basic model of economics is the supply-and-demand graph. As we saw in Allie's case, it assumes that the supply curve slopes up, with more of any good becoming available as the price increases. The demand curve slopes down, demand falling as prices increase. Where the two meet is the market clearing point: the lowest price at which sufficient supply exists to satisfy demand, and the highest price at which demand will keep up with supply. The clearing price is a laboratory version of the market price, pure and unpolluted by real-world factors; supply-and-demand graphs present an idealized version of what the world might look like if we assume away the gritty irregularities of real life.

Kaserman and colleagues set about building a model to establish a clearing price for the right to harvest someone's organs after their death.[8] Their method was to simulate supply and demand curves, to make up for the fact that no actual data are available, as the market does not actually exist; their great assumption is that it does exist, and that everyone is happy to sell their organs, or at least the right to collect their organs after their death. You will remember the circularity of Erica Field's apparent demonstration that property rights lead to better law enforcement in the slums of Peru. The same problem threatens here: if Kaserman and company succeed in demonstrating that organ markets function well, they have done so using the assumption that nobody objects to a market's existence, and in doing so they provide the context in which such an assumption becomes valid.

Demand, at least, appeared to be straightforward: with transplant operations a cheap alternative to prolonged dialysis the economists assumed that the demand would be 'elastic' – that insurers and health services would continue to fund the purchase of an organ, irrespective of price fluctuations. Supply, on the other hand, was more problematic. Kaserman and colleagues made use of a strategy known as the 'contingent valuation method', a model pioneered in environmental economics to establish prices for things such as clean air. In outline, this method is ingenious and simple. A questionnaire asks individuals how much they would be willing to pay to obtain a good and how much they would accept to forfeit the good, and from those responses it is possible to calculate a supply curve.

I'll come back to Kaserman and his colleagues. Let's focus for a moment on the methodology. The 'contingent valuation method' is notorious for its unpredictability. It suffers, for example, from what is known in the trade as 'anchoring bias'. In layman's language, this means that the responses or valuations offered by participants will be swayed by the construction of the survey itself. It will be even more pronounced for the value of something like clean air, where we have no natural anchor. For example if I ask you how much you would pay for a second-hand family car, you might have a fairly good idea, and the value probably would not change much if I gave the range between nothing and £50,000, or the range £5,000 to £100,000; but if I offered you dinner with the film star of your choice or a nuclear-war-free future for your children, moving the top end of the scale would drastically change the results. In addition, the fact that it is a hypothetical transaction causes problems. I might pay a huge amount of imaginary money for an equally imaginary date or a nuclear-free future, but imaginary money clouds the water of policy debate. For this reason, despite the best efforts of economists and careful guidelines offered by regulators, the method remains tricky to use.

The method is also inescapably political, because asking individuals how much they value something changes the nature of that thing. Asking me to set a price on something currently priceless, such as clean air, *makes* it priced, a commodity, a thing in which we can transact. Going through the methodology and using its outcomes to eliminate policy responses institutionalizes this transformation. A high-profile example will illustrate the point. In March 1989 the *Exxon Valdez* oil tanker ran aground in Prince William Sound, an area of extraordinary natural beauty in Alaska. The magnitude of the spill was made worse by the inaccessibility of the area, and the result, as is well known, was an environmental catastrophe only eclipsed by BP's spillage in the Gulf of Mexico in 2010. Less well known is the mechanism used to justify the billion-dollar settlement awarded to the State of Alaska. An economic team assembled by the state argued for a loss in 'use value' of $2.8 billion, a vast sum derived from a contingent valuation model applied across the whole of the United States.

The enormous settlement had nothing to do with the cost of treating oil-coated birds or animals, a relatively small sum that had in the most part already been spent. The state's lawyers argued that even for people who would never visit Alaska, there is value in the knowledge that it exists, and that it is available for the use of future generations. Furthermore, they argued that – and here is the contentious part – the 'use value' can be expressed in dollar terms.

To put a cash value on the benefit that each household derives from knowing Alaska exists, the team simply asked them how much they would pay to preserve the resource and how much they would demand to let it slip away. Each household would be willing, the team determined, to pay $31 to keep Alaska beautiful; multiplied by 91 million households, the total value attached to the Prince William Sound came to $2.8 billion. Marion Fourcade, who analyses the settlement, remarks that the study 'revealed' the value of the wilderness, and her choice of words must be deliberately ironic, for the vocabulary of revelation suggests that a transcendental truth is being made clear.[9] The method, with its surveys, samples and statistical analysis, is presented as a scientific endeavour, discovering a set of preferences and values that always existed but were never properly recognized. It assumes that the natural and proper means of valuing a wilderness is to treat it like any other article of property that can be bought and sold at will: what is shocking, when you really think about it, is how *little* people actually seem to value the wilderness. A cheap dinner for one, a single trainer, or a prime habitat for ever; it does not seem very much, but once the link between consumer sovereignty and wilderness is made it becomes very hard to undo.

The organ market advocates made the same moves in their study, with similar results. A class of undergraduate students at Auburn University – perhaps not best placed to attach a value to their own demise – were asked how much they would pay to hold on to their organs after death, and how much they would accept to sign a contract allowing posthumous retrieval. These youngsters must have been keen on the idea of cash in their hand for something so far in the future; the resulting supply was very 'responsive to incentives', and the price of $1,000 per donor was enough to clear the market. Medical science can get two kidneys, a liver, bowels, pancreas, a pair of corneas, bone marrow, tissue and other body parts we barely recognize ourselves, from a single cadaver, so the authors concluded that the price per individual organ would be 'trivial'.[10]

Yet a rerun of the Auburn experiment with an older, broader survey group produces a clearing value of $1.2 trillion. This 'inflated' figure, we are told, was owing to the tendency of these respondents to offer a value of zero when asked how much money they would accept in return for their bodies as an expression of their unwillingness to accept the question.[11] Where Kaserman and colleagues' student respondents were happy enough with the thought of dollars, an older and perhaps more reflective public attacked the basic assumption of the questionnaire through their answers. Their instruments of calculation struggled, in the end, to remain uncontaminated by real-world, personal ethics, and where the first survey obliquely demonstrated that markets would be acceptable if they did exist, the second quite clearly did not.

The moral status of posthumous organ markets remains unclear, at least when one examines the footnotes. But this investigation does more than just set a price on a kidney. Kaserman and colleagues' supply-and-demand analysis treats the cadaver as a commodity, and in doing so, it *makes* the cadaver a commodity. Remember J. L. Austin's concept of the performativity of language, where the speaking of a phrase changes the world. In a similar way the models enact a world in which a cadaver, as well as being the last remains of a much-loved relation, is also an artefact worth $1,000. After all, a scientifically estimated value can exist whether the apparatus needed to produce it is legal or not.

However, now that there is a price, there is another way – an economic way – of asking whether we should have markets in transplant organs. The circumstances through which the price – the economic fact – has been produced fade into the background, taking methodological uncertainties and complexities with them. Like Frankenstein's monster, the $1,000 cadaver slips its chains and begins to travel. In subsequent papers Kaserman and his colleagues claim that a market in organs would see the end of organized crime and the black market, because organs would be so cheap that it would not be worth the criminals' while. In a discussion over education as a means of encouraging donation, the authors conclude that education is expensive and inefficient, and that the $1,000 cadaver is a better solution. This is no longer a moral argument, or a discussion about the kind of world we wish to live in; it has become a matter of technical simulation, where education and donation can be justified only by a superior economic model.

An economics of living bodies

Simulating supply and demand is one way of deducing a price for an organ, and thereby legitimizing payment for cadaveric 'donations'. But there remains one clear obstacle to a market in cadaveric organs: the unfortunate individual concerned must die before their time and in generally good health. Such things as improved intensive-care techniques, the use of seat belts in cars and generally better road safety have all eroded the supply of useful corpses.

An economist schooled in the exchangeability of bodies and capital might reason that a more reliable supply could be gained from legitimizing live organ sales, and set about working out the value of a living kidney. A sophisticated valuation might come from analysing the consumption behaviour of individuals, following the logic of the Value of Statistical Life, which we met in the last chapter: the rate at which a population will exchange wealth for small increases in survival probability. The premium we demand for risky work, or that we are prepared to pay for a safer toaster, can be used to infer a fair value for our bodily organs. In other words, the analysis might consider how much we would demand to run the risk and discomfort of parting with a kidney.

Inevitably, Gary Becker has done just that. Together with Julio Elias, he has calculated a price for the sale of living kidneys and livers.[12]

Becker's calculation assumes that the 'reservation price of an organ has three main additive components: a monetary compensation for the risk of death, a monetary compensation for the time lost during recovery, and a monetary compensation for the risk of reduced quality of life'. To put that another way, he infers the price from attitudes to death, reduced quality of life and lost earnings. As we saw in the previous chapter, these values are in free circulation already, and Becker can make use of them. Economists spend a lot of time inferring people's preferences from other sources: for example by comparing otherwise identical houses in areas with different schools, crime rates, or cultural activities, it is possible to calculate how much families are willing to pay for better schooling, lower crime, or increased culture. Similarly, by comparing the extra money received for risky work, it is possible to infer the price at which people take risks, or 'risk premium'. But, as my experience in the demolition gang made clear, risk does not necessarily pay that well, and some people just have to take it.

Nevertheless, even the best calculation has an element of guesswork. Risk of reduced quality of life proves difficult to assess, and Becker accords it a 'generous' (which means arbitrary) $7,500 value. The costs of a lay-off while recovering from surgery are taken as a month's lost earnings for an individual earning $35,000, just under £23,000. Compensation for risk is derived from existing 'value of statistical life' figures, the same that determine pricing of safety measures in factories and public works. Based on these figures, Becker and Elias estimate that a payment of $15,200 would procure enough kidneys to clear the market. Liver donation is a more dangerous procedure, with a longer lay-off and a larger quality-of-life impact, and so the price is higher: $37,600 is the going market rate for two-thirds of your liver.

The sophistication of Becker's model obscures not only the arbitrary nature of some of the values, but also the many assumptions that are hidden within the mathematics. If the pricing of risk depends upon the real-life employment choices of those who are most likely to take on risky work – because they are undereducated, unskilled, economically distressed, or simply unable to calculate an appropriate value for the risks involved – then the resulting price mandates that it is these very same individuals who are likely to consider vending a part of their anatomy. Becker's maths acknowledges that much when it takes $35,000 as the annual wage from which to set compensation levels; the same calculation run on the basis of the risk prefer- ences and earnings of leading American economics professors might look quite different. It is still a big number, big enough to be tempting, big enough perhaps to pay the college fees; but it will always be the poorest and the most disadvantaged who are tempted most.

Such valuations and ways of talking creep into everyday life. When a Chinese teenager known as 'Little Zheng' checked into hospital and sold his kidney to purchase an iPad, the global news coverage seemed more outraged at his choice of purchase than the sale.[13] Had he instead chosen to purchase a university educa- tion, I doubt whether he would have made the headlines. Many people would have understood and sympathized with his choice.

It is thirty years since Richard Titmuss argued that setting up markets in blood would drive away the donors that kept the sys- tem operating. In 2011, the Nuffield Council for Bioethics, a leading UK think-tank, published the results of its consultation on human bodies and incentives, which asked whether it is mor- ally acceptable to use incentives to increase supply. In other words, it now *presumed* that incentives, if used, *would* increase supply. A senior official in the UK's transplant service suggested to me that some small payment could greatly increase supply, because 'that's what people are like'.

Just as payment crowds out donors, so economic logic, powerful and straightforward, crowds out other less tangible considerations: equity and justice, for example, or the doctor's first principle of 'do no harm'. Taking an organ from a living body, carving into the healthy flesh, is difficult enough in the case of altruistic donations to friends and loved ones; the mo- tivation of economic exchange would be a step too far for many surgeons. Such difficult moral issues wither in the face of economic models' claimed objectivity. The health economist Anthony Culyer remarks that economists these days speak like philosophers. Having spent time with philosophers myself, I suspect this is because philosophers have caved in to economics, unable to spot the assumptions and the idiosyncrasies in the economists' technical arguments. But the arguments over transplant organs show that economics does more than just describe: that it performs, acting out its descriptions on the stage of real life. And if that is the case, what economics analyses really matters.[14]

Positive economics and the price of sex

Milton Friedman, in his *Essays in Positive Economics*, advocated a dispassionate science, disinterested and separate from value judgements. Economics, wrote Friedman, deals with what is, not what should be. Central to this science is the use of inaccurate assumptions.

Friedman asks us to imagine the leaves of a tree, which grow thickest where the sunlight is strongest. We might assume that leaves are sentient, can move freely, and that they will deliberately position themselves to maximize the amount of sunlight that they receive. This assumption will allow us to make certain predictions about leaves on trees, which would be correct. Friedman asks whether the hypothesis is rendered invalid because leaves do not think, and argues that it is not. The economist does not assert that leaves are sentient and that they do position themselves accordingly, merely that the outcomes are the same *as if* they were and did.

From there, he says, it is only a step to examining a hypothesis that firms behave *as if* they were seeking rationally to maximize expected returns. And we find that they *do* behave in this way, even if, says Friedman, business people do not run through the full range of cost and demand calculations, calculating marginal cost and marginal revenues, for example.

But business people do behave in this way, now. Since Friedman's essay, sixty years of business administration classes have taught young executives to weigh up marginal costs and marginal revenue and push production to the point where one touches the other. Steady innovation among consultancy firms and business gurus has produced a plethora of devices to help managers make economically informed 'scientific' choices. Despite Friedman's best intentions, positive economics are not set apart from normative judgements – they *create* normative judgements. Economic assumptions are so normalized in the world, transmitted through our curriculum, through popular literature and ways of speaking, that they become accepted as a guide to how we should act. It seems that wherever we find economic calculation in the laboratory, we will soon enough discover its fearsome, feral cousin in the wild.

Another 'contested' market that has fascinated economists is the sale and purchase of sexual services. There is a well-developed market in such things, so analysts have no need to extrapolate laboratory prices, but can go to work on real data. One question in particular bothers analysts: why, when one needs no qualifications or particular skills, no financial capital or special equipment to become a prostitute, are the earnings systematically higher than for workers in other sectors? Data from the UK indicate that prostitutes earn twice as much as non-manual workers, and three times as much as manual workers: in London, for example, weekly earnings for manual work were £278, for non-manual work were £465, and for prostitution, £1,024.[15]

Where wages in one area are particularly high, but barriers to entry low, we expect that workers will move to the more lucrative area, increasing supply and bringing prices down. That does not seem to happen in the case of prostitution. It may be that the risk and unpleasantness attached to the profession limit supply, or lead the women (and it is primarily women) to demand higher wages. But that explanation does not stack up. It is the women working on the street that run the highest levels of risk and endure the most unpleasant working conditions, yet they earn the least. Allie's anecdotal evidence indicates the same – high prices do not drive down demand either – and presents the intrepid economist with a puzzle: what is sustaining these high prices?

Here it is useful to remember George Akerlov's 'market for lemons'. Akerlov uses the example of the second-hand car market to show the effects of an unequal distribution of information about the goods on sale. On the second-hand car lot, only the seller knows which cars have been patched and bodged and which are good quality and good value, so the buyer is always at a disadvantage. Buyers therefore react by offering lower prices to protect themselves against the possibility of buying dodgy goods, and so the sellers of good-quality cars go elsewhere. Soon, all the cars that are left on the lot are the patched and bodged 'lemons'.

In these circumstances, one way out is for the seller to charge *much* higher prices, as a means of signalling the high quality of the service. Another is to invest in guarantees and reputation, or to generate long-term relationships which stabilize economic exchange and dull competition. Allie appears to have done all these things: she increased her prices to indicate 'quality', and took block bookings from 'loyal customers'. Moreover, in this exchange, as the prostitute is personally vulnerable, the buyer's willingness to pay a high price might also be seen as an information signal, implying that he is reliable and safe. Allie, at least in the hands of Levitt and Dubner, seems to have come to this conclusion.

Economists refer to situations such as these, where the buyer does not know as much as the seller, as 'informational asymmetries'. The availability of information is central to economic analysis of real-world phenomena because, as we have seen, it can affect pricing, supporting prices where we might otherwise expect them to fall.

The other mainstay of economic analysis alongside information is cost. Alan Williams, the health economist mentioned in the last chapter as a leading architect of the QALY, writes that 'to an economist, what will it cost means what will have to be sacrificed, and this may be very different from how much money will we have to part with'.[16] A powerful – at least in terms of producing testable hypotheses – way of modelling the market for sexual services is to assume that there are 'opportunity costs' – things given up – attached to being a prostitute, and that wages must compensate for these sacrifices, to model, in other words, the exact trade-off that Levitt and Dubner suggest their belle has made.

Yes, that's right. The model of prostitution that has gained most currency in the discipline, understood in terms of publication in pre-eminent academic journals, is based on the assumption that a woman can be *either* married *or* a prostitute. She cannot be neither, nor, for that matter, can she be both.[17] If she is married she derives earnings from her own work and from marriage; if she is a prostitute she enjoys only her earnings from work. Wages from prostitution must therefore always be higher than wages earned from other work, because they must compensate the woman for the lost benefits of marriage. The economic benefits of marriage, understood in terms of happiness and other utilities, have been estimated elsewhere at £70,000; it follows, in outline at least, that a woman who chooses not to be married should expect an additional £70,000 a year in earnings to compensate.[18]

If these assumptions seem a little extraordinary, remember that economic models are praised for their parsimony and their predictive power, rather than their complex description of real life. In this light, simplification is a virtue, and from the economist's perspective the strength of this model is that it can offer genuine insights into wage differentials: prostitution does remain an uninviting occupation and wages do remain high – Why? Because there are costs attached.

The model can make additional predictions on the basis that earnings from prostitution remain tied to other macroeconomic factors; for example if the wages earned by women as a whole rise, then the opportunity cost of being a prostitute also rises and wages from prostitution must increase to compensate. Increased wages for prostitutes mean increased prices for those who employ them, which would mean less demand and fewer prostitutes; the corollary is that poverty will lead to low prices, high demand and therefore higher levels of prostitution. An increase in male wages will lead to a higher 'wife premium' and the necessary compensation will drive up prices and reduce numbers of prostitutes.

This model really does demonstrate the tension between what economics means when it claims to 'explain', and what everyone else understands by the term. The predictions listed above – 'wife premia' and so forth – are true in the very limited sense of being empirically testable. When Friedman says that economics explains, he means that it makes predictions and that we can test those predictions further. When the popular literature of economics claims to explain the world, the word is deployed in this sense: economics does not understand, but predicts in ever-increasing detail.

For most other people, however, explanation is a process that gives an insight into the rich and varied relationships of cause and effect in the world. The notion of a 'wife premium' is inaccurate enough to be untrue by any meaningful standard of the word. It is the case that prostitution is rife in poor societies, but we have a sense that there is more to the explanation than the absence of significant opportunity costs. Economic explanations appear to be self-sufficient and complete, while real-world explanation is usually incomplete; nonetheless we endeavour to understand, for if we do not understand, we can never know whether predictions are correct in more than a temporary way. The philosopher Robert Long offers a clear illustration of this problem:

> Let's say that in early 2001 I formulate a theory to the effect that there is a Constant Tolkienian Force in the universe that produces a Tolkien film every year. When Austrians complain that my theory ignores the fact that films are products of human action and not of constant impersonal forces, I reply: 'Oh, I know that. My theory isn't supposed to be realistic. The question is whether it's a good predictor.' So I test it in 2001, 2002, and 2003. Lo and behold, my theory works each year! . . . But unless I pay some attention to the true explanation of this sequence of film releases, I'll be caught by surprise when the regularity fails for 2004.[19]

The ridiculous concept of a 'Constant Tolkienian Force' shows the nature of the conclusions we might draw if we stay in the laboratory, hiding from the complexities of the real world in unrealistic assumptions. Unfortunately, the narrow understanding of economics' explanatory power spills over into real life. In the case of the economic theory of prostitution sketched out above, we might not accept the balance of the wages and opportunity costs of sex work as an 'explanation', and would rather see a fine-grained descriptive explanation of why a woman takes up this particular occupation. But when Levitt and Dubner wonder why more women do not follow Allie's example and enjoy the high wages which more than outweigh the costs in terms of missed husband opportunities, they really do seem to think that positive economics 'explains'.

The economics of prostitution does not stop there. The model of opportunity cost and high wages, perspicacious as it may be, casts little light on how participants actually value encounters of the flesh. It is analogous to the free-trade models of the organ market enthusiasts, where the level of analysis is the market in aggregate, and predictions are made at the level of group behaviour. Just as Becker and Elias's imaginative simulation made use of risk premia to infer much more specific prices from wage data, so the economists Peter Moffatt and Simon Peters have analysed prices to establish what it is that users really value when it comes to visiting prostitutes.[20]

Moffatt and Peters make use of data recorded on 'Punternet', an online reporting site where buyers of sexual services can write up their visits, including prices paid, the duration of the visit, and give an indication of whether they would return. It is a version of a travel review website for gentleman callers. Through Punternet, Moffatt and Peters uncover the preferences of clients, displayed as always through the medium of price.

I will summarize for the prurient reader: the women who earned the highest fees are aged twenty-three and three-quarters, and 'very thin'. Apart from 'kinky extras', which cost rather more, prices reflected time rather than service provided. And in findings that support the theoretical predictions of the opportunity-cost model, services cost most in the affluent centre of London and least in Scotland and the north-east. Long encounters lead to happier clients, as do more experienced women, with those aged thirty-one and a half years supplying the most satisfaction. Moffatt and Peters speculate that these slightly older women value repeat business more and therefore pay attention to their quality of service. The most unlikely finding of all is that being attractive (on the basis of the description provided by the client) results in lower prices, while higher prices are charged by *unattractive* women. Again, a speculative explanation is posed: it may be that these women do not expect a return visit and therefore extract the highest price that they can, exploiting the 'sunk costs' that the client has put into search, travel and expectation: the punter, having invested so much into his visit, prefers to be overcharged than to walk away empty-handed.

Moffatt and Peters conclude that 'in a smoothly functioning market, any feature of the service that increases client satisfaction should attract a price premium . . . this and other findings suggest that market signals are not functioning perfectly and there exist unrealized profit opportunities'.[21] In other words, the costs of searching are a problem, as they are if we are seeking a university course, or a perfect coffee. Search costs may be caused by poor information or by the difficulties of obtaining information. A more smoothly functioning market, where high-quality information flowed freely, would see a good match of quality and price and a general rise in social welfare: everyone involved would be better off.

In the case of prostitution, as legalization of commercial sex would greatly improve information flows, there is a policy argument that can be made on the grounds of social welfare alone. What is true of one commodity is true of another, be that frozen concentrated orange juice, a kidney still warm, or intimate relations exchanged for cash: free markets and personal choice are the mainstays of national prosperity. All this may seem sufficiently absurd to be irrelevant. But economic simulations may influence policy, entering debates over the legalization of markets in body parts and sexual services, just as they do in debates over markets in harmful or controlled substances – tobacco and alcohol, for example. The economic analysis of prostitution, with its emphasis on information costs, may in time change the way we talk about and regulate the oldest profession.

Economics oppresses

In the meantime, the economist's commitment to a smoothly functioning market, where information is freely and widely available, prices may be compared and value for money established, spills into the wild. We have already seen how consumer review and price comparison sites are relentless in their assertion that we conform as consumers to economic norms of value for money and price competition, and in doing so they force those who wish to supply us to accept those same rules as the preeminent terms of business. I am sorry to say that many such devices exist even in the world of sexual services, and in the UK at least, Punternet is merely the most famous.

This charming online institution, which covers the UK only, claims that since inception in 1999, 110,170 'field reports' have been published representing some £14 million worth of purchased sex. Over 90 per cent of these reports have recommended the 'Lady' (sic). You can, should you wish, consult a ranking of the most heavily recommended workers – current leader 'Rosina of Newcastle' ('formerly of Sunderland') with 125 reports stretching from 2001 to 2011.[22] I have already made clear that rankings – of cities, of educational establishments – have the ability to reshape the institutions that they describe. You can see the same process at work on Punternet's grimy pages, with the 'working girls' or 'ladies' working to manage and curate their status on the site, to be the most recommended, most visible provider of client satisfaction and value for money.

Punternet makes the evaluation processes of the 'punters' visible. It allows the community of users to settle among themselves what counts, what to value and how to value it. The site's field reports are detailed and make sordid reading. Fortunately, for those of us with a weaker constitution, Lynne Pettinger, a sociologist at the University of Essex, has analysed how the punters talk about their experiences and how they articulate value. They use different ways of qualifying the service – perhaps customer care at a premium price level, or value for money at the bargain-basement end of the scale. Here are two, typical, examples from her paper:

> Frankly for this sort of money I really do expect someone to take a bit of time and trouble and at least try to relax not hurry me. I am not 18 and not a machine and cannot orgasm to deadlines. Really am very disappointed . . .

> HR, oral or sex were included in the price, but for an extra £10 I could combine any two services . . . started by putting the condom on with her mouth, a very nice touch, then on to one of the best blow jobs I've ever had . . . very good VFM!!!!!!![23]

VFM is clearly value for money, and HR, apparently, is 'hand relief'. A footnote to the paper translates the Punternet acronyms, all the more toe-curling for Pettinger's dispassionate, scholarly prose. She argues that the stories in these field reports present the purchase of sex as a legitimate consumer activity, where the punter is entitled to service and value for money. Consumer sovereignty – the customer is always right – is implicit in all of these reports. Moreover, the site defines how a customer should act: the good customer researches and makes rational, utility maximizing choices, and the site exists to facilitate those choices.

According to its self-description, the website was 'created to facilitate the exchange of information on prostitution in the UK' and 'aims to promote better understanding between customers and ladies in hopes that everyone may benefit, with less stressful, more enjoyable and mutually respectful visits'. Another page says, 'The guys will be able to get an idea about whether they'd like to visit a particular lady. The ladies who have favourable reports posted should see an increase in business as time goes on . . .'[24] Pettinger is right to see Punternet as a device through which valuations of good service and customer entitlement – moral claims – are negotiated and made explicit, but it also serves another, more simple purpose. It does exactly what it claims to do, facilitating the exchange of information in a market: between buyers and sellers, buyers and buyers, and sellers and sellers. It enables those who intend to visit the 'working girls' to compare prices, ascertain the market rate and get a sense of good service or value for money. It allows the women to compare themselves with their peers and rivals. It establishes market prices and enacts a particular classification of activities, determined by its unspeakable acronyms. The site welcomes replies to negative reviews, and discussions over the quality of service can be heard in open spaces. Taken as a whole, as Pettinger says, it legitimizes the buying and selling of commercial sex; more than this, it demonstrates through action the commensurable nature of the services that are being sold and the commodified, interchangeable nature of those who are selling.

There is much debate over the status of commercial sex as an occupation. For some it is a form of repression, a very particular kind of labour that makes peculiar demands on the very identity and person of the service provider. For others it is not existentially different from other kinds of work, or indeed marriage and domestic labour. It can be seen as an opportunity for women to regain some kind of control over their lives, to assert an identity as active and entrepreneurial, where sex work is a career and profession.[25] As the neo-liberal insistence on autonomy as a primary virtue colonizes discussions about what can and cannot be sold, the latter group of arguments seems to have the upper hand. Happy Allie is in this respect exemplary: charging high prices, choosing her clients carefully and selling her personality as much as her body.

Punternet undoes all of this. While Allie strains to make

herself singular, to de-commodify herself, a website such as Punternet works hard in the opposite direction, to turn the 'Ladies' into commodities, interchangeable objects subject to the logics of value for money and customer service. Punternet reminds us that market devices are powerful, for what can one woman do in the face of calculation accumulated across tens of thousands of users, the collected experience of £14 million of purchased sexual encounters? Just as travel experience sites have become new mechanisms for disciplining hotel owners and enforcing particular expectations and standards of service, here too service providers are simply powerless in the face of mass opinion calibrated and directed by an online engine.[26] What is true – what is most widely accepted – is determined by a device that gains its great power from the networks it gathers around it. The sellers of sex are ruthlessly configured as economic men and women, bound by economic laws and protocols. There is no dignity, no autonomy, no emancipated identity; only the grinding assessment of value for money and open, bitter competition.

Money has been the villain of the piece so far. By making it possible to trade off each and every aspect of the human condition against benefits and costs, it has been central in coordinating the economic understandings that I have discussed in the previous chapters. It is equally possible, however, for us to become economic men and women without the help of money. One such transformation has come about through an institution increasingly naturalized in contemporary society, online dating. In the next chapter I shall explore how this twenty-first-century phenomenon has managed what Dennis Robertson hoped: it has economized love.

8. It's Not the Money, Honey

Online dating is serious business.[1] The major dating corporations turn over hundreds of millions of pounds. The European firm Meetic has revenues of roughly €200 million each year, representing, I would estimate, more than half a million lonely hearts. Meetic runs some of the largest European sites, including the European operations of Match.com, in a deal struck with the American firm in 2009. Its founder, Marc Simonici, said in a rare interview that he 'loved to help people find love', but I think it a fair guess that he loves it even more when they each pay €30 a month. eHarmony, one of the handful of giant dating firms that dominate the United States market, claims responsibility for 5 per cent of American marriages each year. Clearly, there are huge economies of scale that help the bigger firms get even bigger: infrastructure costs will be broadly stable, and so more customers mean more profit, and more money to spend on advertising and expansion. Network effects kick in as well: if everyone who is anyone is looking for a partner on Match.com, then there are still more reasons to join. As with any social media, a few firms at the top effectively control the whole industry.

The big firms have expanded the industry, as well as dominating it. There are scores of mid-range sites; every magazine or newspaper worth its salt seems to have its own dating service. You might suspect that it is only a matter of time until the big supermarkets pile into the market, and indeed, in 2011 the UK grocer Asda launched a dating service that claimed to match people according to their shopping habits. (Inviting an avalanche of one-liners: 'Have you heard about the new [*supermarket name of choice*] dating site? My mate tried it and ended up with a bag for life.') The market has fragmented as sites pursue those seeking more specialized encounters than the online giants can provide. There are, for example, websites for country lovers, classical music enthusiasts, sporty types and former Oxbridge students, sites for people seeking affairs, or for those of a 'fifty shades' persuasion. Whatever your passion, you can probably find a dating site dedicated to your needs, because online dating is unwavering in its assertion that finding a partner is all about what is right for you.

It is tempting to think that contemporary dating services are just a modern manifestation of an old problem. After all, throughout history we have had arranged marriages, debutante balls, clan alliances and all sorts of other ingenious mechanisms for matching people together. Shiona Chillas and I have spent the last couple of years watching them closely. We have analysed interfaces, read patents and interviewed founders, and we are sure of one thing: they are not.

Mobility, sexual liberation and gender equality may have changed much, but many of the basic mechanisms for meeting partners offline remain the same. Schools and universities continue to act as huge, informal meeting places, conveniently sorting individuals by age, interest and social grouping. Academics who study relationships have known for a long time that people tend to marry others of similar age, education and background, and geography plays a part too; the 'one and only' invariably lived within a reasonable driving distance.[2]

At the same time, such factors do not actually determine the success of relationships as much as we might think. Similarities in social group and demographic do not seem to play a vital role in making long-term relationships function, but are a side-effect, the result of what economists call 'search frictions'. If you meet your spouse at school or university, as many still do, you are likely to be the same age and of similar educational background; if you meet on the running track, in the garden centre or at the pedigree dog show, you are likely to share interests. Such commonalities certainly can help kick-start a relationship, by giving people a pool of shared experience from which they can develop their partnership, but they are not the be-all and end-all. The shared experiences of time spent together will soon offer a far greater commonality.

There are also the strange genetics of attraction, which we barely understand. In 1995 the Swiss geneticist Claus Wedekind performed his famous 'sweaty T-shirt' experiment; volunteers sniffing T-shirts that had been worn for two days by members of the opposite sex preferred the scent of those whose immune system differed most from their own. Wedekind's experiment demonstrated that human attraction may be driven by subconscious, evolutionary factors that scientists are just beginning to unpick.

Now, thanks to the Internet, people can form relationships halfway round the world, and can make their choices, in theory at least, unburdened by factors of age or demographic. There is no need to be burdened by search frictions; information flows perfectly and search costs should be limited. In itself, this luxury of choice focuses attention on the act of choice, suggesting that finding the right person to begin with is the essential foundation for a successful relationship. It is in this central claim, the implicit, ever-present sense that online sites will find you the perfect partner, the one and only, who will arrive pre-specified like any other consumer good, that online dating differs from previous matching and marriage systems.

Is it true? Is there a Mr or Mrs Right without whom you will never be happy? Or is it the case that there are lots of possible matches, and that good relationships are built over time through the efforts of both involved? Here, psychology can offer solid answers. We know that flourishing relationships are successful in the long run because partners learn to behave in an empathetic and mutually supportive manner. It is certainly true that some people will never make good spouses: they are just bad at relationships. The reverse is true, as well. Some people are good at relationships, *irrespective* of the pairing. There are some old-fashioned, non-scientific words that describe this kind of person: nice, kind, caring, the sort of words your mother might use when describing your ideal spouse. (For that matter, there are some even older words that describe the first category of partner.) So, in sum, relationship science tells us the following: find a kind-hearted partner, one who excites you in a hearty, primal sort of way, and stick with them. Share experiences and be prepared to compromise. Change.

Dating sites, on the other hand, suggest almost the opposite: find a partner who likes the same sort of things as you, and who has the physical characteristics that you usually find attractive. Get the person who is right for you as you are now. Do not change, and do not expect primal fireworks. Leave the whole problem of compatibility to the experts.

It is my pet theory – and nothing more – that online dating works as a commercial possibility because it occupies a liminal space between two understandings of relationship formation. On the one hand, it benefits from contemporary notions that somewhere in the world there is someone who will be perfect for you, right now, to be hunted down as you might a particular pair of shoes. Finding a partner like this is just an extension of the business of shopping. On the other, psychologists agree that one thing online sites *can* do is sort out the people who are good at relationships from the people who are not. The rhetoric of the dating site must therefore be that they can, due to some particular bit of scientific intellectual property, make matches in a way that real life and other websites cannot; the practice is to put kind-hearted, sane people in touch with one another and let them do the hard work.

It is a fine trick if you can get away with it, like selling flat-pack furniture. Your customers drive to the shop, collect the boxes, spend the weekend hammering and cursing; they do all the work, and yet the shop takes all the money.

How to sell romance

Another possibility is that online dating offers something to those seeking what the psychologist John Alan Lee called 'pragmatic love', a mutually rewarding, stable and profitable connection.[3] A pragmatic approach to relationship formation underlies the economic account of matching, where men and women will seek to maximize their future benefits, understood in terms of the combined outputs, and the likely share of those outputs each can take. So those individuals with the greatest assets, be they intelligence, good looks, charm or wealth, will tend to get together, as the combined benefits are greater, just as five times five is much more than three times three. Underlying the economic account is the usual assumption: people are self-interested and will seek the best return on capital at their disposal.

Online dating can claim a much more direct heritage to economic thinking than, for example, Punternet. While the latter is a manifestation of general economic principles, dating sites have been actively designed around the principles of social science, which themselves are founded on theories of rational choice. There is not much room for primal fireworks here, but there is lots of room for choice and the efficient flow of information. A senior manager at one of the global dating services – I will call him Michael – put it like this: 'Instead of a local match-maker where there was 200 or 500 people, it is a system that allows you to have millions of people, to be able to make the choices even better . . . I think we can help people find choice and make better choices.'

Michael and his colleague – whom I shall call Norman – explained how their own firm's algorithm had been built. The firm's founder enlisted Norman, a psychologist, to help him assemble the data necessary to develop matching algorithms. No one had assembled meaningful predictors of long-term rela-tionships, so the pair set about doing it themselves. Prediction, after all, is an essential part of any dating algorithm; in order to sell relationships one has to be able to predict which will work. So the entrepreneur and psychologist set out to establish what factors were common to successful relationships. They went straight to the survey methods of traditional social science; they conducted a large-scale survey of married couples, asking extremely detailed questions. Into this mix they threw a meas-ure of marital happiness, introducing questions commonly understood to indicate marital satisfaction.

The pair could then use statistical analysis to see what factors were common to those couples hitting high happiness scores. It was a clever idea. Their particular insight was to treat *combin-ations* of traits *across partners* as constitutive of successful relationships, to analyse the relationship at the level of the pair; once this had been done, finding partners became a problem of matching co-dependent variables, of sorting. This itself is a very economic notion, that finding appropriate matches is a case of organizing the static characteristics of individual personalities. It is the rational choice and smooth information flow of a well-organized economic market, brought into being by survey mechanisms and some heavy-duty computing; bilateral match-ing across a database of several million is no mean computational feat. Those who are considered incapable of forming long-term relationships (who fall into lower quartiles of the marital happiness ranking) are screened out at an early stage. Tourists fare equally badly – during our researches, one of these clever engines spotted I was married, or perhaps I somehow admitted it, and kicked me straight out.

Norman told us that developing effective indicators required a large investment of laboratory time, validating measures, analysing and re-surveying. He recalled the results as being surprising, and that the factors identified by the survey could not have been easily determined from raw data. Contrary to the wisdom of the time, like-for-like matching appeared unimportant, and hobbies and pastimes were barely relevant. Instead, Norman and Michael agree that stable matches are predictable on the basis of certain personality traits. At the end of all this algorithmic work there may be little choice left open to the user. Making the right choices involves accepting what the algorithm recommends. Dating sites have harnessed the methods of economics – surveys, statistics (regressions and factor analysis, to be precise) and algorithmic matching – to lay claim to a particular scientific knowledge about what makes a perfect relationship.

At this point, we might feel a little uncomfortable. Scientists demonstrate the strength of their findings by publishing them and letting others imitate. Of course, that would be difficult for dating services because the sorting mechanism is the central intellectual property of the site. Pharmaceutical companies face a similar problem, but regulation forces them to disclose their compounds and the results of trials, so they rely on patents and legal action to protect their intellectual property. Dating services simply don't disclose the nuts and bolts of the algorithms, instead preferring half-measures designed to keep those of us on the outside happy, but the secrets secret.

To give one example, the online dating site TRUE.com

published a 'technical manual' to demonstrate in thoroughly scientific language the 'reliability' and 'validity' of the 'measures' used, and to 'support the perception of TRUE and its contractors that there is an increasing need to enhance and maintain the status of online relationship research and cyber psychology in general'.[4] In this technical manual we find that TRUE's compatibility test covers ninety-nine key attributes, some of which are based on complementarity (opposite traits) and others similarity. It is based on an adaptive questionnaire, where particular answers lead to different strands of questioning. It contains 616 items. Some of these are administered to all users while others are used on those respondents who are inconsistent or whom the algorithm suspects of fibbing. In a moment of luminous clarity the manual tells us that the site's matching algorithm uses a 'compatibility matrix' that includes: 'compatibility levels of individual traits using similarity, dissimilarity or complementarity algorithms depending on the issue; interactions between specific traits; gender-specific weighting of traits; relative importance weighting of traits; bidirectional algorithms for completing the final index'. In fairness, I must stress that the manual remains one of the more comprehensive acts of disclosure I have seen. The opacity of the industry worries even those on the inside, as this extract from an industry paper makes clear:

> The prospect that millions of singles are making life-changing decisions based on compatibility tests that are not scientifically sound is a sobering one. Indeed, medical patients would not take a drug that has not been approved by the FDA . . . and likewise people looking for relationships should not so willingly trust online psychological tests and matching systems that have not been independently proven to meet professional testing standards.[5]

The questions that confront new joiners can be just as opaque. You might be asked to identify your favourite colour, or holiday destination. I am sure I came across inkblot patterns at one point. Users attempting to second-guess the algorithms may be floored by some of these:

> Your personal ad in one sentence [is]
>> 'Wild horses will take us to the edge of the world to fetch a star – with me, each new day is a new adventure.'

> [Or]
>> 'Your rescue remedy, your parachute and your lifeboat – I'll be there to catch you when you fall.'

As I have argued throughout this book, calculative power is manifested by knowing more, or knowing better. Scientific knowledge is an invaluable assistance here. One site asks users to compare finger lengths on the left hand, and to see whether their index finger is longer or shorter than their ring finger; this, it is claimed, is a measure of testosterone levels experienced by the individual as a foetus and therefore acts as an indicator of 'director' or 'negotiator' personality status, where directors have a longer ring finger.[6]

There is, as it happens, a substantial amount of scientific literature investigating the relationship between finger length and personality characteristics. Hundreds of papers have been written on the topic, and while it is commonly supposed that these differences occur as a result of prenatal hormone exposure, the implications are very much under discussion.[7] In the midst of such scientific complexity, we might be forgiven for feeling that a direct association between digit length and the possibility of a harmonious relationship is, at the very least, something of an oversimplification.

Despite the occasional gimmick, such as finger-length comparison, dating entrepreneurs are honest about the problems of biological attraction; as Norman put it, 'We don't know the magic spark,' while his colleague admitted that physical chemistry is 'hard to model'. So dating sites are more careful in what they promise: not love at first sight but a probability of developing a long-term relationship. eHarmony's pioneer, Galen Buckwalter, remarks: 'Long-term satisfaction is not the same as short-term attraction. A lot of people, when they see their initial matches, it's like, this is crap.'[8]

Buckwalter's argument is typical of those put forward by dating services, be they online giants or bespoke agencies: you have to trust science, to trust the algorithm, because the algorithm knows better than you do. Limited shortlists of potential matches restrict the ability of users to browse independently. eHarmony offers 'scientific matching' and Match.com 'dating you can trust': the absence of immediate attraction can be justified on the basis of long-term compatibility.

When Shiona spoke to bespoke dating agencies she heard them say the same thing, emphasizing the need to work on and grow the attractiveness of a partner. They encourage clients to get to know the individuals who are being introduced to them via telephone calls before actually meeting, to work hard at making attraction work. One tells her clients that, 'even if you may not initially find them especially beautiful, that person will become more and more beautiful as you get to know them, if they have all the other qualities that you are looking for'.

So if we don't *know* what we really want, how does the dating site? Economics has an answer here, too. The theory of revealed preference, pioneered by the great economist Paul Samuelson in the first half of the twentieth century and a staple of economic theory since, assumes that the true preferences of individuals may be inferred from their consumption choices. A former chief executive of Match.com describes the site's 'revealed preference' mechanism as follows:

You may specify that you'd like your date to be blond or tall or Jewish or a non-smoking Democrat, but you may have a habit of reaching out to pot-smoking South Asian Republicans. This is called 'revealed preference,' and it is the essential element in Match's algorithmic process. Match knows what's right for you – even if it doesn't really know you. After taking stock of your stated and revealed preferences, the software finds people on the site who have similar dissonances between the two, and uses their experiences to approximate what yours should be.[9]

In other words, economic assumptions about the way that individuals move through websites, that profile browsing can be modelled like any other consumption activity to disclose preferences unknown even to the user, are embedded in the site. Basic economic axioms – that individuals act in a self-interested way and respond to stimuli in a consistent way – are invoked in the use of one individual's outcomes and behaviour to model that of another person with 'similar dissonances'. In other words, online dating sites are designed on the premise that we are all economic men and women, and for this same reason the online dating site, which has greater calculative power and economic expertise, can indeed claim to know best.

Fungibility, or making things the same

Little wonder, then, that online dating resembles the more overtly economic activity of shopping: partners become commodities to be compared and consumed, and the task of the marketer is to provide products that best meet the demands of buyers (even if, when we meet them, we have to learn to like the product that is on offer). Users browse through large numbers of profiles, looking for a perfect partner, treating the profiles with the same sophisticated cynicism that they might any other form of advertisement, and the relationships on offer as they might any other goods. The emphasis on easy consumption as opposed to long-term effort has led one group of writers to nickname the process 'relationshopping';[10] users view 'the profiles as if they had a shopping list where they would tick off which products met the specifications they were looking for'.[11] In place of the slow disclosure and mutual learning of real-world relationships, online there is a premium on upfront and immediate information; people offer intimate information online far more quickly than they would do in real life. In the seamier parts of the dating world, full disclosure means just that, too often without the merciful touches of Photoshop.

Of course, such demand for information leads soon enough to deceit. We know that people really do get taller, younger and slimmer online. Researchers have discovered that such misdescriptions are not even regarded as a lie, so long as there is an *intention* to get to the ideal self you promote online. If you promise yourself that you are going to lose three stone in the New Year, it is quite legitimate to give your post-diet weight in your profile, a kind of electronic IOU.[12] It is quite common for users to construct multiple versions of a profile, or to offer the promise of a casual relationship in order to test the 'market'.[13] I am reminded of stock market traders who 'fish' with small orders before they commit real money; it seems that once we are in a market the range of accepted behaviours changes markedly. We heard similar stories from dating agents, passed on from clients who had moved off-line in pursuit of more reliable introductions. One told us that there is often more than a few pounds or a couple of years at stake: 'There are guys, they say to me, "Oh, I shave ten years off online." Women do it too. People have turned up and they have gone, "She is size twenty, she's never a twelve!"'

To be freely traded, then, goods must be *fungible*: identical with other goods of that kind and easily substituted. Fungibility usually applies to standardized items that are frequently traded, such as frozen concentrated orange juice, bushels of wheat, wine *en primeur*, crude oil and banking securities. Standard qualities, weights and measures are one of the great achievements of economic organization and allow for the easy trade of goods worldwide. The word fungible comes from the medieval Latin term *fungibilis*, itself from *fungi*, meaning to perform or enjoy. The medieval theologians understood that the ease with which a commodity could be exchanged is intimately linked with its consumption in use: the most fungible goods, such as foodstuffs and also money, are the most consumable and exchangeable of all commodities.[14] Look again at my examples of fungible products: frozen concentrated orange juice, wheat, casks of wine, crude oil and banking securities. All but one are consumables, while the last is a variety of money; all exist for the satisfaction of man's appetites.

This is, perhaps, the central reason why more women do not take up high-class prostitution. The wages are high, even if it does mean passing over certain 'opportunities'; many women, I'm sure, would settle for the money in place of a man if that were all that was at stake. But to be a prostitute, as Punternet makes so clear, is to become fungible. It is to be *consumed* in use, used up in the provision of a service. A woman demeans herself, says Immanuel Kant, by handing over her body to a man and making herself 'a thing on which another satisfies his appetite, just as he satisfies his hunger upon a steak'.[15] She becomes a commodity, replaceable by any other and indistinguishable from the rest.

Kant's criticism is perceptive because it hinges upon exchangeability, rather than money itself. Money is a useful medium, for sure, but it is possible to achieve economic relations – competitive, market exchange – without money. A barter market, for example, is clearly economic, as participants struggle to take home the most goods in return for the smallest outlay. One of the greatest of living economists, Alvin Roth, has pointed out that a well-functioning barter market can deliver all the benefits of a money-based market, without the attendant problems.[16] Roth won the 2012 Nobel Prize in economics for his innovations in matching transplant organs, constructing barter markets for kidneys that have enabled many more people to receive transplants. Roth's work shows where twentieth-century economics is going: computing power and the technical sophistication of econometrics have reached a level such that economics, and not the market, is the best available calculator.

If computer-aided barter can reproduce the positives of a free market, then such a barter system can also reproduce the negatives: taking cash out of the picture does not necessarily change the moral content of the exchange. When a man seeking an escort browses a website, he is likely to act economically: he will want to maximize the return on his expensive fee. We all know that the sale of sex is an economic transaction and we might expect a user to pursue value for money. But what about another kind of website, one where there is a sophisticated barter of one set of goods for another? In the case of online dating it is quite possible that we find ourselves in a situation where we face the problems of market exchange though we never even take out our purses. If we go shopping for love we should not be surprised when we ourselves achieve the status of commodity.

Let me give you a particular example. Many online sites allow users to search for potential partners using a mechanism that will be familiar to anyone who has ever used the Internet to search for a second-hand car or a house. These interfaces offer a detailed menu of choices, allowing users to select partner attributes such as age, height, type of figure, hair length, hair colour and interests (the last site I looked at offered some fifteen categories including different types of music, movies, animals, gardening, cooking), marital status, ethnic origin, religion, education, children, and where you stand on drinking and smoking. At the top of the screen, a counter lists the availability of matches. The user begins with a pool of all the men or women available in the country at the time, perhaps thousands. Second-hand car websites have this mechanism too, a dial in the top corner listing available vehicles. One makes a few adjustments – the distance you are prepared to travel, and a suitable age range – and the counter tumbles downwards. Then the real fun begins. Brunette or blonde, and the counter clicks downwards again. Do you prefer warm and well-upholstered, fun and bubbly, or sleek and sporty? The choice is yours as you design your perfect partner online.

Let me settle for blonde, curly haired; a home-lover with a full-time job who enjoys cooking and partying and travel yet goes to church regularly. Eyes should definitely be hazel, and hair shoulder length. Tall, curvaceous, but slim. A postgraduate education finishes the list. The order of my wish list does not betray any prejudice on my part; it is the interface that places education after the physical attributes and interests. All the while I have been designing my perfect woman the clock has been ticking downwards, and it has now reached zero. So I must make some compromises, some trade-offs. The economist might say that I am enacting my 'dynamic preferences'. I must start to question which of these various categories I consider more important, and begin to investigate the relationships between each category and availability. There may be some attributes that matter more than scarcity. The layout of the page itself suggests that age and location are deal-breakers, while other categories may be more open to compromise. Even in the latter group there is a hierarchy suggested by the interface: hobbies and hair colour seem much more important than religion and education.

How does a user behave when presented with such an interface? There is no alternative but to try to maximize one's preferences in searching for a potential partner. We seek the best that we can get from the available supply, making decisions as to the relative merits of available attributes. For the moment, I don't want to go into the complexities of online matching or even open up the discussion of whether or not we are actually able to choose partners online. The important thing is to recognize that a kind of economic behaviour – maximizing dynamic preferences – has been brought into being through the use of a technical interface. The user, in combination with the dating website, has become the individual economic agent, the instrumentally rational, maximizing actor of economic theory.

But the website does so much more than simply help us make the choices we already would have made; instead, it specifies the choices that we can make, and articulates complex relationships between them. It focuses our decision on qualities alone, rather than the bundles of qualities we meet in everyday life, otherwise known as persons: we will choose him, or her, because we desire slimness, red hair and a love of rock-climbing, a process very different from coming to love someone who is slender, red-headed and a rock-climber. In the first, we must already be a rock-climber ourselves: in the second, we may try climbing for the first time and whole new vistas of life might open out. A friend jokes that she did not know she wanted a Jamaican salsa dancer until she found him.

The protocols of online dating make individuals fungible in the sense that they are replaceable, and exchangeable. They are constructed by the machine as goods to be consumed in use. The systems do everything in their power to erode the fundamental differences between persons – that they are different people – and render them as comparable. When a user sets out her list of preferred attributes in a partner, it is the characteristics she is choosing, not the person to whom they belong; one tall, handsome man with a penchant for the Arsenal is every bit equivalent to another.

There is some psychological evidence to support this conclusion. Scanning through lots of profiles fosters the illusion of abundance and causes us to act in an offhand, casual manner.[17] We are much better at identifying characteristics that are generally considered to be attractive than we are at spotting what appeals to us in person, revealed preference or not. The way in which we identify attractiveness online is likely to mean that a few profiles receive much of the attention, and indeed this seems to be the case, with empirical studies of dating sites showing attention clustering around 'hot' individuals.[18] Algorithms highlight popular daters, which only exacerbates the problem, focusing attention on a few and excluding many.

This state of affairs is almost a parody of Becker's utility-maximizing partnership. He suggests that we can usefully analyse how couples form partnerships by assuming that they maximize their utility; we do not need to know what it is that they value. In the case of a search and rank interface we have moved from 'as if' to fact. While Becker's analysis can accommodate any preference under the sun, we have limited our options to fifteen different types of leisure.

This process of selection works both ways. As we begin to make explicit our preferences and systematically evaluate those looking for love online, so we will come to a nuanced appreciation of our own worth and how it compares to others. We have, after all, filled out exactly the same questionnaire, and know where we stand on each point. We will, as the economic models suggest, select the best partner we can afford on the basis of our own attributes. When we do so, the world comes to look more like another theoretical model, this one known as the 'matching hypothesis'.

The 'matching hypothesis' has been a staple of relationship psychology since it was proposed in 1966. It suggests that individuals actively seek out partners of equivalent desirability or 'quality' to themselves. The motivation of individuals is to find the best-quality partner who is likely to be attracted to them in return; the pursuit of excessively high-quality partners is unlikely to yield results, and is effort and time wasted. The hypothesis is well accepted, resonating with the insights of evolutionary biology, itself a cost–benefit paradigm. Yet its predictions are counter-intuitive, for while it suggests that wealthy, intelligent, attractive, charming, educated (or whatever other proxies of quality we choose) people will be attracted to equally wealthy, intelligent, attractive, charming and educated individuals, it also suggests that those less fortunate will actively seek out partners to whom nature dealt a less generous hand. Over time, the hypothesis has been increasingly associated with physical attraction to the point where it suggests that the unattractive will pursue only the unattractive. Yet people refuse to be cowed by theory: empirical evidence overwhelmingly suggests that individuals aim for attractive partners irrespective of their own personal merits. Indeed, I am myself one of the short, oddly shaped yet hopeful men who pursue, or in my case pursued, tall, beautiful women. Admittedly, with mixed results, but the thesis of evolutionary biology was useless in the face of my youthful enthusiasm: the theory doesn't stack up with reality.

Despite the theoretical success and wide acceptance of the hypothesis, there is no scientific, empirical evidence to support the claim that unattractive individuals will prefer unattractive partners. Or at least, there was none until 2011, when a group of psychologists at the University of California at Berkeley reported on their study.[19] Four sets of experiments showed that individuals *did* target those of equivalent social desirability, a broad measure including looks. What makes these results so striking is that Lindsay Shaw Taylor and colleagues chose the medium of online dating to conduct the experiments. Three of the experiments were conducted under laboratory conditions, with the subjects completing mock profiles before searching through profiles of others. The fourth used real data from an online site and took the numbers of contacts elicited from other members of the site as a proxy for desirability; it showed that popular men and women contacted one another, and less popular individuals contacted less popular individuals.

It is possible that the matching hypothesis is correct, and this experiment simply confirms it. But it is equally possible that the mechanisms of online dating encouraged the participants to conform to the hypothetical patterns of behaviour that underpin the design of the software itself: in other words, that completing a profile makes people's evaluation of themselves sufficiently concrete for them to choose others of equivalent worth, and that the pressure to find a match led them to do so. The experiment would need to be done again with a control group to be sure, but a comparison with the findings of other experiments does suggest that online dating enacts the theoretical hypothesis, deduced from an economic conception of self-interest and cost–benefit; that it makes economics real, in the wild.

Once again, how we decide what counts – what matters, what is of value – really matters. The process of selecting a potential partner through a particular search mechanism will shape behaviour accordingly. At the very least, in the words of one study, 'the features of a person that Match.com presents as salient to romance will begin to have some psychological and cultural influences if 40 million Americans view them every month'.[20] If the mechanism directs us to height and weight first of all, that is what we will choose; if it neglects things that we might have considered important, then we will neglect them too. The mechanism cannot even begin to cope with the way we might usually speak about partners: judgements of worth – 'He has lovely eyes' – are replaced by statements of fact – 'He has blue eyes'. We pare ourselves down to a list of characteristics and the bargaining commences: economic men and women, seeking the best deal we can get for the credit we have available.

A question of method

The objectivity and rigour of scientific method are a central part of online dating's appeal, and this is critical, because there do appear to be some significant problems with the principles on which online matching is based. It is difficult to talk about the mechanisms themselves, because they are shrouded by secrecy; there are no publications in leading journals explaining the precise mechanisms of matching. Nonetheless, we are able to consider the general principles on which matching methods are built, as Eli Finkel and his colleagues, academic psychologists from the United States, have done.[21]

First of all, there are some difficulties with prediction, a vital part of online dating, because the product on offer is a relationship, a pairing that can be sustained into the future. Any dating site that offers you a compatibility score or a selection of matches or makes any claims about its ability to identify potential partners is, therefore, making statements about its ability to predict the future.

In some cases, we are quite good at prediction. We know what works in the case of transplantation, for example, where pairing is a well-defined problem of compatibility, lining up genetic codes so a body will accept an organ, and deploying immunosuppressant drugs to keep the body's more tricky mechanisms at bay: doctors have amassed substantial data on success and failure, tested and debated in the public arena. In the case of dating, it is not so simple. Marriage, it seems, is more like the stock market than the human body. We know a great deal about why stock prices move as they do. We understand, with hindsight, the power of economic shocks, and news, and earnings forecasts, and ex-dividend days and all the other little things that push shares up and down. Academic finance has been examining these in ever greater detail for at least four decades. Yet we are still unable to predict share prices: explaining why something *did happen* does not allow you to say *what will happen*, which is why academic finance researchers work in university departments, and not from their villas by Lake Como.

So, knowing what made good relationships work in the past does not necessarily provide us with the mechanisms we need to predict pairings that will succeed in the future. As generations of stock market 'chartists' have discovered, no matter how closely a hypothesis is fitted to past data, its moneymaking powers are weak. In fact, the more retrofitting goes on, the weaker the predictive powers of a hypothesis start to get. This is really a methodological problem. The technique of examining past data to establish factors that *have* influenced existing relationships is valid and fit for *that* purpose, and that purpose only. The accuracy of the factors as *predictors* needs to be established by checking their powers of prediction against another independent sample, a method called cross-validation, similar to those used in the double-blind trial mandated for pharmaceutical research. Industry researchers do not tend to do this, but when it is done, according to one academic study, the difference in results is startling. Predictive power in their sample dropped from 65 per cent to 21 per cent after cross-validation. That is one in five, instead of three in five, and much less satisfactory odds on which to build a marriage.[22]

In the case of stock market prediction the problem is that

share prices are linked to events in the world; as we cannot reliably predict politics, or accident, or even a wet summer, no matter how intelligent or complex our theory of markets, we simply cannot predict how prices will move from one week to the next. The future of marriage is linked to events in the lives of each person, and for the same reason a pair of online tests, taken in just a few minutes and based on proprietary indicators, cannot possibly give much indication of the ability of a couple to survive the ups and downs of a long future, of how they will grow and mature together, and whether their interpersonal dynamics can sustain a flourishing relationship over the long term.

When dating services promise, in the words of a recent advertisement, 'someone special, someone who shares your interests, someone just like you', or encourage you to seek, in the words of one agent, partners with 'exactly the same relationship goal', they create a self-referential, 'metrological' project, where 'love' and 'relationship' mean, as Humpty Dumpty might say, exactly what they mean them to mean. For example, eHarmony claims to make better matches than those occurring 'in the wild'. The site provides evidence for its claim: couples leaving the site register higher compatibility scores than those who have met in other ways. But the site used these scores to match the couples in the first place, and another study comments that eHarmony's data only really show it doing what it sets out to do: putting couples together according to their compatibility scores.[23]

In the end, Finkel and his colleagues suggest in measured, academic prose, that the ability of online dating to deliver what it promises may be limited:

> [T]hese sites imply, and in some instances explicitly assert, that the essential qualities of a relationship can be predicted from characteristics of the potential partners that exist before they

have met. Standing in direct contrast to this suggestion is seventy-five years of scientific research . . . indicating that pre-existing personal qualities account for a very small percentage of the variance in relationship success.[24]

More recently, the University of Chicago psychologist John Cacioppo and his colleagues have reported on a large-scale survey of nearly 20,000 respondents in the US who married between 2005 and 2012. They find that more than a third of marriages in America now begin online, that online marriages tended to be between more educated, working individuals, and that levels of satisfaction are slightly higher and divorce rates slightly lower. Their survey comprises social networking sites and gaming sites, online messaging and chat as well as online dating, which represents 45 per cent of the marriages. Yet, we still do not know why these differences exist; Cacioppo and colleagues suggest that causes could include differences in personality, the initial intention to form a long-term relationship, a larger pool of spouses, or more honest, open self-disclosure online.[25]

Online dating presents us with a distinctively economic way of understanding love. It demands that we treat falling in love as a moment of active and rational choice, where personal attributes and compatibility form the basis of attraction. Advertisements tell us to take control of our own future, and not to rely on chance or Lady Luck. Those sites which allow users to search for potential matches configure individuals as no more than a conjunction of attributes, working out the value of each attribute available, relative to each other and to what the user has to offer. The behavioural economist Dan Ariely has argued that online dating is unrelentingly miserable because this basic mechanism – breaking people into attributes – is flawed. Like a fine wine, or a holiday, he says, people need to be experienced as a whole rather than a collection of traits. But Ariely, perhaps because he is an economist and is wedded to notions of instrumental exchange, misses the point. People are not like a fine wine or a holiday; they are not things to be 'experienced', as dating services would have us believe. Experiencing is a self-centred occupation, and a glass of wine serves no purpose beyond the temporary gratification of the drinker's senses. Flourishing human relationships, on the other hand, are mutually rewarding, ongoing endeavours.

Where the first part of the book investigated economics as a political discourse, these last four chapters have explored the construction of economic man, examined the boundaries of the economic and seen economics at work in the world. I have argued that a particular kind of rationality has been brought into being through economic language and calculation, embedded into the devices that we use to navigate the shifting passages of daily life. I hope to have shown that the self-interest that organizes our society is far removed from the innate selfishness of personal survival, even from the virtuous self-interest of Adam Smith; it is an instrumental, rational, strategic and calculative set of actions that depends for its existence upon the theories and instrumentation of modern economics. To see how this manifests itself, we have had to go beyond monetary exchange and look at the technical, organizational arrangements that make economic behaviour a reality. There are now just two real questions: why does all of this matter? And what, if anything, can we do about it?

PART THREE

9. The True Cost of Economics

The evidence that global temperatures are rising is incontrovertible, and it is clear the effects will bite hardest on the poorest and most disadvantaged regions of the world. We are using up the world's resources of fossil fuels and rare metals, polluting the oceans and making a mess of our hospitable planet. Science fiction Utopias may be back in vogue, with talk of the colonization of Mars. Even if this takes place, for all apart from those plucky few, there is nowhere else for us to go, and nothing else to use. When everything has been exploited, there will be nothing left. That terrifying prognosis introduces many moral questions: is it just that we use up the world's resources, ignoring the claims of future generations? Is it right to restrict access to the high standard of living that we enjoy, and which the populations of rapidly industrializing countries are seeking to share? Are we responsible for harm inflicted on less-advantaged parts of the globe by our actions, even indirectly? Despite the complex and highly problematic nature of any actions we might take, these are moral problems, questions of justice and obligation. They ask: what should we do?

In October 2006, the eminent British economist Nicholas Stern published a report on the subject of global warming, commissioned by the British government. His conclusions were alarming: increased risk of floods in low-lying countries as temperatures rise and glaciers melt; a decline in food production, especially in Africa; a possible 40 per cent extinction rate of global species; and the permanent displacement of 200 million people. An economist through and through, Stern also attempted to make the 'business case' for dealing with global warming. He concluded that 'the total cost over the next two centuries of climate change . . . involves impacts and risks that are equivalent to an average reduction in global per-capita consumption of at least 5 per cent, now and forever'.[1]

Stern's report might have been met with a stunned silence. A respected figure, an expert, a pillar of the global establishment, tells us that nearly half of the world's species may cease to exist if temperatures rise by as little as 2°C, and that there will be 200 million refugees sleeping out on Europe's collective lawn.

That didn't happen. Instead, a row began over the methodology Stern had used to derive these conclusions. An economist himself, and fully aware that economic forecasts are the only discourse of any real power in public life, Stern made the case in economic terms. Unfortunately, in doing so he opened up a battle of calculation. Arguments focused upon his estimation of cost, and the methodology used to derive it. In particular, attention focused on the 'discount rate', where he was accused of making basic errors in his calculations.

The discount rate is a method for taking account of the 'opportunity cost' of spending in the present. Remember that the cost of any course of action is the action it precludes, and in the case of expenditure that cost − the alternative course of action − will be the investment revenues forsaken. Economic theory supposes that capital can be invested risk-free and will bear a safe, though low, return. A course of action carries risks, so we compare them with this risk-free alternative, to work out how much our risk is paying. As an example, I put money in the stock market and make a profit in a medium-risk stock; to really understand how much that risk is paying I should 'discount' by the money I could have earned risk-free. Usually, this is understood to be the 'return' available on assets such as United States government debt.

This model implies that if returns elsewhere are good, I will be less inclined to spend today. Imagine that I must spend

£100 on a product, now or in the future. I have the cash in my hand, to invest or spend. If I invest the money and predict that it will be worth £110 in five years' time, I am losing £10 by acting today. By the same logic, an expenditure of £100 in five years' time is equivalent to spending £91 now: it is cheaper to act later because our money could be working elsewhere. But, of course, we do not know what money will be worth in the future, and we must choose to 'discount' at a rate that matches our estimated risk-free return; the higher the discount, the more costly action becomes today. So if we assume that the global polity remains the same, that global economies are fizzing and good returns are to be had elsewhere, the cost of spending today is high, and we should wait until tomorrow.

Stern was accused of taking an unduly cautious discount rate, exaggerating the cost of acting tomorrow while underestimating the cost of acting today. A vigorous debate sprang up among academic economists, all experts in their fields and reputable scholars, as to the correct way of costing climate change.

But the argument can be built in many ways. There is no universally agreed standard for this discount figure. If you wish to show that action should be taken now, perhaps because you consider environmental catastrophe a pressing problem, you could build an argument that supported a low discount rate. On the other hand, if you are a citizen of a rich developed-world country and feel, with good reason, that your countrymen would be made less affluent by short-term expenditure, you would argue for a higher rate. This too can be seen as a moral statement: Robert Mendelsohn, Professor of Environmental Economics at Yale, argues that 'the *ethical justification* for intentionally overspending on selective projects with low rates of return is weak indeed'.[2]

The argument over Stern's report shows two things. First of all, as I have been arguing throughout this book, once the discussion has been dragged onto economic terrain it can only be settled with calculators and spread-sheets. The second point is that economic reasoning is not objective: not in the sense of having recourse to some higher scientific truth, nor in the sense of treating everyone the same. In the argument over global warming, economic tools become vehicles for existing political wrangling, as the immediate interests of two quite different groups come into contact. One statement of objectivity benefits the poor, and another the rich. Which is more objective? We must go back to our calculators in a dispute that can never be settled.

So it isn't the case that economics is necessarily objective or fair, or that it has no moral content. It is as political, as morally freighted, as any other of our contemporary discourses.

But the real crux of my argument is a third point: economics makes the world it describes. The very foundation of this calculation, the notion of a world where what we *should* do is tied to measures of wealth, where all our decisions are most properly addressed in the language of the social welfare and returns on capital, is a product of economics, of a long process of historical and social adjustment to a set of theoretical laws. Economics and our contemporary society are deeply, irretrievably, intertwined; that is the fount of economic power, the reason that economics explains so well. The collective action that global crisis demands will require an entirely different kind of social contract, with self-interest perceived as inextricable from global survival. Achieving that will take time and effort.

Economic virtues and vices?

Twentieth-century followers of Adam Smith – those same who have thrust smallness upon the Scottish intellectual – have always considered self-interested competition to be the basis of human motivation, and a market to be the natural arena in which that self-interest is expressed: 'A market may be defined as a set of competitive relationships in which agents strive, within the limits set by ground rules, to better their own economic positions . . . a degree of indifference to the market fates of others is, manifestly, an inevitable feature of the market practice.'[3] By this view, there is nothing remarkable in people taking on a competitive, economic persona, while remaining a moral citizen; in fact, if markets are thought to be the most efficient means for allocation of goods, then competitive behaviour is essential. Democracy and liberty flow from the market, which depends upon competition, so the ability to be selfish in a market situation is as much a social skill as good conversation. Such a view is expressed, for example, in Friedman's claim that the sole responsibility of business is to pursue profit: for Friedman, managers may be as moral as they like in the evenings, on the golf course, or when they take the children to church on Sunday, but at work they must adopt the persona of ruthless competition in order to offer the maximum social benefit.[4]

By this account, selfishness and strategic competition are confined to market situations. There is an impermeable division between the cut-throat entrepreneurial persona of the office and the genial, generous parent, spouse and neighbour of the weekend. Those who are prepared to follow Jeremy Bentham and justify action on its outcomes alone distinguish between reasons for entering the market and activity within it: the most self-interested behaviour within the market might be justifiable on the basis of a worthy purpose outside it. (Is it ethical to use the profits from sweatshop labour to build an orphanage? Discuss.)

For Deirdre McCloskey, who has written so persuasively on the rhetorical power of economics, the virtues of the market tread a middle path between the two great traditions of European ethical thinking.[5] On the one hand was a tradition epitomized by Friedrich Nietzsche, who looked back to the aristocratic heroes of the Homeric stories, warlike, disdainful, proud, yet bound by honour and duty; Nietzsche railed against the slave mentality of religion that had kept men in chains for so long and exhorted us to transcend ourselves, to become super-human – *Übermensch*. On the other was the Christian ideal of world renunciation and service, the humble, frugal peasant virtues of St Francis. These cultures together made possible, and were destroyed by, the battlefields of the First World War. Now, in their place, we have the market. McCloskey suggests that we are all 'bourgeois' now – neither aristocrat nor peasant – and we should take – we do take – 'what the market gives – polite, accommodating, energetic, enterprising, risk-taking, trustworthy people; not bad people'. McCloskey's arguments are descended directly from the Enlightenment view that the virtues of trade are preferable to the strife and pillage of aristocratic rule.

I would suggest that these arguments are two hundred years out of date. They fail to recognize the role that economics has taken in governing and shaping our world, and the extent to which economic relations, epitomized by self-interest, have colonized our lives. And here's the rub: the self-interest of contemporary economic man is *not the same* as the native selfishness of small children, of the pre-industrial villager, or mankind in the Hobbesian state of nature. It is self-evidently, trivially true that people have always been interested in their own advancement; contemporary self-interest, on the other hand – the calculative, instrumental rationality of the twenty-first-century economic agent – is a complex, technical achievement, a far cry from the bourgeois virtues listed above. It is the intrusion of this technically mediated, cold-hearted rationality into the most private, personal spaces of our lives and bodies to which I have been pointing throughout.

Moreover, it would be a mistake to think that this self-interest is manifested purely at the level of the individual. It has become part of a social apparatus of governance, by which we are all encouraged to become entrepreneurs of ourselves, viewing our whole lives as a string of personal projects, each of which should be assessed in terms of investment required and the possible return. Cost–benefit, identified by philosophers such as Daniel Dennett as the unique motivating factor of humankind, has become a systematic rule of governance from our persons to our institutions. It has its place, I'm sure. The historian of science Ted Porter has argued that cost–benefit grew in popularity throughout the twentieth century as a means of building trust in bureaucratic administration. Numbers had the appeal of fairness and scientific objectivity.[6] But, as I have argued throughout, calculations such as the QALY or the VSL, of investment returns, or the publicly worked-out value-for-money standards of Punternet, are socially and temporally specific artefacts. They are made, and we should be able to understand and, should we wish, to dispute that making.

To give one final example: liver surgeons and NHS statisticians in the UK are running complex models to see whether outcomes are best if transplant organs are offered to the sickest, the healthiest or those who will benefit most. Outcomes are judged by the difference between patients' life expectancy with and without surgery. These experiments calculate the 'population life years' saved across the three groups, taking into account mortality of those not treated as well as the benefits accrued by those who are treated. It is proposed that the allocation regime offering the greatest savings in population life years will be adopted as a guide for treatment. In other words, the successful treatment regime will be the one that maximizes collective social welfare, a perfect economic solution.

This 'thought experiment' (in the words of the supervising consultant) only makes sense if 'population life years' *has already been taken as the appropriate measure*, and why should it be? There are other possible considerations. A sickest-first rule, for example, will yield fewer life years but will do much to alleviate the terrible suffering of those in the later stages of chronic liver disease. By prioritizing younger people and paediatric patients we can do something to offset natural injustices, when people are struck down before their time. There is a certain strand of public moralizing that would have 'self-inflicted' liver failure, the result of alcoholism or obesity, denied treatment. Some people are seen as more deserving than others; on more than one occasion a student suggested to me that the late Steve Jobs 'deserved' a liver transplant on account of his services to industry (Jobs received one in 2009).[7]

Such considerations, just a few of many possible claims on a possible donated organ, show why cost–benefit analysis is so powerful and prevalent in any organizational situation or public debate: it is straightforward, transparent and apparently objective. It is able to gather people around it: it provides administrators in different offices with a common language, makes organizing easier and allows us to compare the incommensurable in policy debates. But the example also shows that transparency and objectivity are at best relative concepts. Behind any transparent and objective statement of costs and benefits are swathes of calculation, hidden from view; here they take the form of medical data and clinical scores, manipulated through the statisticians' models. Moral work is built into the foundations of any such project. And anyway, what good is objectivity – which here means maximizing life years saved – if it is not the outcome we choose? In fact, research shows that the public values fairness and equity of access over and above total life years as a guiding principle for allocation.[8]

We should not allow ourselves to be lured by the easy answers that cost–benefit analysis provides. When presented by an economic fact, a cost–benefit trade-off, we must ask how and why it was made. Cost–benefit efficiencies are only one of a possible universe of virtues, and we must decide where they are appropriate and where they are not. The economic approach will impose a ruthless utilitarianism of cost–benefit at any possible opportunity, but not all situations are the same. I have offered Nicholas Stern's work on global warming and the response of other economists as evidence of the ability of cost–benefit analysis to subsume pressing moral questions, and it remains the elephant in the room; in the case of global warming, questions such as justice, stewardship and our responsibility to future generations, not to mention to the biosphere, really do trump appeals to cost–benefit. They are not easy questions, but the difficulty of engaging with them does not mean that we should shy away from the task.

I have endeavoured to show throughout this book that all economics is normative, in the same way that all language, according to J. L. Austin, is performative. It is inescapably bound up in the construction of the world that it seeks to describe. Economic behaviour can be learned in formal settings, as economics undergraduates learn to be self-interested and learn to free ride, or private investors learn to tackle the market in particular ways. When we understand the world *as if* people respond to incentives in a self-interested, instrumental manner, then we build institutions which *make* people respond in that manner. Economic thinking, embedded in language and devices, constitutes us as economic subjects; we are shut into the panopticon of economics. The assumptions upon which economic analysis are based are so thoroughly normalized, and validated by further tests and hypotheses and associated assumptions, that they become part of the fabric of our knowledge; a grand unified theory of everything, based on simple, elegant suppositions about 'how people are', constitutes those very same people.

Where the natural sciences celebrate an endless multiplication of theorems and proofs, of data and evidence, economics sets its sights on a single universal algorithm, the trade-off of costs and benefits under conditions of scarcity, and works hard to bring it into existence.

If the central question of economic analysis is the trade-off of costs and benefits, then the central virtue of economic reason (and any decisions, policies or regulations associated with it) is efficiency. It is an explicitly moral claim, a statement about how the world should be: if we can do more with less by following a particular course of action, we are obliged to act in that way. It is certainly true that where the causes of action are identical, apart from cost, it makes sense to pursue the cheaper one; in that case we are all, indeed, better off. But where in our complicated lives are we to find courses of action that are otherwise identical? We soon enough have to choose between efficiency and other beneficial outcomes, and we have seen that pursuing efficiency above everything else leads us to some pretty tight corners: that we should treat failing hips rather than failing kidneys and prefer any kind of low-intensity outpatient treatment to the intensive treatment of chronic or terminal illnesses; that we are not obliged to make changes to faulty or defective equipment, should the benefits of those changes outweigh the costs; that, in the face of coming environmental catastrophe, action is morally wrong, and inaction is right. We have seen how a cost–benefit analysis of our own persons draws certain conclusions: that an education is best understood in terms of the future benefits it will bring as against the costs in the present, where the only measure of value comes from the perspective of the student; that future partners should be determined by the maximum return available on the basis of one's own personal assets.

So I return to my central question: how did economics become so strong? How did it move from an ambitious, but highly specialized and professional laboratory science to a systematic mode of social engagement that can organize the world around it? How did it manage to give rise to a new species – *Homo oeconomicus* – whose bodies we inhabit so completely, despite our discomfort and misgivings? The answer: through the things we own and use. At large, in the wild, whether in care or safety, investment, education or romance, in the shop or at home, economics lurks in devices, in the mundane, material artefacts by which we navigate the world around us. These simple, innocuous artefacts take away the effort of doing, of thinking, of being, and distribute it among databases and scores, systems and rankings. They shape the way we speak, and what matters to us when we have to make a choice. Even the humble shopping label plays its part, a tiny gateway between our money, our desires and chains of labour and production stretching across the globe. The label tells us what matters, it stabilizes complex choices, real, moral questions – what *should* we do – as tiny numbers, prices per kilo or litre.

Through these devices, the insistent, instrumental logic of self-interest has been imposed on the central activities of our lives: in work, in consumption, in buying a home, in getting an education, in finding a partner. It has found its way into the collective activities that distinguish the kind of society we are, that we want to be. So we seem no longer to be able to provide adequate care for the sick, the old or the infirm, because it is not cost-effective. We insist that the students themselves are the only ones who receive the benefit of an education: true if they become investment bankers, perhaps, but not if they become teachers, social workers, doctors, clerics, or 'social entrepreneurs'. (And there is a self-fulfilling effect even here: by forcing those receiving education to pay a price that is ranked in cost and quality, we ensure that the best and brightest do become investment bankers and lawyers.) Even in the formation of our relationships we have come to expect a partnership that is immediate, efficient and effective; that can be severed at will; that requires no investment or commitment from ourselves. These changes have been brought about through simple, ordinary devices: the lists, rankings, scores, tabulations and algorithms that populate our lives.

So, economics' power lies in its ability to hold things together. Divergent networks of people and material devices are coordinated by a common language and worldview, itself embedded in a machinery of calculation. Disparities of power in markets, institutions and organizations can be attributed to calculative superiority as much as political or financial advantage. Consumers are weak in the face of the tools wielded by the supermarket, from labels and shopping trolleys to sophisticated databases and pricing strategies. Consider the earnest young Dennis Gioia, recall coordinator at the time of the Pinto explosions, unable to make change happen. His story showed the punch of calculative power: he did not battle as an angry, powerless rebel against a faceless bureaucracy; quite the reverse, a diligent, apparently caring young executive, struggling to do his best at all times, still decided that the appropriate choice of action – the *moral course of action* – was to leave the cars on the road. And he did so not once, but *twice*.

Yet, efficiency is not queen of all virtues. Others are nobler, though less splendidly clothed; even the knaves of waste and inefficiency may play their part. Not every relationship has to be perfect, nor does every partner have to be just right for you, now. Risks, dead ends and failures contribute much to who we are. Arduous though it may seem, the fact that the process of finding that an individual is not straightforward, and that some effort may be required on both sides, may itself be enlightening. Indeed, the whole dance might even be fun. Frivolity and flippancy struggle to make a mark in the dour world of cost and benefits.

What of our obligation to the weak, the infirm, the less fortunate; to the generations not yet born? Are there things that we simply cannot tolerate – sweatshop labour, perhaps, or exploitative lending, or the suffering of a terminally ill person, or the fact that, at a time of unprecedented human wealth and consumption, there are still children growing up in absolute poverty even in the richest countries in the world? Might it not be that the pages of Punternet are so relentless in their economizing and commodifying that they impoverish us all?

In 1785 Immanuel Kant published his *Groundwork of the Metaphysics of Morals*, a slim volume which has become one of the foundational works of moral philosophy. In this book Kant suggested a 'categorical imperative' for human behaviour, and from that comes the maxim that we should: 'treat humanity, whether in your own person or in the person of any other, never merely as a means to an end, but always at the same time as an end'.[9]

Kant's ethics is of oughts, obligations and duties, rather than outcomes and calculations. It cannot tolerate the felicitous calculus of the market, where the sum total of good may outweigh some significant hurt. It focuses on the singularity and dignity of persons. Economics, on the other hand, makes associations, and the broader it casts its net, the more elaborate these associations become. It is possible, for example, to follow a golden thread of calculation from the overburdened borrower in Florida to the nearly bankrupt city administration in Europe. Economic association makes things fungible, linking borrowers and investors in a way that demonstrates the ease with which some constituents may be substituted for others. It is not personal trust, goodwill or reputation that matters, but credit scores and interest rates. The social roots have been torn from trade and replaced by economic facts, questionable though these may turn out to be.

When we come to value something in economic terms, like a kidney, or a body for hire, we demonstrate in practice the possibility of substituting one person for another, disregarding what it is that makes them special as persons. We signal our willingness to subject them to the rules of exchange. But, as we have seen, we do not need a market to achieve the same outcomes: we pursue commodification through sophisticated systems of barter ruled by economizing algorithms. When we flick through profiles on a dating site, when we trust the science of matching to provide us with a perfect partner, we disregard everything save our own purposes and our own ends. The others on the site become perfectly interchangeable commodities, stripped of all dignity and singularity.

Humans are not distinctive because we truck, barter and exchange. We are distinctive because we can treat others as persons, distinctive in our ability to empathize with, commit to and understand one another, and to build relationships that are strong and mutually nourishing. Through its systematic assertion of self-interest, economics has undone our capacity for relationship; in an age of unprecedented wealth, we are unhappier than ever before. This is the true cost of economics.

10. Let's Occupy Economics

Recycling and 're-purposing' are the buzzwords of the decade. They signal the recognition that new ways of shopping, and new modes of consumption, are not going to go away; if we are wedded to a provision of life's necessities in cardboard and plastic packaging, the best we can do is make sure the packaging finds a new life. Perhaps we should say the same about economics. After all, economics is now ubiquitous, and has changed the way we think and feel about our work, our leisure and even our romance. How then should we go about reclaiming economics? Is it possible to imagine an economics turned back on itself, one that uses the vocabulary and materials of economic life in a way that develops human flourishing, rather than corroding it?

Occupy, the leaderless anti-capitalist uprising of 2011, which allowed a younger generation – those whom neo-liberalism has failed most substantially – to express their anger against the 'system', and created a global news bonanza, hardly made an impression on the carapace of global finance. This was, perhaps, because it misunderstood the nature of economic power. It chose to be high-profile and deliberately disorganized, but the power of economics is not rooted in the media, or in the political cronyism that Occupy sought to avoid through its leaderless structure.[1] It comes instead from the habitual use of economic devices to structure the world in which we live, and of economic language to organize the way that we think. Any serious resistance must come from the ground upwards. It must be grass-roots in a meaningful sense; if economics changes the way we think, then we need an economics that can help us think clearly once more.

We need to discover – to recover – an economics that can invigorate, rather than corrode, our personal relationships; an economics that avoids the instrumental, self-interested evaluation of others. We must leave behind the failing model of a dispassionate science and develop an economics that integrates its ends with its means. And finally, we must seek out an economics that is directed at human flourishing rather than efficiency. No small order, it seems.

Re-imagining economic exchange

Movements that manage to reclaim economics tend to be specific, parochial and democratic, growing out of local settings and community effort. Such movements have been with us since the industrial revolution gave rise to market society. In nineteenth-century Britain the social reformer Robert Owen, appalled both by industrialization and by the poverty that followed the repeal of the Poor Laws, established what became known as 'Owenism'.[2] At its peak, Owenism numbered hundreds of thousands of artisans and workers in its ranks, making it one of the biggest social movements in history, and sought to define a new relationship between workers and machines. Workers' cooperatives developed where unemployed labourers could work, and profits were directed towards establishing cooperative villages, or settlements; the British cooperative movement grew out of Owenism.

Another aspect of the Owenite movement was the Labour Exchange, which made use of freely circulating 'labour notes', a currency based on the promise of work. The artisans who made up the exchange believed that by providing for themselves, they could achieve some stability and avoid the worst excesses of the marketplace. Like neo-liberalism, Owen's movement rejected the division between economy and society; unlike neo-liberalism, it refused to recognize profit as an organizing motive. In his New Lanark factory, visited by travellers from all over the world, Owen kept his workers secure, educated their children, offered shorter working hours and provided housing and leisure facilities. The movement was replete with irony all the same: Owen's factories were very profitable, for wages were not high and rest and happiness made the workforce productive. None other than Jeremy Bentham made considerable profits as an investor in the venture.

There is something of the village in the Owenite movement, a recognition of the loss felt by those who moved from the rich, interpersonal exchange of rural life to the abstract, market-driven existence of the contemporary cities. That feeling is shared by many in the developed world today, and has given rise to do-it-yourself economies of local currencies and trading schemes. Such schemes, direct descendants of Owen's labour notes, are the most recent manifestation of a rich tradition that looks back to non-alienated communal labour, and hopes to find a more authentic, complete way of living through the barter of time and the exchange of goods, something of the pristine designs for living that Polanyi attributed to our forebears.

The first local exchange trading scheme, or LETS, was set up in 1983 in British Columbia, by a man named Michael Linton. His 'green dollars' saw half a million Canadian dollars' worth of economic activity in its first two years. Similar schemes have proliferated worldwide, with particular success in Australia and New Zealand, but remain very small in absolute terms: even the largest LETS might have just a few thousand members, many of whom trade infrequently.[3] On the other hand, perhaps size is neither here nor there, as the schemes emphasize locality and community. By this measure, counting the numbers of schemes, of their members or of the volumes traded, is exactly the wrong way to go about understanding their importance, and what it is that they do. LETS allow their members a glimpse into another world, one of strong community, local resilience and where money is stripped of its savagery.

The principle of the LETS is simple enough. Members advertise services, skills or produce that they can offer, and others that they would like to receive. Usually there is some kind of directory, online or printed, and members contact each other to request whatever it is that they want. They agree a 'price' in the scheme's notional currency, and the transaction is recorded by means of a cheque or an online system. All of which sounds very economic, with its talk of bargains and cheques – which is doubtless the point, as these schemes are an attempt to subvert and re-purpose existing market arrangements. The big difference comes in the agreement of the price. This is based around the amount of time it takes to provide a good or service: three hours of one service costs the same as three hours of another, irrespective of the nature of the service or who provides it.

The equivalence of value and time is a foundational principle of any LETS. Organizers understand that there is something fundamentally liberating about pricing everybody's time at the same level; the unemployed, economically excluded individual is valued at the same level as the wealthy professional, no matter what service or product is offered. By participating in a LETS transaction, an individual actively recognizes the value of the other in a communal exchange.

There seem to be two competing accounts of the values of LETS. On one hand, in the tradition of the Owenite labour exchange, there is a narrative of inclusion and autonomy, with participants hoping to shelter themselves from the vicissitudes of the global economy. Commentators see this as workers taking control of their own production and making use of the skills and time that markets have abandoned under competitive pressure.[4] It is an echo of other do-it-yourself economic fixes from desperate times, such as the butter economy of interwar Germany, or the use of cigarettes as hard currency in Europe after the Second World War.

Unfortunately, it seems that the abstract ideals of economic freedom resonate more easily with the wealthy professional than the excluded individual struggling to survive in the economic margins. Empirical evidence shows that LETS tend to benefit the employed, the well educated, well off and physically capable.[5] It is easy enough to sell one's 'side' skills or offer chunks of spare time if one already has steady employment, and participants with steady employment will expect to obtain their necessities through the existing formal market. While the ability to offer evening lessons in Japanese may be a source of delight to teacher and to student, it is of little use to someone who needs to put food on the table. A local scheme may simply be too small to meet the needs of the unemployed, while the availability of cheaper labour through the formal market means that the skills they have to offer may be unwanted. In short, the unemployed and underfed are likely to remain that way, trading scheme or none.

Local tax offices also tend to treat local currency revenues as real revenues, convertible at the official currency level, so the individual who manages to make a living through a local trading scheme will find her benefits cut and receive a tax bill payable in hard currency. Tax offices are only doing what they must in order to avoid an otherwise obvious loophole; the relationship between the formal economy and an alternative, but still formal, economy remains problematic. There have been successes: New Zealand has seen local schemes, termed 'green dollar exchanges', set up with the exact aim of extending inclusivity by building self-esteem among the unemployed, while the bringing of household tasks into a more formal economy can emancipate women and those unable to work.[6] Nonetheless, studies carried out in Glasgow in the late 1990s suggest that LETS have been most successful at delivering social aims in areas where there is a high level of unemployed but educated middle-class.[7]

One stumbling block for these LETS, particularly in working-class areas, has been the peculiar role of debt. Despite organizers' efforts to tinker with the language and rebrand debt as 'commitment' or 'promise', many have been resistant to the idea of accumulating debts of any kind. Such resistance is a serious problem, for the schemes are driven by debt. As the system begins at zero, at least *some* individuals must go into debt to get the system moving. There is a raw Keynesianism to the functioning of a LETS: only prolific spending will expand the money supply and get things going, while accumulation is grit in the cogs of the economic engine. As there is no payment of interest, there is no reason to be in surplus; besides, organizers will examine the records and encourage those who are 'hoarding' credits to spend them. Surplus, it seems, is too close to capitalism's accumulation, and to be discouraged. A store of credits indicates that someone has been prolific in doing tasks for others, but has a reluctance to allow others to do tasks in return, effectively preventing the sale of other members' services.

Proponents of the schemes put it differently. One says, 'With barter credit we are never in debt to the person we trade with. Our commitment is to the community to return value for value received.'[8] They seek to undo the depersonalization of the marketplace, and I speculate that that effort is a reason in itself for the unwillingness of some people to take on 'debt'. Unlike the depersonalized process of spending on a credit card, where one makes an unspecified commitment to repay money – a universal, disembodied medium – at some point in the future, when 'spending' on a LETS one makes a direct commitment, a promise that must be repaid. At the same time one does not know to whom and in what shape that repayment will be made; there is, as Dr Faustus discovered, a very real risk attached to dealing in the currency of promises. This re-personalization of the marketplace, together with the rebuilding of meaningful economic relationships and the re-entangling of economic transaction with community, is central to the purpose of the schemes. A well-run LETS can act as a centripetal force in a community, establishing networks of commitment and allowing them to flourish as the scheme gathers pace.

The ideal of a successful trading scheme is one of abundance. Increased activity directly results in an expansion of credit, and unlike the formal economy there are no worries about overheating or inflation. As each credit represents an economic exchange that has been reanimated with social content, the endless expansion of the scheme becomes a utopian vision. Schemes and transactions become spaces for experimentation, play and self-discovery, with the directory serving as a semi-public space where people can try out new identities, and where the community as a whole can present an idealized vision of itself.[9] Those who join the scheme solely to make money – and the narrative of economic re-inclusion suggests that some might – become a major source of unrest, while those who need the more substantial goods of existence are likely to be frustrated by, as one scheme member said to me, the absence of anything but alternative therapy treatments and cat-sitting.

The success of LETS is mixed. They struggle to exist in a liminal space between the informal and formal economy. They are formal in structure, with accounting records and a currency that is at least nominally convertible into national systems, so they are at the mercy of local tax and benefits offices. On the other hand, formal records are necessary if the scheme is to deliver the transparency and fairness that it promises. Such constraints, not to mention the schemes' complexity, means that their ability to re-empower people at the fringes of the economy is limited, although not altogether diminished. Even successful schemes tend to collapse under the weight of the bureaucracy required to manage them.

Does this mean that they are worthless? I don't think so. Local exchange trading schemes offer a window onto a new way of organizing markets, one that highlights the role of trust and empathy in economic exchange, and makes it possible to imagine that economics could be different: that it could be an economics for us, locally organized and productive, and one which we control in a very local, specific way. It may even be, and I speculate again, that any trading scheme is a necessarily short-lived thing, with the seeds of its own demise sown in its success. For it seems that once the scheme has succeeded in establishing trading relationships among people who were previously strangers, the bureaucracy is no longer needed, and the scheme peters out. It leaves in its place a community.

Rethinking money

In classical sociology, writers such as Marx and Simmel saw money as the central device for evaluating and exchanging any object, person or service, making, as Marx so neatly put it, 'impossibilities fraternize'.[10] They looked back to Aristotle, who believed that money was *only* a medium of exchange, a convention established and maintained by law:

> All goods must therefore be measured by some one thing, as we said before. Now this unit is in truth demand . . . but money has

become by convention some representative of demand, and this is why it has the name money (*nomisma*) because it exists not by nature but by law (*nomos*) and it is in our power to change it and make it useless.[11]

So we could, if we wanted, simply legislate against money – Aristotle's sentiment is not likely to wash with what anthropologists call 'savage money', the circulating, powerful, global capital that has been abstracted from all of its roots in interpersonal exchange.[12] Anyone who would protest against money needs to subvert it, making use of the strengths of a currency and at the same time attempting to re-enchant it with local identity and relationships. Cue the growth of local currency schemes, which take a step further than the trading scheme and print their own money. Local currency enjoys the robust simplicity of cash; where a LETS needs an accounting system to function, the local currency needs, like state money, no means of tracking the exchange of favours except itself.

One of the oldest and best-established of these schemes is the Ithaca Hours currency, which has run in the university town of Ithaca, New York, since 1991. By 2005 there were ten thousand Hours in circulation, which at $10 an hour equated to $100,000. Hours advocates describe them as 'real money' backed by relationships within the community, comparing this favourably with the 'funny money' of the Federal Reserve, which is backed by billions of dollars of debt. Other currencies have appeared: Bay Bucks in Traverse City, Michigan and BerkShares in Berkshire, Massachusetts. In Britain, there are Brixton pounds, Bristol pounds and Totnes pounds, among others.

In principle, the local currencies work much like trading schemes, stressing the direct relationship of time and money – an Ithaca Hour equals $10, or an hour of somebody's time. Local traders can opt to take these in exchange for goods, and in turn might pay their employees, at least in part, in local currency. Unlike trading schemes there are very real problems of money supply and inflation to contend with, and traders will be wary of landing up with a stockpile of local currency; for these schemes to be truly successful, perhaps a buyer of last resort is needed, and local councils could contribute much by accepting them as part of the rates. Some schemes offer a central bank where the currency can be traded for official money, albeit at a discount. But in the end, someone has to pay: local currencies are torn between their official convertibility – where the taxman will demand his cut, but not in Totnes pounds – and their practical vulnerability, backed by relationships and not by fiat.

Local currencies aim to keep money in the area, forcing it to recirculate among local traders and preventing large corporations from siphoning wealth away. Their cheerful notes are money with a conscience: clutching your Brixton pound, you are obliged to act in accordance with your principles, purchasing an organic bloomer and hand-cured streaky from the farmers' market, rather than popping into the supermarket for white sliced bread and mechanically recovered ham. Supporters talk of the Keynesian multiplier effect, where money in the area leads to an acceleration of local prosperity; cynics argue that people who use the local currencies would probably shop in the same stores, and that in the end it makes little difference. In the case of the Totnes pound the currency is part of the 'Transition Town' project, a grass-roots movement that aims to pursue more sustainable ways of living through sustainable agricultural production, local exchange and community involvement.

Movements like this attract enthusiastic supporters, all committed to envisaging and acting out a new mode of economic engagement. They re-imagine money in an attempt to limit its ability to make things abstract and exchangeable. In the face of savage money, however, local currencies remain small change, a symbolic economic resistance to global finance rather than a practical one.

An alternative way of re-imagining money, and thus economics, is to inhibit money's ability to multiply. The distrust of interest is as old as trade itself. Aristotle insists that money's proper use is the provision of goods for the household; he might just accept trade, but absolutely does not approve of interest. In the only joke, so I'm told, in the entire Aristotelian corpus he quips that money does not have children – the Greek words for interest and childbirth are connected.[13] Aristotle argued that money is intended to be used in exchange, and not to be bred like an animal, treated as a means of getting more money without any productive economic activity. The Aristotelian tradition continued into medieval Europe: Dante's Virgil meets the moneylenders with their faces pressed against the earth as a punishment for their fixation with worldly things. A sophisticated branch of medieval scholasticism debated the legitimate use of money, arguing against interest on the grounds that time belongs to God and should not be sold, and that money was a commodity designed to be consumed in use – was *fungible* – and therefore interest was illegitimate. Similar arguments were made much more recently by those who resisted the arrival of life insurance in nineteenth-century America: insurance constituted a wager on death and sale of time, both of which belonged to God.[14]

While Dante was sculpting his verses, Italian bankers were developing the bills of exchange that circumvented the church's prohibitions on interest; by the time life insurance appeared in Europe, the locals were so habituated to these ideas that it was an immediate success. Islam, on the other hand, still forbids lending at interest. The Qur'an thunders against moneylenders: 'That which you give in usury (*riba*) in order that it may increase on (other) people's property hath no increase with Allah; but that which you give in charity (*zakat*), seeking God's countenance, hath increase manifold,' and 'Oh you who believe! Devour not usury, doubling and quadrupling (the sum lent) . . .'[15] Usurious moneylending had been a serious problem in pre-Islamic Arabia, and the Qur'an rules accordingly. The prohibition is more than just a ban on interest. The supplementary body of law provided by the Hadith, or sayings of the Prophet, suggests that *riba* is equally concerned with the making of equivalence across commodities: 'Abu Sa'id al-Khudri reported God's Messenger as saying, 'Gold is to be paid for by gold, silver by silver, wheat by wheat, barley by barley, dates by dates, and salt by salt like for like, payment being made "hand to hand". If anyone gives more or asks for more he has death in Riba.' Another hadith concerns the exchange of dates of differing qualities, also classed as *riba*.

These sura and hadith have always been open to a wide variety of interpretation, and discussions centre on interest, risk and time. The twentieth-century economist Mahmoud el-Gamal sees the neo-liberal creed in the Qur'an's timeless revelations: man is irrational and prone to 'discounting anomalies' and the Prophet's insistence on using the market to establish value avoids error. For el-Gamal, like Adam Smith, market efficiency is a God-given virtue.[16]

Most, however, recognize in the Islamic rulings a prohibition on unjustified enrichment; *riba* is the opposite of charity (*zakat*), one of the pillars of the Islamic faith. So, while trade is encouraged, risk and reward should be shared equally, and the separation between lender and entrepreneur is unacceptable. Various Islamic contracts have evolved to mimic the benefits of traditional banking contracts. A Muslim entrepreneur wishing to mortgage an asset might take on a contract called the *Ijara wa iqtina*. Under this arrangement, the bank pays for an asset, and the entrepreneur pays rent on the bank's share and buys it out over time. A cynic might say this looks very much like a mortgage, and indeed, Timur Kuran, eminent Turkish economist and professor at Duke University, makes just such a point. He argues that Islamic economics emerged in colonial India as a means of resisting the Western separation of economics and society, and that Islamic finance, which emerged in the 1970s and 1980s, exists as little more than a legitimization of petrodollars, a device of political control and symbolic defiance used by Islamic regimes, who at the same time have expectations from their investments more akin to a sophisticated customer of Wall Street than the Islamic risk-sharing ideal.[17]

A more optimistic reading, put forward by the anthropologist Bill Maurer, is that Islamic economics, with all its debates about derivatives, management of risk and the proper means of trade, makes its practitioners reflect upon, and question, the supremacy of the market that goes unchallenged in neo-liberal economics. It is certainly true that, since the beginning of Islam, entrepreneurial Muslims have sought ways round the prohibition on *riba*. Contemporary derivative contracts in Islamic finance may have something of this spirit, but at the same time they may embody the *itjihad* – which means both striving and reasoning – of a community that recognizes the role of economics is to serve and not to be served, and that the role of the all-knowing is occupied by God, not the market.[18]

Let economics be wise . . .

Throughout this book I have made much of the distinction between prediction and explanation, and I have questioned the ability of technical reasoning to tell us how we should act. Technical skill has become the central endeavour and chief virtue of contemporary economics. Being an eminent scientist, a good manager, or an effective bureaucrat too often appears to be a technical challenge: displaying competence in dealing with technical models or making decisions based upon sophisticated calculation is more important than judgement. We have seen rational, economic decision-making instantiated in our own activities through the many devices with which we navigate everyday life. Even in dating, technical skill is a primary virtue. This is not what Max Weber had in mind when he sang the praises of bureaucracy; for him the cultivation of the bureaucratic ideal involved taking on an identity of judgement and expertise as much as it did shaking off passions and personal opinions.[19]

Nor is our contemporary belief that happiness resides in being able to get and do what you want, as and when you want it – the guiding principle of consumer society – distinctively new. It was advanced by Aristippus of Cyrene, who anticipated Jeremy Bentham by two thousand years in his claim that pleasure is the only good.[20] None other than Aristotle gave that short shrift, remarking that a life driven by slavish gratification is 'the life of grazing animals'. According to Aristotle true happiness comes through living in accordance with the special characteristic of mankind, the ability to reason; humans are characterized, not by barter and exchange, but by an ability to employ debate to distinguish between what is right and what is wrong.[21]

The great error of modern economics has been to forget that it is part of the world. As we have seen, it spills into everyday life, shaping and changing. Economics, academic or otherwise, must be a practical science, and its adherents must be wise and thoughtful, and embody the best precepts of their office. Not just economists, but everyone who does economics: managers, bureaucrats, students, shoppers, daters – all of us, all the time. We need – and thankfully have – doctors who are committed to and expert in healing, not administrators driven by cost–benefit; in the UK we still have a health service to be proud of, but its very future hangs in the balance as market-driven reforms are pushed through Parliament. We need lovers who are in love, not rational and maximizing. An economics that takes seriously its role as a careful participant in the world can help us bring meaningful changes and improvements into being.

Here is one final example, from the work of Alvin Roth. It is distinguished by an attention to practical problems; perhaps it is not surprising that his early qualifications were in operations research, not welfare economics.[22] His interest is in the field of market design, recognizing that economic markets do not spontaneously flourish but need to be built for purpose: he is the quintessential economic engineer. Roth has spent much of his career taking advances in matching theory and applying them to real-world markets. One of his early successes was to sort out the application algorithm for the New York high-school system, so pupils actually received places at schools they wanted to attend; badly configured matching algorithms rapidly end up giving everyone their worst choice. Another success was in matching jobs to trainee doctors. Where couples needed to be found jobs, Roth followed the central principle that a person can never be happier than their spouse – different from the competitive relationships of marriage as imagined by neo-liberal economics. In the early 2000s Roth and his colleagues started to look at the problem of kidney transplants, and what he understood as a problem of the 'double coincidence of wants', first proposed by William Stanley Jevons.[23]

It is not uncommon for patients in need of a kidney transplant to have a donor who is willing to spare them a kidney: a friend, or a spouse. Unfortunately, in many cases the transplant is impossible because the genetic characteristics of the donor do not suit the recipient. The problem of the double coincidence of wants – as Jevons saw it – is that in a barter market straight swaps are unlikely, because they involve finding two individuals whose wants and surpluses exactly coincide. For Jevons, the solution is a medium of exchange – money – that allows multiple, heterogeneous wants to be satisfied through multilateral exchange.

Roth did not follow the received wisdom that only the market can sort out the problem of non-coinciding wants and identify Jevons's argument as yet another endorsement of a market in body parts. He was prepared to accept that many people don't want such a thing to happen, finding the whole idea 'repugnant'.[24] That much singled him out from those who insist on efficiency and welfare gains as the only measures to organize society; Roth's economics is a democratic one, taking seriously the state of public discussion and acting accordingly to bring about outcomes that are sensitive to it and informed. Instead, Roth used matching theory to build a 'clearing house' for transplant organs. This mechanism allowed administrators to link compatible donors and recipients in chains. While Patient A's donor might not match Patient A, and the same with Patient Z and her donor, Donor A and Patient Z might match one another, and Donor Z and Patient A might match. Or patient Q might bridge the gap. Single, undirected donations are also able to trigger chains of exchanges, so one additional kidney can result in several patients receiving life-saving surgery. This may sound simple enough in principle, but it is horrendously complex in practice, with a long list of donors and numerous relevant factors. Roth's innovations, discussed and published in leading economics journals, have led to similar methods being put into place in countries such as the UK, where computer scientist David Manlove and his colleagues from Glasgow University have built similar matching systems for the NHS.

How different is this from the blind ideology of the organ market enthusiast? Where one calls for deregulation and expects the invisible hand of Providence to intervene, saving lives, saving money and fighting crime all at the same time, the other confronts a local, technical problem, respects the opinions and preferences of all involved, and delivers a tangible practical benefit. The algorithm does not deal with 'should' – decisions concerning the factors that will be implemented in the matching are taken elsewhere. Moreover, the transparency of Roth's approach, his focus on instruments and outcomes, means that his innovation can be replicated elsewhere; at once validating his scientific method and saving more lives. This is economic engineering at its best.

Meanwhile, the absence of hard cash from Roth's model keeps some of the more toxic aspects of markets at bay. In a freely competitive market for goods – and organs would be no exception – we can expect prices to be forced down and goods to flow from the poorest to the wealthiest. Roth provides us with an intermediary – an algorithm in place of a market – that prevents such effects. Moreover, these mechanisms are such that they do not change the character of the donation that makes the chain of exchanges possible. An altruistic gesture, designed to save the life of a friend, spouse or child, retains that essential characteristic; while it triggers a pattern of exchange, the instrumental rationality of economic transaction does not seep backwards to contaminate the donation.

Roth's work points to a new economics, but some would have him go further. Market design of this kind remains an elite preserve. The sociologist Juan Pablo Pardo-Guerra argues that the designers of economic markets should follow the model of synthetic biologists, whose aim is to produce toolkits and building blocks that will allow anyone to build novel biological structures. Imagining markets based on, and coupled to, biological systems could result in markets that are 'pragmatic, even civic' – Pardo-Guerra imagines a hacker-paradise of contained, made-to-measure markets able to tackle specific problems and bring about certain ends: conservation of the rhino, for example, or ending the trade in illegal substances. Markets could do more than just allocate goods: they could reshape demand, change the value of things we should hold precious, helping us achieve transformational change in the world.[25]

. . . or let it be absent

Local trading schemes and Islamic economics could scarcely be more different. One is a grass-roots movement that has grown through local activism, the other a theocratic endeavour driven by religious revelation. They do have something in common, however: the use of economic mechanisms, embedded in economic devices, to try to achieve social transformation. In their different ways, they re-imagine the world as a place where economic activity cements social bonds, and where social objectives can be pursued through economic means. In each case the intention of the scheme's originator is enacted through the infrastructures they have put in place, and in each case those architectures are naturally economic.

The local exchange trading scheme relies upon transparent bookkeeping and regular reporting – techniques that proved central to the success not only of industrial capitalism in the nineteenth century but also twentieth-century global finance – to achieve its aim of formalizing networks of promise and social relationship. Even debt is reconfigured to serve a new purpose. Local currencies make use of banknotes with a conscience. Islamic economics has invented legal contracts that allow trade to bloom while striking a fairer balance between the entrepreneur and the owner of capital. These things are acts of sabotage, guerrilla resistance to the totalizing nature of neo-liberal economics. Unlike the sudden, furious uprising of the Occupy movement, they are sustainable over the longer term precisely because they employ the same devices that have made economics so strong. They really do occupy economics.

The LETS schemes, local currencies and Islamic contracts have something else in common. They make economic techniques subservient to the visions they pursue, whether of sustainable futures or Islamic societies. In the classic liberalism of our own economic tradition, economics was also a tool, a means to an end, of wealthier, more just and more free societies. Adam Smith himself was motivated by a sense of sympathy to his fellow man and the feeling that free markets and free trade could do much to help society. Smith lived in a different world from ours, where governments raised taxes and waged wars, and much of the population suffered desperate poverty. It is small wonder that he sang the virtues of trade. Milton Friedman and Friedrich Hayek did ultimately believe in democratic freedom above all else, and even if they did not foresee the real consequences of their policies, they did see the market as the tool through which that freedom could be protected, fighting off the state corporatism of fascists and communists alike.

Such sympathy with our fellow humans and democratic freedom are good virtues, the best that we have. But it is at once apparent that contemporary economics struggles to live out the promise of its Enlightenment forebear. A discipline that of necessity reduces moral problems to technical simulations struggles to cope with the complexity of the world outside and imposes a very particular moral compass of its own. In the wild, the economic tools that have colonized every aspect of everyday life drive us to neglect the basic dignity, the personhood, of others, reducing them to inputs in the manifold cost–benefit calculations through which we organize our lives.

In Isak Dinesen's story, Babette, former chef at the finest restaurant in Paris and exiled revolutionary communard, finds herself housekeeper at the residence of two sisters in Norway. These women live a simple life; they are the daughters of a dour, Lutheran cleric who had formed a small ascetic community on the coast. Babette tells them nothing of her past.

After many years she wins the prize in a Paris lottery, and 10,000 francs arrives. She asks the favour of her employers, that she might be allowed to prepare and provide one single meal in honour of the Dean's anniversary, and they agree, worried though they are about the sinful excesses of Parisian cuisine (of which they have heard only distant rumours). After weeks of preparations, the night comes, and Babette produces a feast that has consumed her entire prize. Only one guest, the general who has lived and travelled the world, recognizes the exquisite food. Babette is an artist, and the general is her audience; through being allowed, just once, to show true excellence, to do her utmost, she is complete.

The food transfigures the guests. Even though the citizens of Berlevaag do not know what they are eating, tongues are loosened, old, bitter differences are made up, and childhood sweethearts reconciled. The tipsy elders stagger home through the snow, their sins washed white as wool. They had, Dinesen writes, been given 'one hour of the millennium'. One hour of Paradise: when has economics ever achieved such transformation?

At times, perhaps we should abandon economics altogether. We should not economize on love, care, or even art. Altruism and civic virtue, love and care grow through exercise, and are not scarce resources to be economized. Even waste may play its part: the spectacular excess of Babette's feast bestows an hour of bliss upon a community, healing and mending. A life lived well, to the full, will be replete with dead ends, about turns, experiments and chances, far richer than a neat parade of rational, calculative choices. I would contend that economics has little place in our personal lives: let them be bounteous, generous and overflowing, and be richer for it.

Yet, we should not abandon economics altogether. In public life we need economics' particular expertise for solving problems. We need economics as engineering, but as an engineering that is subservient to principles and decisions made through democratic process. A bold enough economics might arm us with the tools we need to remake the future. Yet we must recognize economics has no special knowledge of how the world should be, and that there remain choices with which we must deal. A good economics will be local, specific and democratic: in matching organs and in building communities, we see glimpses of a more positive economics for the future.

Acknowledgements

I have many people to thank. First there are those without whom this book could never have existed: Juliet Mushens at The Agency Group, who made the book possible, and Will Hammond of Viking, whose patient editing and insightful comments transformed my messy drafts. My thanks also go to Anne Collins of Random House for her enthusiasm and support throughout. Then there are those academic colleagues on whose work this book is based: some are friends, some I know by e-mail correspondence, and a few only through their writing. I came to write this book not least because I believe their excellent work deserves a wider audience. I hope that they agree. I should add that the book's overall argument is my own, and that I remain responsible for all errors and omissions when presenting their work. I would like to thank my splendid colleagues and students at the School of Management in St Andrews for their support, and for providing constant intellectual challenge and stimulation. In particular, I am indebted to Barbara Townley and Shiona Chillas, who read and commented on drafts. I would like also to take this opportunity to thank those whose help has proved indispensable in the past: Carole Howorth, Chase Robinson and Fritz Zimmerman for teaching me good scholarship; the AHRC and all at BBC Radio Three, especially the Night Waves team, for thrusting me into public debate through the New Generation Thinkers Scheme, such fun; Frank Lucas for believing in a young entrepreneur (Frank, I'm sorry) and Gavin Oldham for help when it was sorely needed. Most of all,

I would like to thank my wife Jane for her constant love, support and common sense, without which I would be lost.

St Andrews
September 2013

Notes

1. I Spend, Therefore I Am

1 Dennis Robertson, 'What Does the Economist Economize?', in Robertson, *Economic Commentaries* (London: Staples Press, 1956). Robertson's argument is discussed in Michael Sandel, *What Money Can't Buy* (London: Allen Lane, 2012), p. 127.
2 Relationship economists really do talk like this. For example: 'the wealthy male will not marry the pretty woman since, whichever way they divide their gains from marriage either he is bid away by the less pretty woman or she is bid away by the poorer man', from Yoram Weiss, 'The Formation and Dissolution of Families: Why Marry? Who Marries Whom? And What Happens upon Divorce?', in Mark Richard Rosenwig and Oded Stark, *Handbook of Population and Family Economics* (Amsterdam: Elsevier, 1997), p. 101.
3 Samuel Cameron 'The Economics of Suicide', in Simon Bowmaker, ed., *Economics Uncut* (Cheltenham: Edward Elgar, 2005), p. 241.

2. From Truck and Barter to the Meaning of Life

1 Peter D. Linneman and Isaac F. Megbolugbe, 'Privatisation and Housing Policy', *Urban Studies* 31, nos. 4–5 (1994), p. 635.
2 The Stoke scheme does recognize that the state needs to shoulder some of the risk and is offering loans for restoration work as well: www.stoke.gov.uk/ccm/content/council-and-democracy/communications/2012-press-releases/08-2012/178-12/. Yet commentators

do not think there is much profit to be made by would-be developers in an area with such low residential values: www.dailymail.co.uk/news/article-2184334/Empty-houses-sale-1-Britains-cheapest-street.html.

3 Andrew Leyshon and Shaun French, ' "We All Live in a Robbie Fowler House": The Geographies of the Buy to Let Market in the UK', *British Journal of Politics & International Relations* 11, no. 3 (2009), p. 441.

4 Ibid., p. 439.

5 Adam Smith, *The Wealth of Nations* (London: Penguin, 1997 [1776]), I.2.2.

6 Ibid., IV.2.9.

7 Amartya Sen, 'Adam Smith's Prudence', in *Theory and Reality in Development*, ed. S. Lall and F. Stewart (London: Macmillan, 1986), pp. 28–37.

8 Heinz Lubasz, 'Adam Smith and the Invisible Hand – of the Market?', in *Contesting Markets*, ed. Roy Dilley (Edinburgh: Edinburgh University Press, 1992), pp. 37–56.

9 Joseph Townsend, *A Dissertation on the Poor Laws* (Berkeley: University of California Press, 1971), pp. 37f. When Karl Polanyi investigated Townsend's story, he found little basis for it in the historical records. Gareth Dale, *Karl Polanyi: The Limits of the Market* (Cambridge: Polity Press, 2010).

10 Townsend, *A Dissertation on the Poor Laws*, p. 27.

11 Karl Polanyi, *The Great Transformation* (Boston: Beacon Press, 2001), p. 122.

12 Polanyi's work provoked a fierce debate among scholars as to the correct way to do anthropology. On the one side, 'substantivists' argued that all economic arrangements should be understood within their social and cultural context, while on the other the 'formalists' sought to use the model of the self-interested individual to analyse societies across varied historical and geographical contexts. Of course, an analysis such as this required a loosening

of the definitions of economic language, but the formalists had recourse to a more pragmatic defence. The anthropology of pre-modern man is limited in its scope by historical boundaries and by the practical fact that archaic economic arrangements are 'obsolete'; around the world economies are getting more like our own. See Dale, *Karl Polanyi*.

13 From Polanyi's essay 'Our Obsolete Market Mentality', quoted by Scott Cook, 'The Obsolete "Anti-Market" Mentality: A Critique of the Substantive Approach to Economic Anthropology', *American Anthropologist* 68, no. 2 (1966), pp. 327–9.

14 George Dalton, 'Economic Theory and Primitive Society 1', *American Anthropologist* 63, no. 1 (1961), p. 2.

15 Alan Ryan, 'Introduction', in *John Stuart Mill and Jeremy Bentham: Utilitarianism and Other Essays*, ed. Alan Ryan (London: Penguin, 1987).

16 Philip Mirowski, *More Heat than Light* (Cambridge: Cambridge Univerity Press, 1989).

17 The authoritative account of the Cold War and 'cyborg' economics is to be found in Philip Mirowski, *Machine Dreams: Economics Becomes a Cyborg Science* (Cambridge: Cambridge University Press, 2002). Modern computational econometrics, game theory and algorithmic matching – the cutting edge of contemporary academic economics – has fortunately turned its hand to more humane endeavours, and one of the discipline's great luminaries, Alvin Roth, was a joint recipient of the 2012 Nobel Prize in Economics for his work on the practical application of matching theory processes. See the final chapter of this book for a short discussion.

18 Ibid., p. 233.

19 Friedrich von Hayek, *The Road to Serfdom* (Abingdon: Routledge, 2010 [1944]), p. 32.

20 Milton Friedman, *Capitalism and Freedom* (Chicago: University of Chicago Press, 1962).

21 In full, Hayek writes: 'It is more than a metaphor to describe the price system as a kind of machinery for registering change, or a system of telecommunications which enables individual producers to watch merely the movement of a few pointers, as an engineer might watch the hands of a few dials, in order to adjust their activities to changes of which they may never know more than is reflected in the price movement.' F. A. Hayek, 'The Use of Knowledge in Society', *American Economic Review* 35, no. 4 (1945), p. 527.

22 This and following from Patricio Silva, 'Technocrats and Politics in Chile: From the Chicago Boys to the CIEPLAN Monks', *Journal of Latin American Studies* 23, no. 2 (1991).

23 Timothy Mitchell, 'The Work of Economics: How a Discipline Makes Its World', *European Journal of Sociology* 46, no. 2 (2005), pp. 297–320.

24 Orlando Letelier, 'The Chicago Boys in Chile: Economic Freedom's Awful Toll', *The Nation* (1976), www.tni.org/archives/ act/3712.

25 Carlos Huneeus, 'Technocrats and Politicians in an Authoritarian Regime', *Journal of Latin American Studies* 32, no. 2 (2000), pp. 461–501.

26 In *Newsweek*, 14 July 1976, reported by Letelier.

27 Letelier, 'The Chicago Boys'.

28 Following Silva, 'Technocrats and Politics in Chile'.

29 Gary Becker, 'Latin America Owes a Lot to Its "Chicago Boys"', *Business Week*, 9 June 1997, p. 22.

30 Silva, 'Technocrats and Politics in Chile', p. 394.

31 Dave O'Brien 'What Price Evidence? Identities, Valuation Technologies, and the Problem of Culture', paper presented at 'What Price Creativity? A Workshop on the Valuing of Social/Public Goods', University of St Andrews, December 2012.

32 Lionel Robbins, *An Essay on the Nature and Significance of Economic Science* (London: Macmillan, 1932), p. 16.

33 Ibid., p. 14.

34 Robertson, 'What Does the Economist Economize?'.

35 Gary S. Becker, 'Nobel Lecture: The Economic Way of Looking at Behavior', *Journal of Political Economy* 101, no. 3 (1993). The italics are Becker's.

36 Michel Foucault, *The Birth of Biopolitics*, ed. Arnold Davidson, trans. Graham Burchell (Basingstoke: Palgrave Macmillan, 2008), pp. 232f.

37 Daniel Dennett, *Darwin's Dangerous Idea* (London: Allen Lane, 1995), p. 132.

38 I owe this gem to Gareth Dale in *Karl Polanyi*, p. 105.

3. Economics Does

1 Steven Levitt and Stephen Dubner, *SuperFreakonomics* (London: Penguin, 2010), p. 49.

2 These quotations, ibid., p. 55.

3 Jorge Luis Borges, *Fictions* (London: Penguin, 1998), p. 24.

4 The position on science that I have adopted throughout this book emphasizes the role of calculation and instrumentation. It is associated with the Paris School of science studies, particularly Bruno Latour, Michel Callon, Steve Woolgar and John Law, and exemplified by Bruno Latour, *Science in Action: How to Follow Scientists and Engineers through Society* (Cambridge, MA: Harvard University Press, 1987) or Latour, *Pandora's Hope* (Cambridge, MA: Harvard University Press, 1999). The other important approach in the science studies of the late twentieth century emphasized the importance of expertise in the construction of scientific knowledge; see particularly Harry Collins and Trevor Pinch, *The Golem* (Cambridge: Cambridge University Press, 1993), and Andrew Pickering, *Science as Practice and Culture* (Chicago: University of Chicago Press, 1992).

5 Popper's arguments have achieved a recent popular resurgence at the hand of Nassim Nicholas Taleb, who picked up Popper's example of the black swan to critique the modelling practices of contemporary finance (*The Black Swan*, London: Penguin, 2007). In philosophy of science proper, however, Popper's ideas are largely discredited, particularly by 'Duheim/Quine' arguments that hypotheses tend to be modified rather than discarded.

6 Milton Friedman, 'The Methodology of Positive Economics', in *Essays on Positive Economics* (Chicago: University of Chicago Press, 1966). In fact, Friedman claimed to have worked out his theories independently of Popper before their first meeting at Mont Pèlerin in 1947. See Donald MacKenzie, *An Engine, Not a Camera: How Financial Models Shape Markets* (Cambridge, MA: MIT Press, 2006), p. 10.

7 Mark Blaug, 'Paradigms versus Research Programmes in the History of Economics', in *The Philosophy of Economics*, ed. Daniel Hausman (Cambridge: Cambridge University Press, 1984), p. 360; Paul Samuelson notes the virtue of assumptions, quoted by MacKenzie, *An Engine, Not a Camera*, p. 10.

8 Quotation and the following detail, from Noel Annan, *Our Age* (London: Fontana, 1990), p. 410. Annan is himself paraphrasing an essay by Berlin.

9 Quoted in Alan McKinlay, 'Performativity and the Politics of Identity: Putting Butler to Work', *Critical Perspectives on Accounting* 21, no. 3 (2010), pp. 232–42.

10 Ibid.

11 Judith Butler, *Gender Trouble: Feminism and the Subversion of Identity* (New York: Routledge, 1990).

12 See, for example, Michel Callon, *The Laws of the Markets* (Oxford: Oxford University Press, 1998), or Callon, 'What Does It Mean to Say that Economics Is Performative?', in *Do Economists Make Markets?*, ed. Donald MacKenzie, Fabien Muniesa and Lucia Siu (Princeton: Princeton University Press, 2007).

13 The interested reader will find a useful summary of the arguments in Pickering's edited collection, *Science as Practice and Culture*.

14 Donald MacKenzie, *Material Markets: How Economic Agents are Constructed* (Oxford: Oxford University Press, 2009), p. 8. MacKenzie is talking specifically about financial market 'facts', such as prices.

15 Karin Knorr Cetina provides a detailed ethnographic study of the practice of particle physics and laboratory biology in *Epistemic Cultures* (Cambridge, MA: Harvard Univerity Press, 1999).

16 Bruno Latour, *Gifford Lectures* (Edinburgh: University of Edinburgh Press, 2013).

17 Timothy Mitchell, 'Rethinking Economy', *Geoforum* 39 (2008), pp. 1116–21.

18 Erica Field, 'Entitled to Work: Urban Property Rights in Labour Supply in Peru', *Quarterly Journal of Economics* 122, no. 4 (2007), pp. 1561–602.

19 www.nytimes.com/2003/01/09/business/economic-scene-a-study-looks-at-squatters-and-land-titles-in-peru.html?pagewanted=all&src=pm.

20 www.doingbusiness.org/~/media/GIAWB/Doing%20Business/Documents/Annual-Reports/English/DB06-FullReport.pdf.

21 Mitchell, 'The Work of Economics'.

22 Mitchell, 'Rethinking Economy', p. 1119.

4. *Making Economic Man*

1 There are many books on this topic. Examples from economists well known to the public include George Akerlov and Robert Shiller's *Animal Spirits* (Princeton: Princeton University Press, 2009) or Dan Ariely's *Predictably Irrational* (London: HarperCollins, 2009).

2 Gerald Marwell and Ruth E. Ames, 'Economists Free Ride, Does Anyone Else? Experiments on the Provision of Public Goods, IV', *Journal of Public Economics* 15, no. 3 (1981), pp. 295–310.

3 John Carter and Michael Irons, 'Are Economists Different, and If So, Why?', *Journal of Economic Perspectives* 5, no. 2 (1991), pp. 171–7; Richard Thaler, 'Anomalies: The Ultimatum Game', *Journal of Economic Perspectives* 2, no. 4 (1988), pp. 195–206. The test instruction comes from an experiment conducted by British game theorist Kenneth Binmore, cited in Thaler's paper. Carter and Irons marshal some evidence that economics students are naturally more self-interested than their peers.

4 Robert Frank, Thomas Gilovich and Dennis Regan, 'Does Studying Economics Inhibit Cooperation?', *Journal of Economic Perspectives* 7, no. 2 (1993), p. 159, and Robert Frank and Gunther Schulze, 'Does Economics Make Citizens Corrupt?' *Journal of Economic Behavior and Organization* 43 (2000), pp. 101–13, both cited in Fabrizio Ferraro, Jeffrey Pfeffer and Robert Sutton, 'Economic Language and Assumptions: How Theories Can Become Self-Fulfilling', *Academy of Management Review* 30, no. 1 (2005), pp. 8–24.

5 Ferraro et al., 'Economic Language and Assumptions', p. 14.

6 Dale Miller, 'The Norm of Self-interest', *American Psychologist* 54, no. 12 (1999), pp. 1053–60.

7 Ibid., p. 1057.

8 Michel Foucault, *Discipline and Punish* (London: Penguin, 1977), p. 201.

9 The following detail comes from Harry Braverman's account of Taylor's *Scientific Management* (1947): Braverman, *Labor and Monopoly Capital: the Degradation of Work in the Twentieth Century* (New York: New York University Press, 1974).

10 Brian Price, 'Frank and Lillian Gilbreth and the Manufacture and Marketing of Motion Study, 1908–1924', *Business and Economic History* 18 (1989), pp. 88–98.

11 Petter Holm and Kåre Nolde Nielsen, 'Framing Fish, Making

Markets: The Construction of Individual Transferable Quotas (ITQs)', in *Market Devices*, ed. Michel Callon, Yuval Millo and Fabian Muniesa (Oxford: Blackwell Publishing/The Sociological Review, 2007), pp. 173–95.

12 Ibid., p. 174.

13 The list of governmental technologies comes from Nikolas Rose and Peter Miller, 'Political Power Beyond the State: Problematics of Government', *British Journal of Sociology* 43, no. 2 (1992), pp. 173–205, cited by Frank Azimont and Luis Araujo, 'Governing Firms, Shaping Markets', in *Reconnecting Marketing to Markets*, ed. Luis Araujo, John Finch and Hans Kjellberg (Oxford: Oxford University Press, 2010), pp. 78–96.

14 Brad Barber and Terence Odean, 'Boys Will Be Boys: Gender, Overconfidence and Common Stock Investment', *Quarterly Journal of Economics* 1 (2001), pp. 261–92.

15 Nikolas Rose, *Inventing Our Selves* (Cambridge: Cambridge University Press, 1996), p. 153.

16 The following from my own work, including: Philip Roscoe and Carole Howorth, 'Identification through Technical Analysis: A Study of the Investment Behaviour of UK Non-professional Investors', *Accounting, Organizations and Society* 34 (2009), pp. 206–21; Philip Roscoe, 'Economic Embeddedness and Materiality in a Financial Market Setting', *Sociological Review* 61, no. 1 (2013), pp. 41–68; and 'Constructing the Retail Investor', paper given at the 38th Annual MacroMarketing Conference, Toronto, 6 June 2013.

5. *Economics in the Wild*

1 Edwin Hutchins, *Cognition in the Wild* (Cambridge, MA: MIT Press, 1995).

2 Michel Callon, 'Economic Markets and the Rise of Interactive Agencements', in *Living in a Material World*, ed. Trevor Pinch

and R. Swedberg (Cambridge, MA: MIT Press, 2008); Fabian
Muniesa, Yuval Millo and Michel Callon, 'An Introduction to
Market Devices', in *Market Devices*, ed. Callon, Millo and Muniesa
(Oxford: Blackwell, 2007).

3 There is some interesting literature on the organization of super-
markets, notably Franck Cochoy, 'A Sociology of Market Things:
On Tending the Garden of Choices in Mass Retailing', in Callon,
Millo and Muniesa, *Market Devices*; Cochoy, 'Calculation, Qual-
culation, Calqulation: Shopping Cart Arithmetic, Equipped
Cognition and the Clustered Consumer', *Marketing Theory* 8, no.
1 (2008), pp. 15–44, and Hans Kjellberg, 'The Death of a Salesman?
Reconfiguring Economic Exchange in Swedish Postwar Food
Distribution', also in *Market Devices*. Cochoy, in particular, urges
us to take the material infrastructures of supermarkets seriously.

4 Khorsed Alam and Martin Hearson, *Fashion Victims* (London:
War on Want, 2006) and www.telegraph.co.uk/finance/china-
business/7773011/A-look-inside-the-Foxconn-suicide-factory.html.

5 Cochoy, 'A Sociology of Market Things'.

6 Michel Callon takes a broad view of the discipline. By his definition, economics incorporates many of the functions that we
might expect to find in a modern bureaucratic organization or
corporation. Michel Callon, 'The Embeddedness of Economic
Markets in Economics', in *The Laws of the Markets*, ed. Callon
(Oxford: Oxford University Press, 1998).

7 Jospeh Stiglitz and Andrew Weiss, 'Credit Rationing in Markets
with Imperfect Information', *American Economic Review* 71 (1981),
pp. 393–410.

8 George Akerlov, 'The Market for Lemons: Quality Uncertainty
and Market Mechanisms', *Quarterly Journal of Economics* 84 (1970),
pp. 448–500. For British readers: 'Lemon' is an American slang
term for a second-hand car of dubious quality. Akerlov's metaphor eluded me for some time before I realized this.

9 Mirowski, *Machine Dreams*.

10 This summary is based on the detailed accounts given by Martha Poon, 'Scorecards as Devices for Consumer Credit: The Case of Fair, Isaac & Company Incorporated', in *Market Devices*, pp. 284–306; Poon, 'From New Deal Institutions to Capital Markets: Commercial Consumer Risk Scores and the Making of Subprime Mortgage Finance', *Accounting Organizations and Society* 34, no. 5 (2009), pp. 654–74, as well as a number of personal conversations.

11 www.myfico.com/#your-state?; http://www.myfico.com/HelpCenter/FICOScores/.

12 Ingrid Jeacle and Eamonn Walsh, 'From Moral Evaluation to Rationalization: Accounting and the Shifting Technologies of Credit', *Accounting, Organization and Society* 27 (2002), p. 747; Donncha Marron, ' "Lending by Numbers": Credit Scoring and the Constitution of Risk within American Consumer Credit', *Economy and Society* 36, no. 1 (2006), pp. 103–33.

13 Andrew Leyshon and Nigel Thrift, 'Lists Come Alive: Electronic Systems of Knowledge and the Rise of Credit-Scoring in Retail Banking', *Economy and Society* 28, no. 3 (1999), p. 437.

14 www.bbc.co.uk/news/business-18640101.

15 Extract from commons debate, 11 Sept. 2012, www.davidwilletts.co.uk/content/higher-and-further-education-debate.

16 Kathia Serrano-Velarde, 'Benchmarking for the Greater Good? The New Investment Paradigm in European Higher Education', in *New Spirits of Capitalism?*, ed. Paul du Gay and Glen Morgan (Oxford: Oxford University Press, 2013), pp. 251–73.

17 Robert Frank's notion of the 'winner takes all market' provides a nice explanation of this problem, in *The Darwin Economy* (Princeton: Princeton University Press, 2011).

18 Gill Wyness, Institute for Fiscal Studies presentation, December 2010, http://www.ifs.org.uk/conferences/pe2010_wyness.pdf. My italics.

19 Wendy Nelson Espeland and Michael Sauder, 'Rankings and Reactivity: How Public Measures Recreate Social Worlds', *American Journal of Sociology* 113, no. 1 (2007), pp. 1–40.

20 Robert Frank and Philip Cook, *The Winner-Take-All Society* (London: Virgin Books, 2010), pp. 11–12.

21 Martin Kornberger and Chris Carter, 'Manufacturing Competition: How Accounting Practices Shape Strategy Making in Cities', *Accounting, Auditing & Accountability Journal* 23, no. 3 (2010), pp. 325–49.

22 This example from Rajani Naidoo, Avi Shankar and Ekant Veer, 'The Consumerist Turn in Higher Education: Policy Aspirations and Outcomes', *Journal of Marketing Management* 27, nos. 11–12 (2011), pp. 1142–62, who have written extensively on students as consumers, and on whose account I rely for these details.

23 Alison Hearn, 'On the Violence of the New Branded University of Circulation', paper given at the 38th Annual MacroMarketing Conference, Toronto, 6 June 2013.

24 On this point, also ibid.

6. *The Price of a Life*

1 Details of the case and costings in the next paragraph from the presiding judge's opinion in the 1981 appellate hearing, available at http://online.ceb.com/calcases/CA3/119CA3d757.htm.

2 Ibid.

3 See Matthew Lee and David Ermann, 'Pinto "Madness" as a Flawed Landmark Narrative: An Organizational and Network Analysis', *Social Problems* 46, no. 1 (1999), pp. 30–47 for a detailed account of the complexities of Ford's organization and the case.

4 Dennis A. Gioia, 'Pinto Fires and Personal Ethics: A Script Analysis of Missed Opportunities', *Journal of Business Ethics* 11 (1992), pp. 379–89.

5 Ibid., p. 381.

6 Milton Friedman, 'The Social Responsibility of Business Is to Increase Its Profits', *The New York Times Magazine*, 13 September 1970.

7 This and following from Lee and Ermann, 'Pinto "Madness"', p. 37.

8 Joel Bakan, *The Corporation* (London: Constable, 2004).

9 Lee and Ermann, 'Pinto "Madness"'.

10 Marion Fourcade, 'The Political Valuation of Life', *Regulation and Governance* 3 (2009), pp. 291–7.

11 Theodore Bergstrom, Rodney Garratt and Damien Sheehan-Connor, 'One Chance in a Million: Altruism and the Bone Marrow Registry', *American Economic Review* 99, no. 4 (2009), p. 1316.

12 These figures and the examples in the next paragraph come from Jonathan Wolff, 'Risk, Fear, Blame, Shame and the Regulation of Public Safety', *Economics and Philosophy* 22, no. 3 (2006), pp. 409–27, who provides a thorough discussion of these issues. The 'irrationality thesis' has been most prominently stated by the economist Cass Sunstein. Wolff's argument is that models of risk are inescapable and should be more subtle, taking into account cause, hazard, probability, fear, blame and shame (p. 427).

13 That is to say, we were paid for week one's work at the end of week two; our employer effectively held us in bond for the duration of the job. Payment in hand is distressingly common in part-time occupations.

14 Richard Thaler and Sherwin Rosen, 'The Value of Saving a Life: Evidence from the Labor Market', in *Household Production and Consumption*, ed. Nestor E. Terleckyj (New York: National Bureau of Economic Research, 1976).

15 There is a huge literature on the QALY. For an introduction to the technical issues of health-care economics see Michael F. Drummond et al., *Methods for the Economic Evaluation of Healthcare Programmes* (Oxford: Oxford University Press, 1998).

16 The original quality scale was developed by Rachel Rosser and Paul Kind, 'A Scale of Valuation of States of Illness: Is There a

Social Consensus?', *International Journal of Epidemiology* 7 (1978), pp. 347–57.

17 John Harris, 'QALYfying the Value of Life', *Journal of Medical Ethics* 13 (1978), pp. 117–23; Harris, 'It's Not NICE to Discriminate', *Journal of Medical Ethics* 31 (2005), pp. 373–5.

18 This example comes from John Rawles, 'Castigating QALYs', *Journal of Medical Ethics* 15 (1989), pp. 143–7.

19 Harris, 'QALYfying the Value of Life'.

20 Alan Williams, 'Cost-effectiveness Analysis: Is It Ethical?', *Journal of Medical Ethics* 18 (1992), p. 7.

21 Malcolm Ashmore, Michael Mulkay and Trevor Pinch, *Health and Efficiency: A Sociology of Health Economics* (Buckingham: Open University Press, 1989).

22 Philip Roscoe, 'A Moral Economy of Transplantation: Competing Regimes of Value in the Allocation of Transplant Organs', in *Value Practices in Life Sciences*, ed. Claes-Frederik Helgesson, Francis Lee and Isabelle Dussange (Oxford: Oxford University Press, forthcoming, 2014).

23 *The Lancet*, 17 August 2013, p. 57.

24 Robert Francis, *Independent Inquiry into Care Provided by Mid Staffordshire NHS Foundation Trust January 2005–March 2009*, vol. 375 (London: The Stationery Office, 2010), and Robert Francis, *Report of the Mid Staffordshire NHS Foundation Trust Public Inquiry: Executive Summary*, vol. 947 (London: The Stationery Office, 2013).

25 Huw Davies and Russell Mannion, 'Will Prescriptions for Cultural Change Improve the NHS?' *British Medical Journal*, 1 March 2013.

7. How Not to Pay Your College Fees

1 Jake Linford, 'The Kidney Donor Scholarship Act: How College Scholarships Can Provide Financial Incentives for Kidney Dona-

tion While Preserving Altruistic Meaning', *St Louis Journal of Health Law & Policy* 2, (2009), p. 265.

2 Gerald Dworkin, 'Markets and Morals: The Case for Organ Sales', in *Morality, Harm, and the Law*, ed. Dworkin (Boulder, CO: Westview Press, 1994), p. 155.

3 Here and next paragraph, B. Cohen and C. Wight, 'A European Perspective on Organ Procurement: Breaking Down the Barriers to Organ Donation', *Transplantation* 68, no. 7 (1999), pp. 985–90; Madhav Goyal et al., 'Economic and Health Consequences of Selling a Kidney in India', *Journal of the American Medical Association* 288, no. 13 (2002), pp. 1589–93; Nancy Scheper-Hughes, 'Keeping an Eye on the Global Traffic in Human Organs', *The Lancet*, 10 May 2003, pp. 1645–8; and Javaad Zargoosh, 'Quality of Life of Iranian Kidney "Donors"', *Journal of Urology* 166 (2001), pp. 1790–99.

4 Scheper-Hughes, 'Keeping an Eye on the Global Traffic in Human Organs', p. 1645.

5 Source for UK figure: www.organdonation.nhs.uk/; US figure: www.unos.org/.

6 Richard Titmuss, *The Gift Relationship: From Human Blood to Social Policy* (London: Allen & Unwin, 1970).

7 Kieran Healy, *Last Best Gifts: Altruism and the Market for Human Blood and Organs* (Chicago: University of Chicago Press, 2010).

8 The following section is developed from my paper 'On the Possibility of Organ Markets and the Performativity of Economics', *Journal of Cultural Economy*, 6, no. 4 (2013), pp. 386–401. Readers can find references to the relevant papers there. Despite Kaserman's dominance in the ongoing debate, the original model is found in A. Frank Adams, A. Barnett and David Kaserman, 'Markets for Organs: The Question of Supply', *Contemporary Economic Policy* 7 (1999), pp. 147–55.

9 Marion Fourcade, 'Cents and Sensibility: Economic Valuation and the Nature of "Nature"', *American Journal of Sociology* 116, no. 6 (2011), pp. 1721–77.

10 Adams, Barnett, and Kaserman, 'Markets for Organs', p. 154.

11 Alison Wellington and Justin Whitmire, 'Kidney Transplants and the Shortage of Donors: Is a Market the Answer?', *Contemporary Economic Policy* 25, no. 2 (2007), pp. 131–45.

12 Gary Becker and Julio Jorge Elias, 'Introducing Incentives in the Market for Live and Cadaveric Organ Donations', *Journal of Economic Perspectives* 21, no. 3 (2007), pp. 3–24.

13 www.bbc.co.uk/news/world-asia-pacific-13639934.

14 My thanks to Katherine Wall, one of my students, for pointing out the significance of the 'do no harm' principle in live donation. Anthony Culyer, 'Hic Sunt Dracones', *Medical Decision-Making* 32 (2012), pp. 25–32.

15 Peter G. Moffatt and Simon A. Peters, 'Pricing Personal Services: An Empirical Study of Earnings in the UK Prostitution Industry', *Scottish Journal of Political Economy* 51, no. 5 (2004), p. 685. The figures are for the year 2000. They also exclude street-prostitution, the lowest-paid branch of the activity.

16 Williams, 'Cost-effectiveness Analysis', p. 7.

17 Lena Edlund and Evelyn Korn, 'A Theory of Prostitution', *Journal of Political Economy* 110, no. 1 (2002), pp. 181–242.

18 Edlund and Korn's analysis is complex, and a more accessible summary can be found in Peter G. Moffatt and Simon A. Peters's excellent chapter 'The Economics of Prostitution', in *Economics Uncut*, ed. Simon Bowmaker (Cheltenham: Edward Elgar, 2005), pp. 193–228. The figure of £70,000 comes from Peters and Moffatt, themselves citing A. E. Clark and A. J. Oswald, 'A Simple Statistical Model for Measuring How Life Events Affect Happiness', *International Journal of Epidemiology* 31 (2002), pp. 1139–44.

19 Robert Long, 'Realism and Abstraction in Economics', *Quarterly Journal of Austrian Economics* 9, no. 3 (2006), p. 4.

20 Moffatt and Peters, 'Pricing Personal Services'.

21 Moffatt and Peters, 'The Economics of Prostitution', p. 225.

22 www.punternet.com/frs/fr_stats.php.

23 Lynne Pettinger, 'Market Moralities in the Field of Commercial Sex', *Journal of Cultural Economy* 6, no. 2 (2013), pp. 184–99.

24 www.punternet.com/index1.html; www.punternet.com/frs/fr_stats.php.

25 A pair of papers by Joanna Brewis and Stephen Linstead, ' "The Worst Thing is the Screwing" (1): Consumption and the Management of Identity in Sex Work', *Gender, Work & Organization* 7, no. 2 (2000), pp. 84–97; and ' "The Worst Thing is the Screwing" (2): Context and Career in Sex Work', *Gender, Work & Organization* 7, no. 3 (2000), pp. 168–80, give a good overview of the complicated arguments that surround the sale of sexual services.

26 Ingrid Jeacle and Chris Carter, 'In TripAdvisor We Trust: Rankings, Calculative Regimes and Abstract Systems', *Accounting, Organizations and Society* 36, nos. 4–5 (2011), pp. 357–77, discuss the disciplinary mechanisms of travel review sites.

8. It's Not the Money, Honey

1 This chapter is based on work conducted by my colleague Shiona Chillas and me, partly published as 'The State of Affairs: Critical Performativity and the Global Dating Industry', *Organization*, early online doi:10.1177/1350508413485497 (2013). The paper presents a more focused analysis of online dating as 'perfomative'.

2 Michael D. Botwin, David M. Buss and Todd K. Shackelford, 'Personality and Mate Preferences: Five Factors in Mate Selection and Marital Satisfaction', *Journal of Personality* 65, no. 1 (1997), pp. 107–36.

3 My thanks to Anne Meike Dackweiler for pointing this out.

4 TRUE LLC and Ilona Jerabek, *The Technical Manual of the TRUE Compatibility Test* (2004), true.com/images/tctmanual.pdf, pp. 3–5.

5 James Houran et al., 'Do Online Matchmaking Tests Work? An Assessment of Preliminary Evidence of a Publicized "Predictive

Model of Marital Success"', *North American Journal of Psychology* 6, no. 3 (2004), pp. 521–2.

6   Lori Gottlieb, 'How Do I Love Thee?', *Atlantic Monthly*, March 2006.

7   Elizabeth J. Austin et al., 'A Preliminary Investigation of the Associations between Personality, Cognitive Ability and Digit Ratio', *Personality and Individual Differences* 33, no. 7 (2002), pp. 1115–24.

8   John Tierney, 'My eHarmony Experiment: Can This Marriage Be Matched?' *The New York Times*, 1 February 2008.

9   Quoted by Nick Paumgarten, 'Looking for Someone: Sex, Love, and Loneliness on the Internet', *The New York Times*, 4 July 2011.

10 Rebecca D. Heino, Nicole B. Ellison and Jennifer L. Gibbs, 'Relationshopping: Investigating the Market Metaphor in Online Dating', *Journal of Social and Personal Relationships* 27, no. 4 (2010), pp. 427–47.

11 Monica Whitty and Alan Carr, *Cyberspace Romance: The Psychology of Online Relationships* (Basingstoke: Macmillan, 2006), p. 131.

12 Nicole B. Ellison, Rebecca D. Heino, and Jennifer L. Gibbs, 'Managing Impressions Online: Self-Presentation Processes in the Online Dating Environment', *Journal of Computer-Mediated Communication* 11, no. 2 (2006), p. 433.

13 Whitty and Carr, *Cyberspace Romance*.

14 John Noonan, *The Scholastic Analysis of Usury* (Cambridge: Cambridge University Press, 1957).

15 Immanuel Kant, *Lectures in Ethics* (New York: Harper and Row, 1963), p. 165.

16 Alvin E. Roth, Tayfun Sönmez and M. Utku Ünver, 'A Kidney Exchange Clearing House in New England', *American Economic Review* 95, no. 2 (2005), pp. 376–80.

17 Eli Finkel et al., 'Online Dating: A Critical Analysis from the Perspective of Psychological Science', *Psychological Science in the Public Interest* 13, no. 1 (2012), pp. 3–66.

18 Günter J. Hitsch, Ali Hortaçsu and Dan Ariely, 'Matching and

Sorting in Online Dating', *American Economic Review* 100 (2010), pp. 130–63.

19 Lindsay Shaw Taylor et al., 'Out of My League: A Real World Test of the Matching Hypothesis', *Personality and Psychology Bulletin* 37 (2011), pp. 942–54.

20 Quoted by Ellison et al., 'Managing Impressions Online'.

21 The following paragraphs rely on the excellent survey conducted by Finkel et al., 'Online Dating: A Critical Analysis'.

22 Ibid., p. 39.

23 In full, the argument is that 'the validity of [eHarmony's] methods derives from the fact that the . . . respondents obtained higher DAS [compatibility] scores than the control group. However, by definition, the eHarmony couples exist precisely because their members' predicted DAS score would be optimal.' Houran et al., 'Do Online Matchmaking Tests Work?', p. 513. Houran et al. complain that the algorithm matches couples according to this score, and that eHarmony is guilty of fulfilling its own prophecy in using the same device to measure output as it uses to construct it.

24 Finkel et al., 'Online Dating', p. 49.

25 John Cacioppo et al., 'Marital Satisfaction and Breakups Differ across Online and Off-line Meeting Venues', *PNAS Early Edition* (2013) www.pnas.org/content/early/2013/05/31/1222447110.full.pdf.

9. The True Cost of Economics

1 Nicholas Stern, *Review on the Economics of Climate Change* (London: HM Treasury, 2006), p. x.

2 Robert Mendelsohn, 'Comments on Simon Dietz and Nicholas Stern's "Why Economic Analysis Supports Strong Action on Climate Change: A Response to the Stern Review's Critics"', *Review of Environmental Economic Policy* 2, no. 2 (2008), pp. 309–13.

3 T. G. W. Smith, 'Markets and Morals: Self, Character and Markets', *Royal Institute of Philosophy Supplements* 26 (1989), p. 15.

4 Friedman, 'The Social Responsibility of Business Is to Increase Its Profits'.

5 Deirdre McCloskey, 'Bourgeois Virtue', *American Scholar* 63, no. 2 (1994), pp. 177–91.

6 Theodore Porter, *Trust in Numbers* (Princeton: Princeton University Press, 1995).

7 I encountered the population life years simulation in my own research for 'A Moral Economy of Transplantation'. Public opinion here from M. Johri and P. A. Ubel, 'Setting Organ Allocation Priorities: Should We Care what the Public Cares About?', *Liver Transplantation* 9, no. 8 (2003), pp. 878–80. In fact, for purely clinical reasons, alcoholics have to prove that they have been teetotal for six months before being put on the waiting list to receive treatment in the UK. So extraordinary are the recuperative powers of the liver, some recover during this period.

8 Peter Ubel and George Loewenstein, 'Distributing Scarce Livers: The Moral Reasoning of the General Public', *Social Science and Medicine* 42 (1996), pp. 1049–55.

9 Immanuel Kant, *The Moral Law (Groundwork of the Metaphysics of Morals)*, trans. H. J. Paton (London: Routledge, 2005).

10. Let's Occupy Economics

1 As the legal scholar Alasdair Roberts points out, Occupy also succumbed to the seductive 'faux anarchism' of leaderless business organization, flat hierarchies and flexible, empowered teamwork promoted by the management gurus of the 1990s. These smart new management practices had, of course, been little more than novel ways of squeezing more value from workers, direct descendants of Taylorist working regimes and a source of innova-

tive new types of self-surveillance. Yet, Roberts argues, Occupy took these management practices at face value, and the lack of leaders became a critical problem for the movement as it sought to deal with strife within the camp and develop more meaningful relationships with city officials: when the mayor of Denver asked the camp to provide a representative with whom he could negotiate, it responded by electing a dog. Alasdair Roberts, 'Why the Occupy Movement Failed', *Public Administration Review* 72, no. 5 (2012), pp. 754–62.

2 Polanyi, *The Great Transformation*, pp. 175f.

3 Mark Peacock, 'Local Exchange Trading Systems: A Solution to the Employment Dilemma?', *Annals of Public and Cooperative Economics* 71, no. 1 (2000), pp. 55–78.

4 Finn Bowring, 'LETS: An Eco-Socialist Initiative?', *New Left Review* 232 (1998), p. 99.

5 Peacock, 'Local Exchange Trading Systems'.

6 Colin Williams, 'Local Currencies and Community Development: An Evaluation of Green Dollar Exchanges in New Zealand', *Community Development Journal* 34, no. 4 (1996), pp. 319–29; Eric Helleiner, 'Think Globally, Transact Locally: Green Political Economy and the Local Currency Movement', *Global Society* 14, no. 1 (2000), pp. 35–51.

7 Michael Pacione, 'Local Exchange Trading Systems as a Response to the Globalisation of Capitalism', *Urban Studies* 34, no. 8 (1997), pp. 1179–99.

8 LETS literature quoted by Helleiner, 'Think Globally', p. 47.

9 The Ithaca Hours directory is described by its founder as a portrait of the community's capability, ibid., p. 38. Individuals join LETS to meet people through trade, and for the pleasure of 'symbolic or social interaction', according to O'Doherty et al., 'Local Exchange and Trading Schemes: A Useful Strand of Community Economic Development Policy?', *Environment and Planning A* 31 (1999), p. 1645.

10 Karl Marx, *Economic and Philosophical Manuscripts* (London: Penguin, 1975 [1844]), p. 210.

11 Aristotle, *Nicomachean Ethics*, NI 1133a30.

12 Bill Maurer, 'The Anthropology of Money', in *Annual Review of Anthropology* (Palo Alto: Annual Reviews, 2006).

13 Aristotle, *Politics*, 1.10 1258b4.

14 Viviana Zelizer, *Morals and Markets: The Development of Life Insurance in the United States* (New York: Columbia University Press, 1979).

15 Suras 30.39 and 3.130.

16 Bill Maurer, 'Engineering an Islamic Future: Speculations on Islamic Financial Alternatives', *Anthropology Today* 17, no. 1 (2001), pp. 8–11.

17 Timur Kuran, 'Speculations on Islamic Financial Alternatives', *Anthropology Today* 17, no. 3 (2001), p. 28.

18 Maurer, 'Engineering an Islamic Future'.

19 Paul du Gay, 'Max Weber and the Moral Economy of Office', *Journal of Cultural Economy* 1, no. 2 (2008), pp. 129–44.

20 Alan Waterman, 'The Relevance of Aristotle's Conception of Eudaimonia for the Psychological Study of Happiness', *Theoretical and Philosophical Psychology* 10, no. 1 (1990), pp. 39–44.

21 Twentieth-century ethical thinking became marked by a resurgence of Aristotelianism as philosophers such as Alasdair MacIntyre and Elizabeth Anscombe sought to establish new means of thinking about the common good.

22 http://news.stanford.edu/news/2012/october/nobel-economics-roth-101512.html. Roth sets out an agenda for engineering economics in a famous paper: Alvin Roth, 'The Economist as Engineer: Game Theory, Experimentation, and Computation as Tools for Design Economics' *Econometrica* 70, no. 4 (2002), pp. 1341–78.

23 Roth, Tayfun Sönmez, and M. Utku Ünver have published a number of highly technical papers on the topic: 'Kidney Exchange', *Quarterly Journal of Economics* 119, no. 2 (2004), pp. 457–88; 'A Kidney

Exchange Clearing House in New England' (op. cit.); 'Pairwise Kidney Exchange', *Journal of Economic Theory* 125, no. 2 (2005), pp. 151–88; and 'Efficient Kidney Exchange: Coincidence of Wants in a Structured Market', *American Economic Review* 97, no. 3 (2007), pp. 828–51.

24 Roth urges his fellow economists to treat people's repugnance seriously when designing markets in 'Repugnance as a Constraint on Markets', *Journal of Economic Perspectives* 21, no. 3 (2007), pp. 37–58.

25 Pardo-Guerra's argument is made in an elegant and far-sighted blog: http://socfinance.wordpress.com/2013/08/27/will-the-real-engineers-please-stand-up/#more-4816.

Index